FAIR, SQUARE & LEGAL

FOURTH EDITION

FAIR, SQUARE & LEGAL

FOURTH EDITION

Safe Hiring, Managing & Firing Practices to Keep You & Your Company Out of Court

Donald H. Weiss

АMACOM

American Management Association

New York • Atlanta • Brussels • Chicago • Mexico City • San Francisco
Shanghai • Tokyo • Toronto • Washington, D.C.

Special discounts on bulk quantities of AMACOM books are available to corporations, professional associations, and other organizations. For details, contact Special Sales Department, AMACOM, a division of American Management Association 1601 Broadway, New York, NY 10019.
Tel.: 212-903-8316. Fax: 212-903-8083.
Web site: www.amacombooks.org

This publication is designed to provide accurate and authoritative information in regard to the subject matter covered. It is sold with the understanding that the publisher is not engaged in rendering legal, accounting, or other professional service. If legal advice or other expert assistance is required, the services of a competent professional person should be sought.

Library of Congress Cataloging-in-Publication Data

Weiss, Donald H., 1936–
    Fair, square & legal : safe hiring, managing & firing practices to keep you & your company out of court / Donald H. Weiss.—4th ed.
        p.   cm.
    Includes index.
    ISBN 0-8144-0813-3 (hardcover)
    1. Labor laws and legislation—United States.   2. Personnel management—United States.   I. Title: Fair, square, and legal.   II. Title.

KF3457.W45   2004
658.3'11—dc22   2003024532

Printing number

10   9   8   7   6   5   4   3

Contents

Preface to the Fourth Edition

As I review the earlier editions of this book and think back over the nearly fifteen years since I began my research into the issue of safe management, I'm reminded of the old adage: The more things change, the more they stay the same. Whatever gains women and many racial minorities have made are sadly offset by the stagnation and outright losses they experience in the business world. While a few women have crashed through the glass ceiling, many women have yet to crash through the glass wall that prevents them from entering fast-track positions once they graduate from high school or college—and more women than men are graduating from college today.

African-American men continue to fall farther behind African-American women, white men and women, and other racial minorities (for example, Asians) in high school and college educations, forcing these young men into low-paying jobs. The same can be said for Latino men. Solid doors, not glass walls, keep apprenticeships and entry-level positions in skilled labor jobs beyond their reach. Training programs are available, but often the jobs aren't. In addition, history does shape attitudes, and, given their history, many young African-American and Latino men and women don't believe that opportunities are available to them, so they don't even look for those that do exist.

In the summer of 2003, I experienced firsthand young people's self-defeating attitudes in a summer school workshop for middle-school students in St. Louis. On the first day, I asked the class of twenty-four thirteen- and fourteen-year-olds in the room, "How many of you plan to go on to high school?" Only two—that's right, two!—said they would.

By the end of the six-week workshop, only fifteen children remained. One had been arrested for shaking down the foreign-born students, and the rest of those who vanished either voluntarily dropped out (and no one went looking for them) or had been expelled for one reason or another. Of those who finished the semester, the common denominator among them was the desire to "sleep in" between the end of summer school and the beginning of the fall term. Not one of them had a constructive plan for the nearly eight weeks they had to wait, and the classroom teacher told me that she didn't expect most of the children to return to school at all. As managers, you probably won't find any of them applying for your available jobs at any time down the road either.

A reviewer for the *Chicago Tribune* said of the first edition of this book that I had an obsolete view of affirmative action. Instead, he argued that we must put an end to the old system and create new ways of elevating women and racial minorities through the ranks. That was over a decade ago. In many ways affirmative action programs have been undermined, but no new ways of leveling the playing field have emerged. That is why, as I said in the third edition, the good news is that I have a great deal of material to use for revising this book for a fourth edition. The bad news is that I have a great deal of material to use for revising this book for a fourth edition. My preference would be that there was no longer a need for this book, because all was right with the world. But we do still need this book, and which cases to leave out is a bigger problem than which to include. Despite whatever the gains we have made, we should not kid ourselves into thinking that running a company no longer demands safe management.

My research has uncovered a constant flow of claims, including sexual harassment, age discrimination, hostile environments (sexual, racial, and age-related), race discrimination, discrimination against people with disabilities, abuses of waivers and of arbitration, invasion of privacy, and retaliation. Many of these cases never make it through the courts to become case law because the parties settle out of court, and many of the defendants deny any guilt in settling this way. So, the gains about which we read in the daily newspapers are only feel-good stories.

In this edition, I've added current changes in EEOC and court guidelines with respect to each of the book's main topics of hiring, managing, and firing. I've added newer cases to illustrate older laws and guidelines. I've also added new chapters concerning two now critical laws that I left out in the past: The Uniformed Services Employment and Reemployment Rights Act of 1994 (USERRA, 38 U.S.C. §§ 4301–4333) and The Worker Adjustment and Retraining Notification Act (The WARN Act) of 1989.

The wars in Afghanistan and Iraq have dragged many reservists and National Guard men and women out their civilian jobs and into the military, which makes how to help them reinsert back into their civilian lives an issue of major proportions for quite some time to come. In addition, with more and more companies, including service organizations (for example, bank card offices), moving offshore and with huge businesses such as MCI declaring bankruptcy, the need to assist displaced workers in the United States has become a sleeping elephant in the room. As long ago as 1970, I sounded the alarm that "cybernating" industry (attaching computers to automatic machinery) would vastly increase productivity while displacing hundreds of thousands of workers. We still haven't woken up to or prepared ourselves adequately for a revolution that has moved beyond its infancy into its childhood.

All the underlying issues I discussed in the first edition still remain the same. Middle and executive managers, whether intentionally or unintentionally, frequently violate the law and get themselves and their companies into deep trouble. Only ongoing training and carefully crafted, enforceable (and enforced) policies can provide safe methods for managing a diverse workforce.

I offer you the same caveat about this edition that I gave you in the second and third: While updated cases are valuable and newer cases can be somewhat more interesting, don't discount the value of older cases. Unless recent decisions overturn earlier rulings, the guidelines created by case law apply just as much now as they did when first issued. I did not delete landmark or important cases just for the sake of replacing them, because they are the decisions that set the precedents and create the current guidelines.

Acknowledgments

I would like to thank my editors at AMACOM Books for their help and ongoing support. Most of all, I want to thank the many readers of previous editions for their suggestions and their requests that I continue to update this book.

Introduction

Americans have been suing each other for almost any reason for quite a long time now, and our times can probably now be called the Century of Litigation rather than the Age of Litigation. Some personnel decisions belong in court because they were intentionally harmful. Others, however, result from ignorance of the law or mistakes in judgment.

This book should help prevent your decisions from being challenged in court, but if they are, the suggestions made here should help you to defend them. In short, this book should help make your personnel decisions legally safer than they would have been without it.

Most well-informed managers, once they understand the consequences of some of the decisions others have made, would not make the same mistakes, but the complexity of legal issues sometimes seems too unwieldy for a nonlawyer to grasp. That complexity often restrains managers from learning all they can about laws or procedures that could guide their actions. And often, fearing to make the wrong decision, conscientious managers refrain from taking actions that are entirely legal.

I hope to reduce the complexity and fears by simplifying the issues and taking some of the uncertainty out of the decision-making process. Safe management is an informed and proactive management that follows commonsense rules.

A Management Book

Fair, Square & Legal is written about managers, for managers, by a manager. At the same time, to ensure accuracy, the book has been reviewed by a practicing attorney.

This book should be read by all managers because it addresses managers' concerns and practices in all sectors of economic society— private for-profit, private not-for-profit, and public—and should be useful to policy-making executives and policy-implementing managers alike. References to the "organization" are really to the managers who operate it. They make the decisions that wind up in court. The book is, therefore, written for general managers as well as for human resources professionals.

The legal picture examined in this book affects three basic aspects of personnel decisions: hiring, management practices, and discharging. For our purposes, all people-management activities fit into one of the three analytic categories laid out in the following table:

MANAGEMENT ACTIVITIES

Hiring	Management Practices	Discharging
Advertising	Training	Discharging (with or without cause)
Recruiting	Evaluating performance	
Interviewing		
Testing	Promoting	Downsizing
Selecting	Disciplining	
Compensating (pay/benefits)		

Many organizations (especially large companies or agencies) write policy manuals that govern these management activities. Most do not. Still, managers frequently get themselves in trouble with or without policies to guide them. In fact, the policies themselves can produce more problems than they prevent if they are applied incorrectly.

The Management Activities Table reproduced here simplifies the activities of management, although managing is not simple; it is a rose garden only to the extent that you need to watch out for the thorns.

Fair and consistent application of personnel policies defines safe management and also contributes to proactive management—that is, preventing problems, or at least preventing them from getting out of hand. Explaining your positions on employment contracts, discrimination, harassment, references, disciplinary action, performance reviews, and personal conduct benefits you and your organization by reducing liabilities *and* by inspiring more commitment from your employees to achieve your business objectives.

Even if they are not explicit, your *business* objectives and the employees' *personal* objectives interact in every employment situation. Sound, and therefore safe, management practices capitalize on a blend of those objectives through policies and practices that show a genuine concern for people and their rights, as well as for furthering business objectives. Setting policies where none exist or enforcing those that do can prevent *some* (but not all) legal disasters. Besides, respecting your people and their rights makes good management sense.

When it comes to the legalities that affect management decisions and practices, most people plead ignorance. In many cases, the plea is true; in some, it is not. Most of the time, the law comes into play only after someone simply ignores the dictates of sound management thinking. Effective managers usually do not violate the law even when they do not know what the law itself says. Nevertheless, every manager should be aware of the laws that personnel actions could violate.

Few managers consciously decide to breach a contract, or discriminate, or violate public policy. Instead, they find themselves in trouble because they did not think at all or because they spoke or acted out of ignorance of the law. Still, ignorance of the law is no defense. Managers should know what the laws say they can and cannot do as managers, and senior managers have a legal obligation to teach middle- and first-line managers their rights and duties. If you are a *policy maker,* you should be able to explain the laws that affect management's personnel decisions. You should use the information in this book to examine your existing policies and test them against our models, instead of waiting for warnings of impending disasters. If written policies do not exist, you should be able to devise them. You should then teach your middle- and first-line managers what they can and cannot do under the law. Then, no one can make the futile ignorance plea.

If you are a *middle- or first-line manager,* by taking the steps I describe, you should be able to make day-to-day personnel decisions within the limits of the law. At the same time, do not ignore the policy issues. While perhaps only senior managers or key executives *make* policy decisions, *all* managers can *influence* policy. An informed management is akin to an informed electorate, and armed with the information this book provides, you will be in a better position to protect yourself, the organization, and your employees from unpleasant working conditions, violations of the law, or messy, expensive courtroom challenges to your actions. As you read, watch for how policies could be jeopardizing the organization. If you think that you see ways of preventing the organization from becoming embroiled in time-wasting, money-wasting, or needless courtroom battles, you should notify upper management.

Issues, Answers, and Real-Life Cases

This book addresses many legal issues you could possibly confront when you make personnel decisions: not only civil rights issues *or* contract issues but both. Key terms are defined whenever needed. I make clear what you as a manager cannot do and outline the steps or procedures you can utilize. Each chapter ends with a Casebook.

The section in each chapter on *what you cannot do* as a manager covers legal or common law prohibitions you should be aware of to avoid violating the law out of ignorance and to avoid errors of omission or errors of judgment. A second section in each chapter tells you *what you can do* within the law.

The Casebook section is included for the following reasons:

› To illustrate the legal issues underlying my suggestions and to document the validity of what I have said with judicial, or Equal Employment Opportunity Commission (EEOC), or National Labor Relations Board (NLRB) decisions
› To point out cases in which the courts have defined key terms—for example, "because of sex"—in unusual ways
› To give you a chance to compare your organization's situation with cases that could affect it
› To provide materials for improving management safety—for example, a "safe" employment application

I have framed the cases within both their legal and their management contexts. While the *legal* issues are very complex—even judges and attorneys will disagree over them—the management practices that could have prevented these legal hassles are much more straightforward. You do not need to be an attorney to understand the management issues affected by common or statutory law.

To make the cases useful to you, I ask you to think through the issues to conclusions based on your experience. I ask you to question yourself, your opinions, or the way in which your organization operates. And I provide answers that clarify the issues and also furnish useful tips to help you correct possible problems or prevent them from occurring.

That a particular courtroom scene was played out in some state other than yours or in a specific federal court could be immaterial. Cases from anywhere may be used as precedents on which your case will be decided. These decisions can help you to evaluate some of your own words or actions or some of your organization's policies and procedures. Something you read could possibly lead to positive steps to prevent problems from arising.

The cases are real. Names (but not the essential facts) have been changed to protect the identities of the parties involved. Even though all these cases are a matter of public record, many happened a long time ago, and where penalties were imposed, the people involved—many of whom are no longer employed by the organizations implicated—paid them. To drag them through the court of public opinion serves no learning purpose. I follow this practice, which is followed by other publishers as well, only to prevent needless embarrassment.

By identifying what you cannot do and what you can do, as well as discussing sample cases, I try to answer these important questions:

› What are the limits of your rights as an employer?
› To what extent do the laws grant rights to employees?
› How are your personnel decisions constrained by legal requirements or procedures?
› What does having a policy manual do to your freedom of action?

› What can you or your organization do to protect yourselves from lawsuits (or at least from losing them)?

But the most important question I try to answer is:

› What can you do to be a more effective manager?

The Limits of This Book

I do not cover every possible management decision or every possible legal issue. I do address equal opportunity and collective action, and most other key personnel and legal issues that affect mainly white-collar, nonunion, and industrial- or service-related employments. I deliberately exclude safety problems (under OSHA) and benefits concerns (under ERISA) because they involve too many large technical problems and are too complex to include in this type of book. An organization should have an OSHA officer to monitor safety requirements and a personnel manager to set up the insurance and benefits programs governed by ERISA (and, more recently, COBRA). A sequel about those laws may be in order, but this book already covers more than most single volumes do.

Regarding labor (union) issues, I cover only those aspects of the National Labor Relations Act (NLRA) that concern union organizing and other labor-management issues and stop short of talking about union shops. If a union contract limits your management actions, adapt these discussions to the contracts that bind you.

The book assumes that your organization does not have a set of employment and personnel policies, but if it does, you can check them against our recommendations and, if necessary, make or request revisions. Because of its generic nature, the book does not address your local issues, but it includes ways in which you and your organization can avoid being hauled into court or win in the event that you are. My recommendations could serve as models for writing policies and procedures, but please note that nothing in this book substitutes for an attorney's advice. If legal advice or other expert assistance is required, *the services of a competent professional person should be sought.* (Adapted from *Declaration of Principles Jointly Adopted by a Committee of the American Bar Association and a Committee of Publishers.*)

It would not be honest to say that the book does not have a point of view. I take a long view. With history on which to build and the future as a guide, I take a backward- and forward-looking view of what I think is best for managers, their organizations, their employees, and society as a whole.

The Personnel Climate

Back when I first wrote this book, a new personnel climate drove the book's point of view. Employees (and former employees) had discovered their rights—not only civil rights but also contract and tort rights. And most courts encouraged them by awarding remedies and damages under contract law as well as civil rights and labor laws. That personnel climate still prevails in the main; however, at this writing the U.S. economy is emerging from a recession in a manner that defies economic logic: unemployment lags far behind the rest of the recovery, and those currently employed face a formidable labor surplus. They aren't as likely right now to press the most typical complaints, although they still aren't inclined to let discrimination or harassment on the basis of gender, race, ethnicity, religion, national origin, age, or physical disability simply slide without protest.

Unless your organization protects itself against those protests, it could face claims of breach of contract, wrongful discharge, discrimination, or harassment. There are almost as many possibilities for taking legal action as there are possibilities for making personnel decisions.

What policies govern your organization's hiring and firing decisions? If yours is a nonunion shop, does it exercise its right to employ at will or has it circumscribed its own rights by publishing and distributing a personnel handbook that unwittingly limits how you can manage your employees effectively?

What policies make clear that your organization hires, trains, and promotes people without regard to race, color, creed, national origin, religion, age, sex, or disability? Does your management refuse to give out information about employees or former employees unless the other person has a need or right to know?

The publication and fair and consistent application of such policies may not *prevent* a hassle in a court or with the EEOC or the NLRB, but it may help you win your day.

The following is a *partial* list, a mere sampling, of possible actions against your organization—and you personally—if you have not phrased your rules properly or if you do not follow those that you have:

> › Breach of contract for firing someone without just cause
> › Retaliatory discharge for firing someone after he or she files a workers' compensation claim or a harassment complaint or has been involved in a protected action to protest working conditions
> › Violation of public policy because a supervisor denied an employee time off for jury duty
> › Slander or defamation for telling a caller the reason for dismissing an employee for cause
> › Sexual harassment for failure to take immediate action to remedy an ugly situation someone else created
> › Wrongful discharge and breach of contract because your handbook calls for progressive disciplinary action and a manager skipped a step
> › Sex discrimination because one of your managers promoted an employee who granted sexual favors over an employee of the same gender who refused
> › Age discrimination because your executive management reorganized a division to reduce costs by laying off the highest-paid managers, who also were the oldest
> › Race discrimination because, in the absence of a job-posting system, an African-American person with the proper qualifications did not know of an opening to which he or she could have been promoted

The list neither exhausts all the possibilities nor identifies those that occur most frequently. The situations identified all occur regularly and could occur at any time. Indeed, practically any personnel decision is open to challenge in court or before the EEOC or the NLRB, *or all three at the same time, in the same case.*

The Cost of Management Mistakes

Ignorance of the law, thoughtlessness, and, sometimes, plain stupidity cost U.S. organizations millions of dollars each year, not in production losses, but rather from mistakes in judgment that managers make when they hire, supervise, and discharge employees.

Take the following case, for example. There must be a more profitable way to spend nearly half a million dollars.

Kent Williamson was elated the day Discount Warehouse Sales hired him as a forklift driver. Bill Perry, the supervisor who hired him, had said, "Kent, when you come on board, you've got it made. We want our employees to feel they've found a home here. As long as you do your job and meet our standards, you've got a job for life—at least, until you retire."

Much to Kent's dismay, things didn't work out that way. Without knowing why, Kent found himself out on the street, but once there he went straight to an attorney. He was much too young for early retirement.

Kent's attorney argued that not only did firing Kent contradict promises made to him when he was hired but that he was fired contrary to company policy statements that guaranteed him that he would never be fired without cause or without following a progression of disciplinary procedures mandated by the employee handbook. The employer, Kent's attorney argued, failed to meet any of these contractual obligations, and the Nevada Supreme Court agreed.

The employer, the court ruled, violated its "covenant of good faith and fair dealing." Williamson's payoff came to $382,120 in compensatory damages and $50,000 in punitive damages.[1]

Can your organization afford to waste that much money, too?

Very frequently, the courts agree with the plaintiff in situations such as the one described previously. In fact, more than ever before, state and federal courts now rule in favor of employees who feel wronged—especially when they can pull out the employer's own oral and written statements as incriminating evidence. What better evidence can a victim have than a "smoking gun" in the defendant's hand?

The Future of Lawsuits

The major battles of the day—and this is likely to be the case for many years to come—take place in two different courtrooms. One involves employment at will (or termination at will), wrongful discharge, labor-management relations, and defamation. Most of Sections II and III concern legal situations in which you, your organization, and your employees can find yourselves if you say things or take action outside the constraints of common law as well as statutory law. Since the outcomes may differ from court to court and from state to state, the questions raised by these courtroom sagas serve as warnings—that the cost in resources (money and time) may not be worth the struggle.

Civil rights battles are fought in the other courtroom, with many new issues emerging in addition to the familiar race bias cases. During the 1980s, some people accused the EEOC of falling asleep, but it really didn't. Instead, it actively took up newer types of cases in addition to the traditional race discrimination claims. In the 1990s, the commission expanded its range of issues. According to the Justice Department's Bureau of Justice Statistics, lawsuits alleging various forms of discrimination in the workplace more than tripled in the 1990s: from 9,936 to 21,540.* Whether or not an employer is innocent of the claims, court battles are very costly. Therefore, many employers find it more practical to settle out of court to avoid long legal battles and potentially high jury awards. A large number of supermarket chains, IBM, and other large companies have taken this route for nearly a decade. In spite of employee fears, claims today— sex, age, and disability—kick up quite a ruckus.

In the 1980s, the Reagan Justice Department shifted administration policy by backing or supporting *employers* in class action and

---

*See, Associated Press, "Lawsuits Over Bias Soared in 1990s, Justice Dept. Says," reported in the *St. Louis Post-Dispatch,* January 17, 2000, p. A9; see also, "Survey Reveals More Than Half of Employers Have Been Sued," in *HR News,* the newsletter of the Society for Human Resource Management, August 1999.

"pattern or practice" cases. However, the Civil Rights Law of 1991 and the Clinton Justice Department reapplied pressure on employers, which may explain why we see more companies claiming no wrongdoing but settling out of court (thereby reducing legal fees and the possibility of higher awards in what they perceive to be a losing cause). Examples are the following two high-profile cases: The Boeing Company, in 1999, paid $6.5 million to 3,600 employees, $4.05 million in attorney fees, and $3.6 million on workplace diversity programs. The Federal Deposit Insurance Corporation paid 3,000 current and former African-American employees $14 million in 2000. Since no one can ever be too confident about what the courts will say about anything, especially about civil rights and equal opportunity, prudence must always rule management decisions.

This is especially true since the opportunities for being damned if you do and damned if you don't as a result of social and legal climates in the United States have greatly increased. For example, make room for minorities and women in your labor force through preferential affirmative action programs and white males will howl reverse discrimination. Hire white males and minorities and women will howl bias. What's going on here?

The answer lies in values and perceptions. They play as large a role in legal decisions as they do in management decisions. The activist courts of the 1960s and 1970s valued equal employment rights of all citizens and perceived certain *classes* of people—racial and ethnic minorities, women, disabled people, Vietnam-era veterans, and older employees—as receiving less than equal treatment. The activist court of the late 1980s valued equal employment rights of all citizens as well, but perceived *individuals*, not classes, as receiving less than equal treatment. *Whole groups* of people do not apply for individual jobs, and that they are denied access to opportunities is a social and economic accident. Denial of opportunity is to be considered only case by case.

Herein lies the apparent paradox of the U.S. Supreme Court bequeathed to us by Ronald Reagan. A conservative U.S. Supreme Court values the *liberty* inherent in free speech rights for *all* people, as long as the exercise of speech does not present an "imminent danger" to society and the U.S. government. On the other hand, a conservative Court is not egalitarian and does not value equal economic and employment rights for *groups* of employees.

The denial of equal opportunities in employment to groups of people is not perceived by the justices as an "imminent danger" to society and the U.S. government. The injury, in their opinion, is to individuals, not to the groups to which they belong or to society. Here we see the importance of values and perceptions.

Because perceptions play a major role in judicial interpretation of laws, and because many activist groups and members of Congress share perceptions quite divergent from those of the U.S. Supreme Court, the controversy will continue to affect your decisions for a long time to come.

The pressures of the legal burden of proof may turn off and on, but the management burden of responsibility always remains. I will also discuss the importance of the legal concept of intent, now that claims against unintentional bias have been weakened. Keep in mind that new decisions and new laws, such as the Civil Rights Act of 1991 and the Americans with Disabilities Act, change the rules and that it is important to keep abreast of the latest developments. (This book reflects important decisions and legislation through the spring of 2003.)

Case

1. 2 I.E.R. Cases 56 (Nev. Sup. Ct. 1987).

Section I
Safe Hiring Practices

Selecting one candidate from among a large group of potential employees can be a complicated and tedious process that at any point could become unsafe. Anyone who has ever recruited and hired new employees knows how true that is. Management values and perceptions permeate advertisements and other recruiting materials, applications, and interview procedures or questions, as well as your actual hiring decisions. Those values and perceptions could draw civil rights fire unless they reflect contemporary social and economic necessities.

Chapters 1 through 5 should help make the hiring process safer for management and you. In this brief introduction, I give reasons why civil rights laws are written and justify their social and economic value; I also define key terms, explain the consequences of not conforming to the laws, and explain what you cannot and can do under the law. The following chapters then deal with specific issues: advertising (Chapter 1), applications and interview questions (Chapter 2), making hiring decisions (Chapter 3), preventing sex discrimination (Chapter 4), and preventing negligence in hiring (Chapter 5).

Safe Management and Equal Opportunity Hiring

Thirty-nine years after the Civil Rights Act of 1964 was passed, discrimination as defined in the act still exists—and it is still illegal. Society can try to reform itself through legislation, but the main issue underlying civil rights legislation—prejudice—cannot be erased by laws.

Prejudice means forming opinions or having feelings about a group of people on the basis of *special characteristics,* such as race, color, religion, ethnicity, sex, age, or disability, or making a judgment *in advance*—on the basis of stories, implications, or limited experiences—about people from a particular place or with certain characteristics or a specific background. Therefore, anyone can be prejudiced toward anyone else. Most often, ignorance underlies the prejudice; what you don't know usually does hurt.

What you do not know about a group of people—ignorance—can lead to prejudice. What you think you know, but really do not—again, ignorance—almost always leads to prejudice. Broad, general statements about whole groups of people that impute bad traits or a lack of skills usually express prejudices. You have heard the gospel according to Archie Bunker.

On the other hand, broad or general statements that extol the virtues or favorable traits of a whole group of people usually express prejudices as well. And, too often, hiring decisions are made more on the basis of such prejudices than on applicants' knowledge, skill, availability, or willingness to do or to learn.

Ignorance and prejudice have prevented many productive groups of people—racial minorities, women, people with disabilities, Vietnam-era veterans, and older citizens—from taking full advantage of economic opportunities available to young, healthy white males. Regardless of intent, managers often close out large segments of our population whom they perceive as not "qualified" to hold skilled or professional positions. So laws are enacted to protect people whose opportunities are limited merely because they do not share in the characteristics considered "right" by the people doing the hiring. The seven laws and the executive order are as follows:

> ˃ The Civil Rights Law of 1866
> ˃ Title VII of the Civil Rights Act of 1964
> ˃ Executive Order 11,246
> ˃ Age Discrimination in Employment Act (ADEA)
> ˃ Rehabilitation Act of 1973
> ˃ The Americans with Disabilities Act of 1990 (ADA)
> ˃ Veterans' Readjustment Assistance Act of 1974
> ˃ The Uniformed Services Employment and Reemployment Rights Act of 1994 (USERRA, 38 U.S.C. §§ 4301–4333)

They are all designed to do essentially the same thing: create "protected classes," groups of people whom our legislators have identified as having suffered from economic discrimination in the past.

How Civil Rights Legislation Helps You Manage Effectively

Civil rights legislation produces obvious social benefits, such as social harmony, equal treatment, and political franchise. It also produces large economic benefits, such as more capital in circulation, lower unemployment rates, and so forth. But are there benefits at the micro level, at the level of managing a specific organization? What are the values of civil rights legislation to you, as a manager?

From an effective, as well as safe, management perspective, civil rights legislation makes available to you a pool of human resources you might have otherwise overlooked. It opens the door of your organization to protected classes of people and allows you to select from a larger array of talent. Rather than create barriers to hiring employees, civil rights laws help managers to hire the people best suited to performing a job profitably.

Definitions of Key Terms

Equal opportunity cases often turn on a matter of definition. The terms *protected class* and *discrimination* are matters of legal definition as well as perception and experience.

protected class   A group of people distinguished by the special characteristic(s) that has inhibited its progress: race, color, ethnic identification, national origin, religion, sex, age, disability, and veteran status.

As noted in a 1987 decision, the Equal Employment Opportunity Commission (EEOC) and the U.S. Supreme Court accept the nineteenth-century definition of *race* in the Civil Rights Law of 1866, Section 1981: "any ethnic minority."[1]

You cannot, under the law, discriminate on the basis of a characteristic specific to any protected class, unless the characteristic is a bona fide occupational qualification (BFOQ).

BFOQ   A trait that is integral or essential to the job in question.

For example, except in the state of New York (where state law protects all age groups), you can specify a minimum age requirement. You can require a specific sex when hiring male or female models for photo advertisements for clothing. Organizations representing or doing business for protected groups—for example, religious or racial organizations such as churches or action groups—can fill positions requiring affiliation or membership in the protected class. The important ingredient in your decision is that the characteristic for which you are looking must be essential for the proper performance of the job.

However, laws, as we said earlier, cannot prevent or eliminate prejudice or ignorance. If obeyed, they can only prevent prejudice and ignorance from interfering with a worker's economic rights. And laws do not always mean what we think they mean—or they may mean one thing to one court and something else to another as they undergo judicial review. So what *does* the federal government call discrimination? If you do not know, how can you manage without fear of legal retaliation?

discrimination   With respect to *hiring* practices, the decisions and actions that deny *individuals in protected groups* access to employment, advancement, benefits, training, and compensation permitted to other people in the organization.

What You Cannot Do

Equal employment opportunity laws identify—and the enforcement body, the EEOC, spells out—general guidelines for what managers cannot do:

1. Fail or refuse to hire any person or to otherwise discriminate against any person with respect to compensation, terms, conditions, or privileges of employment because he or she is a member of a protected group
2. Limit, segregate, or classify employees or applicants for employment in any way that would deprive or tend to deprive a person of employment opportunities, or have an adverse effect on the person's status as an employee
3. Fail to provide training to a person because he or she is a member of a protected group

4. Retaliate against any employees or applicants for employment because they made a charge, testified, assisted, or participated in any manner in an action protected by this law
5. Print or publish (or have someone else print or publish) any notice or advertisement relating to employment that may adversely affect members of a protected group
6. Discharge any person because he or she is a member of a protected group
7. Fail to post and keep posted in an obvious place a notice concerning the contents of a civil rights law

Consequences of Intentional Discrimination

› A court order stopping the company from conducting unlawful employment practices and ordering affirmative action, which may include but not be limited to reinstating or hiring employees, with or without back pay, or any other fair relief the court rules is appropriate
› Court action to force an organization to comply (if needed)
› Reasonable attorneys' fees and other costs

As a result of a 1989 U.S. Supreme Court decision[2] that made proving an employer's intent to discriminate in employment or management practices a vital issue, many charges of discrimination that before might have been handled administratively may go directly to court, where they could be tried by a jury and where the penalties could be severe. While it may appear otherwise, intent is not as difficult to establish as you might think.

Most courts rely on the common traditions of case law in which judges or juries define torts and in which intentional torts—that is, wrongful acts or breaches of duties—can result in heavy penalties (especially punitive damages). Although the burden of proof is on the plaintiff to show the accused's state of mind, usually all the person needs to show is that the defendant intended to produce the outcomes in question.

Often only showing the defendant's willful or reckless disregard for the consequences of an action is sufficient to prove intent. All someone needs to show is that the defendant intended to commit the act and *should have foreseen* the consequences. Falling behind a shield of "good intentions" may not be a sufficient defense.

Few, if any, challenged decisions and policies about hiring, promotion, firing, or compensation can hide from the requirement that the employer produce evidence that it did not discriminate. Employers can be called upon to defend themselves by producing affirmative action plans, consultants' studies and minutes of employee relations committee meetings, past histories of internal discrimination complaints and investigations, and many other diverse events or activities.[3–5]

What You Can Do

You personally can take some steps to correct the errors of the past by looking at your own hiring results to see where you can take your own affirmative action measures. You can prevent legal difficulties by doing the following:

> Take care not to discriminate against potential employees; avoid even the *appearance* of discrimination. It is up to you and the other managers of your organization to whip your publications, interview materials, and interview questions into line. If you think your organization errs on the side of unfair employment practices, you might suggest that management seek the advice of counsel. Here, however, I will deal with those things that you, as a manager, can do to prevent discrimination in hiring.

> Base decisions that take into account a person's protected characteristics, such as sex or race, on BFOQs. Produce well-written ("functional") job descriptions based on actual performance requirements; remove irrelevant physical requirements; set criteria that identify the characteristics you need to consider. Then, if you match qualifications with the requirements of the job, other characteristics become irrelevant. I discuss these issues in Chapter 3.

> Consider reasonable accommodations for dealing with someone whose personal situation—a disability, military obligations, a gender difference, or a religious preference—could conflict with usual work patterns, or shift activities to other jobs if possible. If you find

that for sound business reasons the only accommodations available will create an unrealistic and unacceptable burden on you, the organization, or other employees, you can say no to the applicant. I discuss the whole issue of reasonable accommodation in Section II.

> Prior to an interview, provide applicants with detailed directions to an accessible interview site, as well as a detailed description of the job's essential functions.*

> If requested by an applicant, provide a professional interpreter for the hearing- or speech-impaired (or permit the applicant to bring one with him or her to the interview), and make reasonable accommodations for other disabilities.

> Ensure that pay distinctions are not pretextual or the result of deliberate discrimination. The Equal Pay Act requires you to offer equal pay for equal work (and some legislators are still attempting to pass laws requiring employers to offer equal pay for comparable work—comparable worth). However, you can apply different standards of compensation or different terms, conditions, or privileges of employment as part of a legally acceptable seniority or merit system, or a system that pays for piecework or on commission or according to location.

You can set up different compensation packages that affect different job groups if the differences are authorized by the provisions of Section 6(d) of the Fair Labor Standards Act of 1938 (FLSA) as amended. They are allowed on the basis of factors other than the protected characteristics—for example, a seniority or merit system, piecework, or quality bonuses. Often, different types of labor groups are dominated by one sex or one race. Pay disparities created by piecework, for example, could affect one sex and not the other. That kind of disparity has found court support. For more information about equal pay, read the discussion of sex discrimination in Chapter 4.

> Use pre-employment tests as long as they are job-related and tested for bias. Avoid pre-employment physicals if you can. And if

---

*If you have specific questions you need answered with regard to any matters pertaining to hiring practices under ADA, call one of the following agencies or non-profit organizations: U.S. Equal Opportunity Commission (202-663-4900); U.S. Department of Justice (202-514-0301); the Industry-Labor Council on Employment and Disability (516-747-6323); JANA, the Job Accommodation Network of America (800-526-7234); IBM National Support Center for Persons with Disabilities (800-IBM-2133); the Paraquad chapter in your community.

you must make an offer subject to the outcome of a physical, make sure that:

> › The successful performance of the job absolutely depends on the specific health or physical requirements.
> › Everyone applying for that job or similar jobs undergoes the same examination requirements.

Drug screening is a special case with regard to pre-employment physical examinations. Drug screening for *all new hires at all levels,* on which the ADA has a negligible effect, can still be used. Drug screening, as long as it is applied properly, fairly, and legally, can be of great benefit to both the company and other employees, as reported by one company in Oklahoma City. Not only have workers' compensation claims been reduced in number, the company has also experienced:

> › An 80 percent reduction in the rate of "no call, no show" absenteeism
> › A reduction in turnover of new hires from 25 percent to zero
> › A reduction in workers' compensation costs paid to the state

> › Finally, watch what you publish—not only the advertisements you write for job opportunities but also your applications. They, too, can create the appearance of discrimination. A detailed sample application appears in Chapter 2.

Inasmuch as this section deals exclusively with avoiding discrimination in hiring, I have not said anything about preventing breach of contract or bad-faith lawsuits during the recruiting and hiring process. For example, making outlandish promises, such as a promise of permanent employment (discussed in Section III), can often get you in trouble. One preventive step is to include a disclaimer in your application.

Be a positive influence or force for change. Even if you do not make policy decisions, you can influence them if you see something wrong with the way in which your organization goes about making hiring decisions. Communicate your perceptions and thoughts to management. Consider these issues: To be legally acceptable, a system must be based on objective considerations or standards and cannot be used so as to produce either disparate treatment or adverse impact. The system, especially one including subjective criteria, should be based on sound and reasonable business judgments and should not be used as a subterfuge to discriminate, a point extremely crucial to many age discrimination suits.

Discrimination and unfair treatment begin and end with attitudes, values, and perceptions. What you feel or think about other people dictates whether or not you will hire them, regardless of race, sex, religion, national origin, disability, age, or military status—and whether you will treat them fairly in the process. You can take an affirmative action if you put aside many of the common excuses people use to explain away their problems. For example:

› *"They won't let me . . ."* (where *they* means *"the bosses"*). Managers allow their supervisors or prevent them from hiring in accordance with the law if they do not protest illegal discriminatory, or potentially discriminatory, hiring policies or practices.

› *"My peers will be angry if . . ."* Same story. Managers perpetuate and reinforce other managers' prejudices by acquiescing to peer pressure.

› *"My other employees will hassle [them] or quit if . . ."* Managers should strive to achieve a positive, productive work environment, and they have an obligation to guarantee the opportunity to work in that environment to all qualified (or trainable) applicants for a job. Hiring a less qualified (or trainable) person to satisfy the prejudices of other employees will only diminish the productivity of the group and introduce negative pressures into the work environment. Communication, training, and exposure can reduce or eliminate the initial shock of having "different" people on the job.

Legal procedures or rules of evidence may change, but one principle underlies all equal opportunity laws: to protect people who have, for one reason or another, been denied equal opportunity in the marketplace. Had not ignorance and prejudice controlled that marketplace in the past, these laws would not exist today.

Equal opportunity, you see, begins where prejudice or ignorance leave off. With you.

Cases

1. 483 U.S. 1011 (1987).
2. 110 S. Ct. 38 (1989).
3. 679 F.2d 762 (8th Cir. 1982).
4. 95 F.R.D. 372, 31 F.E.P. Cases (BNA) 1359 (N.D. Ill. 1982).
5. 598 F.R.D. 27, 349, 31 F.E.P. Cases (BNA) 1366 (N.D.N.Y. 1983), *aff'd,* 729 F.2d 85.

1

Safe Recruiting Practices

Safe management begins *before* you hire people. How you advertise, what you write about in company publications, the questions you ask on forms, and your interview questions all talk to other people about you and your organization. Sometimes they may tell the truth, perhaps that you *do* illegally or unfairly discriminate or that you *do* pry into matters that are of no concern to you or to the organization. Other times, they say things that you may not want to say or you do not intend to communicate. In this chapter, I describe discrimination in advertising and other recruitment materials and how to prevent discriminatory language from infecting them.

Few managers today directly and openly specify discriminatory characteristics in an advertisement unless these are required by a bona fide occupational qualification (BFOQ). However, they identify age limits and other traits that do discriminate, and they often indirectly discriminate in subtle ways.*

What You Cannot Say

The following list identifies the types of statements you cannot make in print, unless they specify a BFOQ.

Specific age limits:	"17–25," "under 40," "recent college grad," "long-term career-minded people," "recent retiree"
Sex characteristics:	"men only," "lineman," "waiter," "waitress," "barmaid," "Girl Friday," "gentlemen"
Racial characteristics:	"blacks," "Asians"

*See also John P. Kohl and David B. Stephens, "Wanted: Recruitment Advertising That Doesn't Discriminate," *Personnel*, 66:2 (February 1989), pp. 18–25.

National origin:	"American-born," "Hispanic"
Religious preference:	"Christian person"
Physical characteristics:	"good health"
Geographic areas:	If specifying them would isolate specific protected groups (for example, limiting recruits for menial jobs to inner-city neighborhoods, or limiting recruits to predominantly white suburban areas)

You cannot specify protected group traits *even to fulfill the conditions of an affirmative action program*. The laws prevent hiring people *merely* on the basis of a qualification that is not job-related.

In addition, employers are not *required* to have an affirmative action plan—a proactive effort to balance a workforce with regard to the various protected classes in the community—unless they employ fifty or more employees, have federal nonconstruction contracts or subcontracts of $50,000 or more, or it has been determined that the employer has a history of discriminatory hiring practices. In situations covered by affirmative action requirements, employers must produce a written plan that contains:*

> Detailed analysis of the employers' current workforce by race, gender, disability, and/or age
> Statistical analysis of underrepresentation of members of a protected class or more than one class
> Rules for filling positions in job categories in which protected class members are underrepresented
> Timetables for bringing the company into compliance

Advertising copy need not blatantly discriminate to suggest that you or your organization will not hire specific kinds of people. You leave yourself vulnerable if the advertisements *imply* the possibility of discrimination. The main issue is not whether the organization illegally discriminates. Rather, the *appearance* of discrimination can bedevil you more than the act; people go to court on that basis

See Executive Order 11246, 1965.

more frequently than on the basis of actual fact. What you publish can damn you more than what you actually practice.

That is particularly true of the way in which you advertise job openings. Even though few people go to court because of the way an advertisement is written, someone could use your ads as evidence when suing you for discrimination in some other way. The example in the Casebook at the end of this chapter illustrates how what you write could be used against you.

Intentionally or unintentionally, ad writers screen out potential applicants. Few employers blatantly discriminate in their advertisements anymore. In a study of 39,311 advertisements, social researchers John P. Kohl and David B. Stephens found that race bias never appeared; national origin bias occurred only twice (.2 percent); bilingual requirements seemed questionable in about 25 percent of the ads; the predominant violations were sex-based (68 percent), with age bringing up a distant third (7 percent); nearly 50 percent of the ads were aimed at "trade" or "hospitality" (restaurant/hotel) workers; and only 16.2 percent of the ads were aimed at professionals and managers—the better-educated workers.* My own review of help-wanted advertisements supports the findings that there have been improvements in how ads are being written.

What You Can Say

One rule establishes what you can say in a recruitment advertisement: All qualifications or characteristics must be job-related.

As long as what you specify is in fact a BFOQ, you can identify it in your recruitment materials. Let's take a borderline example: Suppose you have an overseas operation in a Spanish-speaking country such as Mexico and you need a Spanish-speaking supervisor to relocate there. "Spanish speaking" (not "Latin extraction") is acceptable in this case, although it might not be if the position were located in the United States. Still, with the enactment of the North American Free Trade Agreement (NAFTA), the rules could change again.

You can avoid writing illegal advertisements by following three steps:

*"Wanted: Recruitment Advertising That Doesn't Discriminate," *Personnel*, 66:2 (February 1989), pp. 18–25.

1. Write a clearly worded description of the job you are trying to fill.
2. Write a list of specific qualifications or characteristics essential for performing the job properly.
3. Word your advertisement to reflect both the job description and the qualifications or characteristics.

Job Profiles

To ensure that you do not write illegally discriminatory advertisements, you need to develop what I call a *job profile*, which consists of two worksheets: a job description and a recruiting guide.

The job description requires a clear statement of the job's objectives and the means for achieving them: what the job is and how the employee filling that job is supposed to do the work. The list of job components defines or describes what you need to include.

Position:	The title of the job to be filled. It should describe what the employee is to do—for example, "drill press operator," "stenographer," "word processor," "cable installer."
Last revision:	The date on which you or the personnel officer (department) made the revision to the job description from which your advertisement will be written.
Pay grade level:	The status of the position within your organization's payroll process—for example, "entry level," "pay grade 8."
Reports to:	The name of the person to whom the employee in this position would report—that is, the person in charge.
Supervises:	The number of people this person would supervise, if this is a supervisory or management position.
Primary tasks:	A list of results for which this employee will be held accountable—for example, "produce and ship twenty widgets an hour."
Essential	What the employee will have to do to com-

| *functions:* | plete the tasks—for example, "wrap wire around a spindle," "tie off the wire on the spindle with a plastic clip," "pack wound spindle into shipping carton." |
| *Skills needed:* | What the employee will have to know or be able to do in order to perform the activities listed above—for example, "color code specific products," "operate a wire winder." |

Under the category of *skills needed,* you can list specific *personal* characteristics if the position calls for them, even if they are subjective (not easily measured). For example, in positions dealing with the public, you can list characteristics such as "comfortable talking with other people" or "good listener." A blank job description that you can copy for your own use appears in Figure 1–1.

Once you have written your job description, you can prepare a recruiting guide (see Figure 1–2). This document will tell you (or anyone else writing the advertisement) just what you are looking for in an employee and why you need it. Our recruiting guide is divided into two columns: *job description* and *requirements.*

The job description categories match the job description in Figure 1–1: *primary tasks, essential functions, skills needed,* and *personal characteristics.* The last category is not essential unless the job requires personal characteristics that you might not find in the entire workforce population available to you. The *requirements* column will then consist of the background, education or training, and skills or personal characteristics you think are necessary for performing this job either with training or with a minimum of orientation.

The sample recruiting guide shown in Figure 1–2 reflects a need for an experienced, skilled, and trained person with specific personal characteristics: minimum *requirements*, not merely preferences. That means that to do this job, you need someone with the credentials listed because you do not have the time or resources available to train someone to do this job. But that will not always be the case.

If you have the time and the resources to develop someone in the position, you could list basic requirements, such as "B.A. in psychology" and other requirements or "training experience *preferred*." The advertisement would then reflect both requirements and preferences.

Figure 1-1. Sample safe job description.

Position: _____ Last revision: _____

Pay grade/level: _____ Reports to: _____

Supervises: _____

Primary tasks: _____

_____

_____

Essential functions: _____

_____

_____

_____

Skills needed: _____

_____

_____

_____

Personal characteristics: _____

_____

_____

Figure 1-2. Sample recruiting guide.

Job Description	*Position:* Training Coordinator *Requirements*
Tasks	*Work History/Skills*
To provide technical training	Experience in technical training
	Experience evaluating technical train- ing needs in an organization like this
Essential Functions	
Needs assessments/technical training	Experience in workshop design
Collect and analyze data	Experience in workshop delivery
Training design	
Write outlines, manuals, aids	*Education/Training*
Prepare, present/demonstrate, pro- vide practice, follow up	Minimum of a B.A. in psychology or related field
Training evaluation	Technical skills training and three
Review trainee feedback, revise	years' experience
Learning evaluation	
Review supervisor's feedback, follow up, revise	*Skills Needed*
	Knowledge of and experience with
Skills Needed	state-of-the-art training equip- ment
Operate AV equipment	Proven writing and oral communica- tion skills
Analyze/evaluate	
Communicate	
Write, design training practices	*Personal Characteristics*
Personal Characteristics	The ability to work without close su- pervision
Outgoing, friendly, open, creative, team-oriented	The ability to communicate well with all levels of employees

Let's look at an advertisement based on the sample recruiting guide.

TECHNICAL TRAINING COORDINATOR

EXPERIENCED Training Coordinator. B.A. in psychology or related human resources field; 3 years' experience in state-of-the-art design and program delivery in electronics environment required. Outgoing, proven skills in communicating with all levels of employees. Exempt position, salary up to $25,000 commensurate with experience.

Obviously other items could be added, such as "good benefits" or "exciting environment," to encourage qualified people to apply. These, however, are not relevant to the points we are illustrating.

This advertisement does not limit the type of people who can apply. Any interested person satisfying the advertised requirements is eligible, regardless of race, sex, age, religion, national origin, or disability. That is the issue at hand. Meet the job-relatedness criterion in all your ad writing, and you solve the puzzle of what constitutes safe recruiting practices.

Effectively designed job descriptions include only job-related qualifications and help to prevent discrimination before you begin your applicant search. Their appropriate use guarantees that advertisements are neutral with regard to protected characteristics. Neutrality should permeate any and all of your organization's publications, which may or may not fall into an applicant's hands and could become the basis for a lawsuit against you or your organization.

Recruiting Materials

Everything your organization publishes—marketing copy, employee manuals, procedure manuals, newsletters, in-house magazines—can be (and often is) used as recruiting material. Especially if you intentionally communicate them, orally or in writing, to headhunters or other adjunct recruiters or to applicants, you leave yourself vulnerable if they imply the possibility of discrimination.

Electronic Recruiting

Companies in ever-increasing numbers have turned to the Internet to recruit employees; some of them now accept only online résumés. This often conflicts with EEOC requirements that companies with more than one hundred employees file résumés for one year and log in demographic data to include gender, age, and race. Since "more than 52 million Americans have searched for a job via the Internet,"* critics complain that this requirement places an overwhelming bur-

---

*Lee, Thomas. "Employers' Shift to Recruiting on Web Brings New Regulation," *St. Louis Post-Dispatch,* (July 31, 2002), pp. C1 and C7.

den on their resources; the EEOC regulations are more than forty years out of date.

On the other hand, many companies have developed specialized screening software to assist in the recruiting process that overcomes the volume objection, only to run into the objection that people applying for jobs over the Internet encounter software that activates based only on key words. Those key words tend to respond to words used only by whites—not African Americans. A test case in 2001 failed to reach a court-mandated conclusion when the company settled with the applicants out of court.*

The best advice is to use the Internet selectively, in cases where you know that the people you want are probably best found online. Since these people usually have special skills, you may want to list on a job-search Web site that specializes in those skills. In addition, carefully parse or have an attorney examine any screening software you might consider using for words that might suggest discrimination, for unnecessary wage and benefits information, for inflated promises about jobs or job security. Finally, include your company's nondiscrimination policy statements and conform to the requirements of the Fair Credit Reporting Act with regard to conducting background checks. So, will no one ever sue you for discrimination? Maybe not, but if you follow all the guidelines, you at least can protect yourself in court.

Remember, the main issue is not whether an organization illegally discriminates but whether there is the *appearance* of discrimination. That is true not only of the way in which you advertise job openings but also of your other publications. That is why the Casebook begins with a sample of the problems biased publications can generate.

──────────────── **CASEBOOK** ────────────────

Employers use many different types of materials in addition to advertisements when recruiting future employees, such as brochures and in-house magazines. What they say communicates more about

*Shaller, Elliot H. (ed.). "E-Recruiting: A Great Idea, but Be Careful," in Washington, D.C., *Employment Law Letter* (October 2001), reprinted in *Hot Employment Issues: 2002 Edition* (Brentwood, TN: M. Lee Smith Publishers, LLC, 2001), pp. 27–28.

your organizations than you may think. Preventing discriminatory language from creeping into these publications is just as important as monitoring your classified advertisements.

Consider this case concerning an edition of an in-house magazine that extolled the company's practice of recruiting recent college graduates. The suit was brought by an employee, not by a job applicant, which underscores the importance of keeping your eye on in-house publications: Anyone who takes exception to language in these publications can bring suit against you. What is that old saying about "an ounce of prevention"?

Can Your In-House Publications Be Used Against You?

Bauder, Inc., prided itself on its open communication, including the corporatewide distribution of a house organ called *The Bauder Review*. When an article in *The Review* proudly proclaimed that Bauder's sales success could be directly attributed to its recruiting policies, one fifty-two-year-old salesperson took issue.

The article, Sam Kowalski charged, lauded the company's "youth movement" by claiming that the company's success was due to a policy of recruiting either recent college graduates or inexperienced salespeople who could learn from the company's more experienced sales personnel. The examples—only *younger* superstars—reinforced the company's image of blatant discrimination against older people.

Bauder's attorney asked that the article not be allowed as evidence against the company. It was too well-written and could unduly persuade the jury against his client.

With whom do you think the court agreed and why? Does your organization publish a newsletter or magazine? If so, pay heed.

Judicial Discretion

The plaintiff's attorney appealed to the appearance of discrimination, but evidence rulings are usually a matter of judicial discretion. The court decides what can and cannot be admitted as evidence.

In the Bauder case, the trial court refused to accept the implication of discrimination the magazine created, and the First Circuit Court affirmed the trial court's decision. The courts agreed that the jury might give undue weight to the magazine when trying to decide if the company's recruiting policies were in fact discriminatory, as the article implied.[1] However, a publication making the same assertions could be used in a different case, especially one in which a rejected applicant sued for discrimination.

Yes, this is a 1982 case, but nothing has happened to change the situation. Therefore, use the case as a barometer for measuring the implications that your organization's publications could create. Consider tone and references to age, gender, race, religion, or nationality. Do they focus on job-related factors such as skills, talents, aptitudes, or achievements, or do they laud irrelevant characteristics such as youth and religious values? Avoiding such possibly incriminating materials in the first place can eliminate the need for a costly self-defense later.

Case

1. 687 F.2d 526, 29 F.E.P Cases (BNA) 1253 (1st Cir. 1982).

2

Safe Interviewing Practices

Have you taken a close look at your organization's employment application recently? What kind of information does it seek? Are all the items necessary for deciding if someone can do the job for which he or she is applying? How about your company's interview questions? Does the company ever ask questions about age, or child care, or where someone comes from?

If the application asks for unnecessary or non-job-related information, or if the interview questions encroach on personal issues, they could be discriminatory. Just how safe are your company's interview practices?

This chapter can be summed up with the same rule we apply to any aspect of the hiring process. To be safe, *ask for job-related information only.*

What You Cannot Do

Questions regarding protected characteristics are unacceptable, period. You cannot ask them. (See Figure 2–1.) Regardless of the area—sex, race, or age—an employment application or interview question without a job-related motive for knowing the information may be unlawful per se.

On an Employment Application

If you cannot refer to specific protected characteristics when you advertise, you certainly cannot ask about them on an application. Three items, in particular, belong on the list of what you cannot include in an application.

Figure 2-1. Impermissible and permissible questions to ask during an interview.

Don't Ask	Ask Instead
Do you have any physical disabilities?	This job requires heavy lifting. Will you be able to do that without some accommodation?
[*Of a woman*:] Which do you think is more important to you, a family or a career?	[*If true and asked of all applicants*:] We need people interested in a career. What are your career goals?
[*Of parents, especially of women*:] What arrangements do you have for taking care of your children?	Sometimes we have to work overtime. How do you feel about that?
Jews don't work on Saturdays. You're Jewish, aren't you?	We often work on weekends. How do you feel about that?
Do you have transportation to work?	We begin the workday at 8 A.M. Would you have a problem getting here on time every day?
Are you Hispanic?	Some of our employees speak only Spanish, and the ability to communicate with them is essential to the job. Can you speak Spanish?
Do you have a high school diploma?	[*If true and asked of all applicants*:] Reading instructions and doing arithmetic are important parts of the job. Are you willing to take an aptitude test?
Do you use drugs?	[*If true and asked of all applicants*:] All applicants are required to undergo drug screening as a condition of employment. Have you any objections?
You're very overweight. Can you get around okay?	[*If true and asked of all applicants*:] The essential job functions require a lot of moving around, carrying things, climbing up and down stairs. How do you feel about performing these functions?

We don't let women do heavy or dangerous work. Okay?	We work around chemicals and radioactive materials. How do you feel about heavy or dangerous work?
[*Of a member of the opposite sex, in particular:*] Will you have dinner with me?	We like to get to know the candidates well, including socially. Would it be possible for you and your spouse or guest of your choice to have dinner with me?

1. *Date of Birth.* Some applications continue to ask for date of birth (DOB), which is the same as asking, "How old are you?" Now it is true that logic and simple arithmetic can help you to determine approximately how old anyone is. Check the dates an applicant lists for attending or graduating from high school, and you can easily figure it out. However, you should not use this information as a basis for making a hiring decision unless you feel you can waste your own and your organization's resources defending yourselves.

2. *Arrest Records.* Never ask applicants *arrest* questions. Arrests without convictions are completely irrelevant and have an adverse impact on minorities (who are often arrested, but not necessarily convicted).

3. *Membership in Religious or Other Groups.* Asking someone what church or synagogue he or she attends would be an obvious no-no, but just as managers sometimes use arrest records to discriminate against racial minorities, they also use membership in social or religious organizations to deny racial and religious minorities access to employment. Membership in the Urban League, for example, usually suggests that a person is black, while members of B'nai B'rith are usually Jewish. Unless the information is pertinent to the job for which a person is applying—as it often is for sales, professional, or executive positions—don't ask for group affiliations of any kind. In the sample safe application at the end of this chapter, you will find out how to obtain information appropriately.

During an Interview

The best advice repeats what was said at the beginning of this section: *Questions regarding protected characteristics are unacceptable, pe-*

riod. You cannot ask them. Regardless of the area—sex, race, or age—an interview question that is not job-related may be unlawful per se.

What You Can Do: Safe Questions

An application should ask only for information that will help you sift through the possibilities when considering several applicants for the same job and help you to make the best or most reasonable hiring decision. It should be divided into three relatively self-explanatory main parts: work history, educational background, and personal information that could affect job performance. You can solicit specific kinds of information that go beyond routine items such as name and address or previous employment. For example, you can ask questions about convictions, about disabilities, and about organizational membership, but only as long as the questions are appropriate to the job.

Questions about convictions for crimes related to the work the person is expected to perform—for example, a conviction for embezzlement in relation to an accounting job—are relevant, and you can ask them. Hiring a convicted felon can leave you vulnerable to a repeat crime or can lead to a lawsuit if a felon convicted of a violent crime harms or injures another employee, a customer, or a member of your public at large. Circumstances make it difficult for employers to offer felons rehabilitation opportunities.

You can ask how a person will perform the essential functions of the job for which he or she is applying, but under ADA and related EEOC Guidelines of 1994, you cannot ask general questions about health or disabilities, or, before offering a job, ask about the following:

> › Medical history (for example, "How did you become disabled?")
> › Prescription drug use (for example, "What medicines do you take during the day?")
> › Prior workers' compensation or health insurance claims
> › Work absenteeism due to illness (for example, "How many days were you sick last year?")
> › Past treatment for alcoholism, drug use, or mental illness

With regard to the last item, you can conduct drug screening tests for all applicants at all levels. Recruiting applicants with disabilities has some side benefits for employers. In some cases, rebates and tax credits of up to $10,250 are available to employers who remove barriers to access. Although subtle differences in permissible versus impermissible questions have confused many employers, ADA hasn't imposed nearly as much burden as many employers feared.* On the other hand, hiring people with disabilities encourages the use of new technologies that benefit the company, such as telecommunications instead of frequent travel or telecommuting (virtual offices), which eliminates the need for employees to travel into an office to work. And, of course, as in any case of opening up avenues to people previously denied access to jobs, you enlarge the pool of candidates from which to draw the talent you need.

As for affiliations, a simple disclaimer solves most of your problems. Whatever you are asking for—previous employment, professional or social membership—just add the following statement:

> *[In response to any relevant question:]* You may exclude organizations that indicate race, color, religion, national origin, disability, or other protected status.

That statement is incorporated in the sample safe application for employment shown at the end of this chapter.

In addition, the sample includes an applicant's acknowledgment, which gives what I believe is a legally safe format that you can compare with your organization's current paperwork for applicants. You may make a copy of the sample format for use in your organization.

This is not the place for a detailed discussion, but you should know that you are obligated to ask for detailed proof of an applicant's eligibility to work in the United States. While it is illegal to ask where a person comes from, you can ask for proof of employment eligibility—for example, alien registration card, U.S. passport, or U.S. Social Security card. Check with your personnel officer to see if your organization is meeting federal requirements, as amended in

---

*Udayan Gupta, "Disabilities Act Isn't As Burdensome As Many Feared," *The Wall Street Journal* (April 20, 1992), p. B2.

1996 by the Illegal Immigration Reform and Immigrant Responsibility Act.

Your personnel officer is also responsible for how your application is written and what it asks for. If you find a questionable item in it, bring that item to his or her attention. That includes asking applicants to acknowledge that they have read and understood the application and the basic terms and conditions of employment in your organization. While not a safeguard against a lawsuit, this can protect you or your organization in some suits for breach of contract, which I describe in Section III.

During an Interview

Although you cannot ask certain questions or solicit specific types of information during an interview, you can ask questions that will allow you to get information you need for choosing among applicants. It is not always the question itself, but the way you ask it, that offends or violates the law. Again, appearances often speak louder than words.

For example, although you cannot ask if a person's religion prohibits him or her from working on a Sabbath, if the position requires weekend shifts, you may say, "We work rotating shifts on Saturday. How do you feel about working Saturdays?" If the applicant objects to working on a Sabbath, and if accommodating that belief would create an undue hardship on the organization or other employees, you can reject his or her application.

A rule of thumb for questioning during an interview: *Keep all your questions job-related and ask them of every applicant.* Any qualifications are acceptable as long as they are clearly job-related, are applied equally, and do not have an adverse impact on protected groups in which members are qualified.

The left-hand column in the chart shown in Figure 2–1 lists inappropriate or illegal comments or questions, while the opposite column lists properly phrased questions that refer to a certain job requirement, condition of employment, or business necessity.

In some cases, an item as phrased may not apply to your situation. You may need to modify it to make it work for you. Therefore, I offer this table as representative and general suggestions and do not assume responsibility for their use or for the manner in which you use them.

──────────────── **CASEBOOK** ────────────────

It should be clear by now that you should avoid saying or doing anything that can be construed (or misconstrued) as evidence of discrimination, such as requesting a photograph, birth date, or birthplace on résumés of applicants. What other kinds of requests are unacceptable?

Are Special For-Women-Only Medical Questions Discriminatory?

Frampton and Sons, Inc., a manufacturer of plastic products, considered good health a prerequisite of employment. It would hire people with disabilities as long as they could perform the duties of the job for which they were hired, but because some jobs presented a health risk in the first place, the company considered it prudent to ask all seriously considered applicants to have preemployment physicals and have their own doctors complete a medical form.

One section of the form, labeled *Women,* requested information about urogenital problems (for example, menstrual problems, disorders of the ovaries or uterus, and number of pregnancies). No one had ever refused to complete the form until Sally Stevens and her physician objected to completing the for-women-only section. Instead, the physician wrote "healthy female" on the form, and Sally returned it signed but incomplete.

The company then sent back the form with a cover letter asking for the omitted data. Rather than submit, Sally filed a sex discrimination complaint charging that the company's application procedure treated women differently from men because it did not ask men to answer questions concerning their urogenital health as well.

The company replied that the difference in treatment was merely apparent, driven by the concern that women usually resist intrusive pelvic examinations. Sensitive to women's concerns, they merely accommodated women's sensibilities.

Do your job applications include separate health questions for women only? How do you think the employer fared in this case?

The Danger of Generalization

According to the Connecticut Supreme Court, the issue is not a matter of health but rather one of making generalizations about the preferences of a whole group of people, in this case women. Even a true generalization, the court said, is not sufficient reason to disqualify someone to whom the generalization does *not* apply. The employer's medical history procedure illegally discriminated because it did not give a woman the option of completing the questions or demonstrating her good health through a physical examination, an option male applicants received.[1]

This ruling does not prevent employers from setting reasonable health screening procedures. Instead, it warns them that health forms or other medical policies should not discriminate on the basis of any bias. It outlaws medical questions that require one gender to supply information not requested of the other, a principle applied to race- and age-related questions as well.

Interview Questions

The way in which you treat different kinds of people during an interview, rather than the specific questions you ask, may cause problems.

Can You Ask a Woman About Pregnancy, Childbearing, or Child Care?

During a job interview, major U.S. corporations usually do not make potentially sensitive inquiries about pregnancy, childbearing, or child care. But when a major airline did just that, the applicant, Donna Sales, took the company to court alleging sex discrimination.

"No," the company protested, "we did not discriminate against the woman on the basis of those questions." Although it admitted to not asking them of all applicants, it claimed that Donna's poor references, her close relationship with one of the airline's employees, and her history of excessive absences were the reasons for not hiring her.

What kinds of questions do you ask during an interview? How do you think the Eighth Circuit would rule on your questions?

Equal Treatment for All

A federal court of appeals ruled that the applicant had shown clearly that the airline had discriminated against her in its hiring *process* by conducting her interview differently from the way it conducted others.[2] The employer, on the other hand, could not show that its questions about child care and childbearing were in any way job-related. The court also decreed that the several lawful and otherwise undisputed criteria for not hiring the plaintiff were irrelevant and possibly pretextual.

The specific questions—

"What arrangements can you make for taking care of your children?"

"Do you plan to have more children?"

"Will you be able to work when you're pregnant?"

—are not as important as the charge the woman leveled at the airline company. It *treated her differently during the interview process from the way it would have treated a man,* which is not the same as charging it with illegally refusing to hire her. Those are two different matters: (1) discriminatory treatment during the interview process and (2) making the ultimate hiring decision. If the questions or their answers had played a role in the ultimate hiring decision, then the plaintiff would have been entitled to damages; nevertheless, the company was liable for violating Title VII merely in terms of its hiring process.

As I said at the outset, questions regarding protected characteristics are unacceptable, period. Dwelling on gender- or race- or age-related questions or issues during an employment interview without a job-related reason could be seen as biased or discriminatory (unlawful per se). An employer should not have two interview policies for job applicants, one for men and another for women, or one for whites and one for nonwhites, or one for young people and another for older applicants. In 1971 the U.S. Supreme Court outlawed such dual systems when it held that an employer's policy of accepting applications from men with pre-school-age children while rejecting those from women with children of the same age violated Title VII.[3] Questions or discussions should be pertinent to the job in question and should form a part of every interview, or they could land you in court.

Our sample case violates the EEOC's Sex Discrimination Guidelines,[4] which prohibit sex-based preemployment inquiries unless based on a BFOQ. Questions concerning child care arrangements may in themselves be neutral, but they could have a disparate impact on female applicants and reflect the bias that women have more child care responsibilities than do men.

The sample case not only distinguishes between two forms of hiring discrimination claims (the process and the decision) but it also underscores the fact that you must prove that legal considerations led to a decision not to hire. In the event that you cannot prove this, you could be held liable for damages (or relief), as was the airline in the case.

See the last section of the sample safe employment application at the end of this chapter for an example of the Voluntary Data Record Survey that should be attached to your organization's employment application.

Cases

1. 188 Conn. 44, 32 E.P.D. 33 (CCH) 791 (1982).
2. 738 F.2d 255, 35 F.E.P. Cases (BNA) 102 (8th Cir. 1984).
3. 400 U.S. 542 (1971).
4. 29 C.F.R. ß1604.11(e) (1983).

[Sample safe application for employment]

APPLICATION FOR EMPLOYMENT

[PLEASE PRINT]

_____

Last name   First name   Middle name   Soc. Security no.

_____

Address   City   State   Zip   Phone no.

Position(s) Applied For: _____

_____

Employment History   Begin with current or last job. Include military service assignments. If you include volunteer activities, you may exclude organizations that indicate race, color, religion, national origin, disability, or other protected status.

1. _____   _____

     Employer   From   To   Duties or responsibilities

     Address

                 Hourly/salary: _____

                   Start/final: _____

     _____   _____

     Job title   Supervisor

                 Phone no.:   _____

_____

Reason for leaving

2. _____   _____
   Employer   From   To   Duties or responsibilities
   _____
   Address

                 Hourly/salary: _____

                 Start/final: _____

   _____   _____
   Job title   Supervisor

                 Phone no.:   _____

   _____
   Reason for leaving

3. _____   _____
   Employer   From   To   Duties or responsibilities
   _____
   Address

                 Hourly/salary: _____

                 Start/final: _____

   _____   _____
   Job title   Supervisor

                 Phone no.:   _____

   _____
   Reason for leaving

4. _____   _____
   Employer   From   To   Duties or responsibilities
   _____
   Address

                 Hourly/salary: _____

Start/final: _____

_____ _____
Job title   Supervisor

Phone no.: _____

_____
Reason for leaving

IF YOU NEED ADDITIONAL SPACE, PLEASE USE A SEPARATE SHEET OF PAPER.

Education   Years Completed: 6 7 8 9 10 11 12 13 14 15 16 17 18 19 20 +

School	Location	Diploma Degree	Studies
Elementary			
High School			
Trade/professional school			
College/university			
Graduate school			

Specialized Training, Apprenticeship, Extracurricular Activities _____

_____

_____

_____
Honors, awards, copyrights, or patents

Special Job-Related Skills and Qualifications from Employment or Other
Experience _____

_____

_____

Foreign Languages	Fluent	Good	Fair
Speak	_____	_____	_____
Read	_____	_____	_____
Write	_____	_____	_____

Professional, Trade, Business, or Civic Organizations/Offices

You may exclude organizations that indicate race, color, religion, national origin, disability, or other protected status.

_____

_____

_____

Military History

_____
When   Release/type

_____
Job-related training

_____
Current status

Personal

Yes _____   No _____   If under 18 years of age, can you provide proof of
                                        eligibility to work?

Yes _____   No _____   Have you ever applied to us before?

  If yes, when? _____

Yes _____   No _____   Have you ever been employed with us before?

  If yes, when? _____

Yes _____   No _____   Do you have a relative or friend employed with us?

  If yes, who?_____

Yes _____   No _____   May we contact your present employer?

Yes _____   No _____   Have you ever been convicted of a crime (other than a traffic violation)? Conviction will not necessarily disqualify you from employment.

  If yes, please explain _____

  _____

Yes _____   No _____   If applying for a position that requires driving, do you have an appropriate license? [Unless using public transportation is acceptable.]

Yes _____   No _____   If applying for a position that requires driving, have you ever been ticketed for a moving traffic violation?

  If yes, please explain _____

  _____

Yes _____   No _____   Are you a citizen of the United States?

Yes _____   No _____   If no, does your immigration status permit you to work? Proof must be provided: Visa, green card, Social Security card, and driver's license.

Yes _____   No _____   Are you currently on "layoff" status, subject to recall?

On what date will you be available for work? _____

Availability:
_____ Full Time _____ Part Time _____ Shift Work _____ Temporary

Yes _____   No _____   If required, are you available for travel?

Yes _____   No _____   If required, are you available for relocation?

References Other than Previous Employers or Relatives

Providing this information means that you give this organization permission to contact the references listed.

1. _____
   Name   Address   Telephone No.

2. _____
   Name   Address   Telephone No.

3. _____
   Name   Address   Telephone No.

4. _____
   Name   Address   Telephone No.

APPLICANT'S ACKNOWLEDGMENT

(This application shall be considered active for no more than 45 days. After that time, applicants will be required to resubmit a completed application. The applicant understands that neither this document nor any offer of employment from this employer constitutes an employment contract unless a specific document is executed in writing by the employer and employee.)

I certify that answers given in this application are true and complete to the best of my knowledge. I authorize investigation into all statements I have made on this application as may be necessary for reaching an employment decision.

In the event I am employed, I understand that any false or misleading information I knowingly provided in my application or interview(s) may result in discharge and/or legal action. I understand also that if employed, I am required to abide by all rules and regulations of the employer and any special agreements reached between the employer and me.

For Personnel Department Use Only

Arrange Interview: _____ Yes _____ No   Comments: _____

_____

If employed, start date: _____   Hourly/salary: $_____

Department:_____   Title: _____

Notes: _____

_____

_____

_____

_____

_____

_____

_____

_____

_____

_____

_____

_____

_____

_____

By: _____

                                        Name and title   Date

Sample Voluntary Data Record Survey

[*Use this document only if your organization has affirmative action obligations or if it is required to submit the information collected for some other reason. This information should be kept separate from the application.*]

Voluntary Data Record Survey

Date: _____

(Applicants and employees are treated equally, without regard to race, color, religion, sex, national origin, age, marital or veteran status, medical condition or disability, or any other legally protected status. At the same time, as an employer with an affirmative action program, we comply with government regulations, including affirmative action responsibilities and reports where they apply.

Government agencies periodically require reports on the status of protected employees. The purpose of this Voluntary Data Record is to comply with government record-keeping, reporting, and other legal requirements. These data are for statistical analysis with respect to the success of the organization's affirmative action program only.

Completing this Voluntary Data Record Survey is optional. All data records are kept in a confidential file and are *not* a part of your Application for Employment or Personnel File.)

NOTE: THE DECISION TO SUBMIT THIS INFORMATION IS VOLUNTARY.

Job Title

Check one: Male: ___   Female: ___

Age: ___   Vietnam Era Veteran: ___   Disabled Veteran: ___   Disabled: ___

Check one of the following (ethnic/racial background):

White: ___   Hispanic: ___

Native American/Alaskan Native: ___

Black: ___   Asian/Pacific Islander: ___   Other: ___

3

Safe Employment Decisions

Civil rights laws *do not say* you *have to* hire minorities, women, older people, people with disabilities, or veterans. They *do not say* you *have to* hire them in proportion to their numbers in the community's general population. Rather, they say that *if you do not hire* protected individuals, *you must exercise sound business judgment* and base your decisions on a BFOQ or some other valid business reason.

You have read how to avoid accidental or intentional discrimination by wording your advertisements appropriately, asking only for work- or job-related information on your applications, and asking only work- or job-related questions during your interviews. But you are not out of the woods yet.

You still need to make the hiring decision, choosing the one candidate from the many to fill any one job opening. Here, all your safeguards against even the appearance of discrimination can be breached by a decision that seemed safe at the time you made it but was not as safe as you thought. To prevent any such mishap, you should be aware of what you cannot and can do at this point in the hiring process.

What You Cannot Do

Here, the edges between *cannot* and *can* blur. For example:

› You cannot refuse to hire someone whose personal religious practices conflict with work schedules, unless—
› You cannot apply subjective criteria for judging a person's ability to do the job, unless—
› You cannot underemploy women or minorities, unless—

You cannot do anything that would exclude protected individuals from certain jobs—*unless you have reasonable business grounds for doing it.*

What You Can Do

You can do anything you need to do to run your business efficiently, effectively, and productively, as long as you can justify your actions on valid, reasonable business grounds. The courts are quick to perceive pretexts and subterfuges that attempt to hide the truth. If you carefully evaluate your hiring criteria and procedures and take a proactive stance toward hiring, you can prevent unnecessary court appearances or at least give yourself a solid defense if you are hauled into court.

Subjective Hiring Criteria

I have said that you should base your job descriptions and other selection aids on objective, measurable criteria. Subjective ("soft") criteria can be too easily used as a subterfuge for discrimination. Yet not all job descriptions fit neatly into an objective and measurable mold.

How do you measure "ability to relate well to other employees and to customers"? "listens well"? "motivates others"? "receptive to new ideas"? "creative"? "innovative"? You may be able to pull together *indirect* measures—low absentee rates, increased customer activity, or improved productivity—but you would be hard-pressed to *prove* that any one thing a new employee does would necessarily produce those changes.

Still, some positions—for example, supervision/management and sales—by their very nature require that you consider the candidates' ability to work well with others, to motivate them, or to relate to them as hiring criteria. You have to judge applicants for these positions (whether moving within the organization or coming to you from the outside) on the basis of soft standards. In the past, employers used lie-detector tests in an attempt to screen applicants for a variety of personality characteristics, but the Employee Polygraph Protection Act of 1988 prohibits using preemployment polygraphs. Many employers have now turned to integrity tests, personality tests, and clinical measures as screening devices.

Integrity Tests. Tests like the Trustworthiness Attitude Survey do the following: (1) measure attitudes toward theft, and (2) question applicants about their own past behavior related to theft or wrongdoing. Longitudinal studies have demonstrated the test's validity and predictive power.

Personality Tests. Personality assessment devices, such as the California Personality Inventory, have been used for many years, but must be used with caution because, unlike integrity tests, their validity and predictive power are limited to items such as honesty, absenteeism, tardiness, and disciplinary problems. Their intent, however, is to identify counterproductive work behaviors, such as reliability, conscientiousness, trustworthiness, and sociability.

Clinical Measures. Borrowed from the diagnostic tool bag of clinical psychologists, clinical tests such as the Minnesota Multi-Phasic Inventory (MMPI) have been successfully interpreted by psychologists to predict an applicant's trustworthiness and integrity.

Legal Issues with Regard to Integrity Tests, Personality Tests, and Clinical Measures. Under Title VII, Section 703(h) of the Civil Rights Act of 1964, an employer may lawfully give these tests and act on the results of professional interpretation. However, employers leave themselves open to possible attacks for disparate treatment if members of protected groups believe that the tests have had a disparate impact on them.* It is best to discuss the validity and usefulness of such tests with your human resources people and/or an attorney before using these tests or continuing to use them.

Most courts[1] and the EEOC will accept decisions based on soft criteria if they pass the following two tests:

1. The same criteria are applied evenhandedly to all applicants for a position.

---

*See Shaffer, David J. and Ronald A. Schmidt, "Personality Testing in Employment," in *Legal Report* (Society for Human Resource Management, September-October 1999).

2. The subjective criteria are job-related—that is, they meet the standard of business necessity.

The courts merely ask managers to manage well when making personnel decisions. One way to prevent soft criteria from becoming illegally or unfairly discriminatory is to hire by committee.

Hiring by Committee

Now committees do not always make a camel from the blueprint of a horse. Especially when making a hiring decision, a committee can give the kind of input or feedback that prevents subjective factors from interfering with an appropriate choice. Unless your organization's culture and climate interfere with good management judgment, more than one person's opinion undermines blinders—personal biases and preferences.

An effective committee will function well if its composition incorporates at least one person from a protected class, especially if at least one candidate is from the same protected group. There is no need to worry that just because that person is a member of a protected group, he or she will decide in favor of a "protected group" candidate, as one of the Casebook studies shows.

When minorities or women participate in the selection process, you get the benefit of the perspective they bring to the situation. You see how well the new employee will fit in with the other employees with whom he or she will have to work (an important point in this day of increased interdependence among workers). And, most important, by including minorities or females on hiring or promotion committees, you create a safeguard against errors that also blocks charges of discrimination. In short, participatory hiring makes good management sense by ensuring that you hire the right people into the right jobs and by making a defense against bias charges easier.

Proactive Action

I wrote this book, in part, to provide readers with tests, such as the three below, that courts apply to discover if reasons for not hiring someone are pretextual or bona fide.[1-3]

Test 1: Is a given criterion a *requirement* for the productive, proper, and safe performance of the job?

Test 2: Are criteria evenhandedly applied?

Test 3: Has every reasonable effort been made to recruit or to accommodate members of protected classes?

From a management perspective, all such tests force managers to give careful thought to their job analyses and criteria for hiring people. Not a bad management practice, really.

You can refuse to hire a member of a protected class, the courts have said, but you must be prepared to defend your decision. Nothing prohibits you from saying no to applicants who cannot perform the duties of the job if, in fact, you do not have the time or resources for training them. If you need to hire someone competent to perform up to or close to the standards of the job, and you hire someone from a nonprotected group to do that job, then your hiring policy falls within civil rights guidelines. If you hire a nonprotected person *to train,* you could be in trouble.

Proactive managers should make business necessity their main concern—for example, safe and efficient operation. If a situation makes it impossible for a person to perform the job's duties or perform them safely, you are preventing problems and can defend your decisions on the basis of a BFOQ. But you should be able to prove in court that *sound criteria* defining a BFOQ exist, if you deny employment to members of protected groups.

Affirmative Action

Adhering to an acceptable affirmative action plan, something with which your personnel administrator should be concerned, remains the most proactive approach to safe hiring practices. All government agencies and government contractors and their subcontractors are required to have one. Many organizations have adopted voluntary affirmative action standards as well.

However, employers are not *required* to have an affirmative action plan, a proactive effort to balance a workforce with regard to the various protected classes in the community, unless they employ fifty or more employees, have federal nonconstruction contracts or subcontracts of $50,000 or more, or it has been determined that the employer has a history of discriminatory hiring practices. In situations covered by affirmative action requirements, employers must produce a written plan that contains:*

> Detailed analysis of the employers' current workforce by race, gender, disability, and/or age
> Statistical analysis of underrepresentation of members of a protected class or more than one class
> Rules for filling positions in job categories in which protected class members are underrepresented
> Timetables for bringing the company into compliance

If your organization has published a plan, you should ask to read it if it has not been disseminated to everyone with hiring responsibilities. If you do not know what the plan requires or where the organization stands with respect to its affirmative action goals, you cannot be expected to abide by the plan.

The effectiveness of affirmative action as a socioeconomic and business tool has been brought into question by many white males and also by some African Americans. Public policy decisions haven't helped to clarify the issues, either. In November 1996, California's Proposition 209—which generally prohibits discrimination or preferential treatment based on race, sex, color, ethnicity, or national origin in *public* employment, education, and contracting—passed by referendum and was upheld by the Ninth U.S. Circuit Court of Appeals. On November 3, 1997, the Supreme Court refused to hear challenges to the circuit court's decision, thereby sustaining it; however, at the same time, in Houston, Texas, voters overwhelmingly refused to repeal that city's affirmative action ordinances. Decision makers thought they'd get some help from the case known as *Piscataway v. Taxman*, in which a white teacher (Taxman) claimed her school district illegally discriminated against her in order to promote its diversity policies. After several years and three appeals, during which the Justice Department wavered back and forth between sup-

---

*See also John P. Kohl and David B. Stephens, "Wanted: Recruitment Advertising That Doesn't Discriminate," *Personnel*, 66:2 (February 1989), pp. 18–25. See also Click, Jennifer, "AA Reporting Can Be Waived, but Employers Must Follow Rules," *HR-News* (May 1999), p. 10.

porting her and not supporting her, the case was settled out of court, settling nothing for the rest of us and creating an ongoing battle.*

———————————— **CASEBOOK** ————————————

This Casebook highlights problems that could arise when you hire new employees. Situations such as denying promotions or unemployment benefits may not seem to have a direct bearing on hiring decisions, but courts apply legal definitions and conclusions from them to a wide range of cases. Pay as close attention to them as you do to situations involving immediate hiring decisions, as in the following case.

Does an Older Employee Have to Accept Your Offer?

Although she knew that she would be the oldest person applying for the job, Sally Johnson applied for an entry-level position advertised by a printing company because, in spite of her age, she met all the conditions stipulated by the employer, including extensive prior work experience. Imagine her shock when she was told that there were no openings. She was even more shocked when the company asked her to come to work for it *in the cafeteria.*

When Sally answered, "No, I have more skills and experience than you need in the cafeteria, and I'm really not interested in that line of work," the interviewer shrugged and thanked her for applying.

Sally, however, could not shrug off her rejection. She took the company before the EEOC, and when the company refused to settle, the EEOC took it to court.

In court, the company argued that it had offered the woman a job that she refused, and therefore it was not guilty of discrimination; Sally was not entitled to a settlement that included back pay. She was the unreasonable party in the affair.

*See Associated Press, "High Court to Hear Reverse-Bias Case," *St. Louis Post-Dispatch* (June 5, 1997), 1A; see also "Supreme Court to Hear Affirmative Action Case," *The Wall Street Journal,* (June 30, 1997), p. B8; Associated Press, "Administration May Join Affirmative Action Case," *St. Louis Post-Dispatch* (October 4, 1997), p. A4; Associated Press, "Civil Rights Groups Help Fund Settlement for Reverse Discrimination Case," *St. Louis Post-Dispatch* (November 22, 1997), p. 3A; Eva M. Rodriguez, "Rights Group's Settlement Settles Little," *The Wall Street Journal* (November 24, 1997), p. A3.

How would you have treated Sally if she had applied to you for an entry-level position? What does your organization say about hiring older employees?

The Right of Refusal

In a similar case, an appeals court, ruling in favor of the applicant, answered that she was not unreasonable in turning down a job that was not substantially equivalent to the one for which she applied. Prior U.S. Supreme Court decisions[4] do not require a person to go into another line of work, accept a demotion, or take a demeaning position just to protect his or her claims or rights. Here, the *printing company acted unreasonably* in assuming that an applicant should accept whatever it wished to offer her just because she was older than the average applicant for an entry-level position.[5]

Several mistakes made the company's managers liable for back pay. In this case, two simple steps could have prevented this outcome:

First, they should have hired the plaintiff at the outset, but failing that, they should have offered her a position that approximated her skills, background, and experience. The Eighth Circuit Court made it clear that the closer the approximation, the less likely it is that the employer will be held liable if the person refuses the offer. An older worker should not be asked to accept less than a younger person would just because he or she is older. The company's hiring criteria could not pass the tests of job requirement and evenhanded application.

Second, the company should have properly conveyed the offer to her. They offered Sally a job and merely shrugged off her rejection. With proper documentation—a written, dated offer and a written, dated acceptance or rejection—they would have demonstrated that they took the application seriously, but that a legitimate business reason prevented them from hiring the applicant into the position for which he or she applied. Courts demand a *legitimate business reason*, not a pretextual excuse.

The next case involves judgments that affect hiring decisions insofar as the situation involves definitions on which hiring decisions are made.

Can You Refuse to Hire Someone Whose Personal Religious Beliefs Prevent Him or Her from Working on a Sabbath?

Frank Williams was laid off in 1984. When he turned down an offer of a temporary retail store job that would require him to work Wednesday through Sunday, the manager understood. Explaining the situation to the state's unemployment officer was a different matter. "Why won't you work on Sunday?"

"It's against my faith to work on Sunday," Williams answered.

"What faith is that?"

"I'm a Christian."

"What kind of Christian?"

"Presbyterian."

"But the Presbyterian Church doesn't forbid work on Sunday."

"No; just as a Christian, I feel it's wrong."

The officer studied the man's face for a long, silent moment. "Since you refused to accept a position when it was offered, we have to deny your claim for unemployment insurance."

Supported by the Rutherford Institute, a nonprofit organization that litigates cases involving religious freedom, Williams took the state of Illinois to court. The appellate court upheld the official's decision, ruling that constitutional protections extend only to "a tenet or dogma of an established religious sect." The plaintiff then carried his case to the U.S. Supreme Court.

How do you think the Court ruled, and what difference would that ruling make in your hiring decisions?

"I Believe" and the Law

The Court cited an earlier, 1963, U.S. Supreme Court decision extending the First Amendment clause on the free exercise of religion to cover observants of established minority sects, such as Seventh-Day Adventists and Jehovah's Witnesses, and protecting them from having to choose between practicing their religion and forgoing government benefits. Turning down a job offer requiring work on the Sabbath, said the 1963 Court, clearly conforms to the teachings of such churches.

But this case involved a matter of *personal* conscience or faith. Did the law's protections extend to it as well? The Anti-Defamation League of B'nai B'rith (a Jewish group), in a friend of the court brief, had warned that the Illinois decision to deny the claim threatened the rights of American Jews, more than one third of whom observe Jewish holy days even though they are not formally affiliated with any of the religion's organized branches.

Justice Byron R. White, writing for the Court, said that the law does not stop at protecting only formal doctrine. "We reject the notion that to claim the protection of the free-exercise clause, one must be responding to the commands of a particular religious organization." The belief need be only "sincere" and of a "religious" rather than of a secular or "bizarre or incredible" nature to qualify for protection.[2]

So what does a case involving unemployment insurance have to do with hiring or not hiring someone who refuses to work on a Sabbath?

What constitutes a religious belief? is a crucial question for First Amendment and civil rights laws. Although it left ambiguous the meaning of *religious*, the Supreme Court ruled that personal convictions mean as much to the law as do formal doctrines. A large, diverse group of religious organizations (representing millions of evangelical Christians and many Jews) hailed this decision because it supported the same rights enjoyed by members of recognized churches for devout but nonaffiliated religious people.

This case provides two steps you can take to prevent risking a day (or many years) in court if a person's religious practices present barriers to hiring him or her:

1. Be sure that working on a Sabbath day is a *necessary* condition of the job in question, and, if it is, make that information known either in your recruitment information or early on in the discussion; let the applicant rule him- or herself out of the job.
2. If working on a Sabbath day is not essential, but desirable, and if a person is otherwise qualified, see what you can do to accommodate that person's needs.

These proactive steps could prevent a possible lawsuit.

The issues of religion and national origin have taken a center-stage position in the post-9/11 business environment, but, while some situations are merely transitory, others have left a permanent landmark on the scene. Not only must employers do whatever they can to prevent hostility toward Arabs and Muslims, they must do what they can to prevent discrimination against anyone on the basis of national origin and religion.

According to the Society for Human Resource Management (SHRM), more of the workforce in the United States will be foreign-born in part because the H1-B visa program, which provides temporary visas for nonimmigrant workers, and increased permanent immigration are bringing more and more foreign nationals into the workforce. Title VII of the Civil Rights Act of 1964 prohibits employers of as few as four employees from discriminating on the basis of national origin; the Immigration Reform and Control Act of 1986 (IRCA) prohibits such discrimination by employers of fourteen or more employees of noncitizen applicants as well as citizens as long as they have the proper work documents: a certificate of alien registration or alien registration receipt card.*

The EEOC says that religious discrimination complaints increased more than 20 percent between 2001 and 2002, primarily because of complaints of harassment by Muslims. Still, according to some reports, during the 1990s complaints involving a broad range of religions rose by 85 percent† in which employees charged they were denied time off for religious observances, were prohibited to dress or appear certain ways, or were denied promotions. To avoid such claims, a company should:

> Have people requesting accommodation explain their restrictions or requirements at the time of their interviews

---

*See "National Origin Discrimination: A Tip for Small Employers," *Missouri Employment Law Letter* (Brentwood, TN: M. Lee Smith Publishers LLC, February 2000), pp. 5–6; "Trends in Immigration," *Workplace Visions* (New York, NY: Society for Human Resource Management, #5, 1999), pp. 5–6; "Immigrant Employee Denied Promotions," "Recent Cases Provide Guidance on National Origin Discrimination," "Avoiding National Origin Discrimination," *The EEO Review* (New York, NY: Panel Publishers, Inc., February 2000), pp. 1–8.

†"A Dispute About Faith," "A Question of Undue Hardship," "Religious Discrimination is a Continuing Issue," "Awareness Is Important for Managing Muslim Employees," in *The EEO Review* (Panel Publishers, November 1999), pp. 1–8; "Religious Accommodation: Accommodation Ideas That Work," *Fair Employment Practices Guideline* (New York, NY: Panel Publications, July 15, 2000), p. 6; Geller, Adam, "Workplace Gets Religion Through a Test of Fire," *St. Louis Post-Dispatch,* January 19, 2003, p. E8.

> Document in writing the accommodations they request and your responses
> Document in writing all discussions that have been conducted to resolve any problems
> Document in writing any undue hardship accommodations might cause the company or other employees

These are all simple preventive measures, but too many employers tend to neglect them. Here is another, seemingly different question: Since the courts expect you to recognize your employees' needs (such as accommodating religious preferences), how far can you go to protect what you perceive to be their needs?

Can You Discriminate to Protect Women from Toxic Environments?

Because studies of the work environment in a manufacturing plant showed that a high level of exposure to lead existed and since medical evidence indicates that exposure to lead can produce birth defects, the managers of the plant closed positions in that part of the process to women. "The union is sure to grieve," the CEO cautioned.

And grieve the union did, alleging discrimination against both men and women under Title VII. In federal district court, the union argued that lead poses a reproductive risk to *both sexes. To exclude only women from those jobs was discriminatory.*

The company countered with medical evidence showing that the risk of lead exposure to an unborn fetus was greater than the risks to fertile men: Damage to the fetus's central nervous system, retardation or learning disabilities, and possible stillbirth were cited.

On which side do you think the court came down? Which side would your organization support? Why?

Imminent Danger

The U.S. Supreme Court reversed the district court in this case. The district court had supported the employer by saying that it had met the following three-part test:

1. Does substantial risk of harm exist?
2. Is the risk mainly to members of one sex?
3. Is there no acceptable alternative that would produce a lesser impact on the gender affected—for example, protective clothing?

In review, the Supreme Court agreed that substantial risk of harm exists, but to the members of both sexes. "Fetal protection" policies barring women of child-bearing potential from certain hazardous jobs, even in the absence of malevolent intent, violate Title VII, as amended by the Pregnancy Discrimination Act (PDA). Excessive exposure to lead causes risks to both sexes and their offspring. Since "fertile men, but not fertile women, are given a choice as to whether they wish to risk their reproductive health for a particular job [and the company does not seek to protect the unconceived children of all its employees], the result [is an obvious] facial classification based on gender." Business necessity and BFOQ are both overturned by a facially discriminatory policy, regardless of how benign it may be.[3]

In this action, the Supreme Court supported the lower courts that have applied more stringent tests, including the PDA, which makes it illegal not to hire an applicant (or to fire someone) merely because she is pregnant.[6] It is just as discriminatory to treat a pregnant applicant or employee differently as it is to treat someone differently just because he or she is black or Jewish or disabled. The district court, in the case on which this discussion is based, required an employer to pass at least one of three tests:

1. A nondiscriminatory reason exists, such as incompetence.
2. The discrimination results from a BFOQ, such as a job as model for maternity clothing.
3. The policy satisfies a business necessity.

In sum, you must have sufficiently good reasons, such as safe and efficient operation of the employer's business, if you refuse to hire members of protected groups, for example, pregnant women who are qualified or competent to do or learn how to do the job.

If you proactively apply such legal tests to your job analyses and criteria for hiring people, you will be prepared to defend your decisions in court. As I said before, nothing prohibits you from saying no to applicants who cannot perform the duties of the job, if in fact you do not have the time or resources for training them. If you need to hire someone competent to perform up to or close to the standards of the job, and you hire someone from a nonprotected group to do that job, then your hiring policy falls within civil rights guidelines and administration if qualified protected individuals are not available. If you hire a nonprotected person *to train*, you could be in trouble.

By making business necessity—safe, productive, and efficient operations—your main concern, you can defend your decisions on the basis of a BFOQ. But you should be able to prove in court that *sound criteria* defining a BFOQ exist, if you deny employment to qualified members of protected groups. The issue of what constitutes sound criteria, especially with respect to supervisory or management positions, was settled in the next case.

Can You Use Subjective Hiring Criteria?

Francine, a black woman, worked long and hard at doing her job well and could not understand why, whenever it came time for promotion, she was passed over. Explanations about communication skills, the ability to interact with all levels of employees, appearance, and ability to take command made little sense to her. "No one does the job better than me, and I have the evaluations and letters to prove it," she argued when she took her employer to court for racial bias.

"Yes," the employer agreed. "Francine does her job well, but she is talking about technical skills, and we are talking about different, more subjective skills important for supervisors to have. She is just not qualified for a supervisory position; we have told her so and what she can do to improve herself."

Is the use of *subjective* criteria, by itself and in the appropriate situation, per se discriminatory? What do you think?

"Soft" Criteria

That this case involves a promotion rather than a new hire is irrelevant. In the court's perception, promoting someone from within is a hiring procedure because you could have hired someone from the outside to fill the same position. In effect, the promotion is hiring someone to perform new duties.

In this case, the decision not to promote the plaintiff was upheld because it passed the tests of job requirement and evenhanded application. A job function integral to a position is definitely required, even if it is not necessarily measurable by a numerical test.[1]

In the model case, the employer had another defense. Blacks and women participated in the selection process. Including minorities and women on the committee served as a safeguard against errors and blocked charges of discrimination. Francine was a black woman, but blacks and women turned her down for the job. Their decision, in the court's view, was fair and proper.

Hiring decisions often appear biased in spite of safeguards because social history has created situations for today's managers over which they may not have any control. It may seem from this discussion that the courts presume your guilt until you prove yourself innocent of wrongdoing. But consider the following case before you come to a final conclusion.

What Hurts More: Hiring or Not Hiring a Pregnant Woman?

When Anita Stone applied for a job at the retail giant where she had worked once before, she told the personnel manager that she was pregnant but that the doctor had placed no restrictions on any activities. She and the personnel manager discussed three positions for which Stern was qualified, and they agreed she should work in the layaway department where receiving department employees could help her if heavy lifting was required. Three days later, when Anita called the assistant store manager to schedule a drug test, the manager told her she would not be hired "because of the conditions of [her] pregnancy," which supposedly would prevent her from lifting boxes.

Not so, said the EEOC, which filed suit on Stone's behalf for the store to pay compensatory and punitive damages. The jury in the initial trial agreed, but the trial judge didn't believe the evidence showed "malice or reckless indifference," which is required for *puni-*

tive damages. Stone and the EEOC took their case to the Ninth Circuit Court of Appeals for a ruling on the punitive damages.

What do you think the Ninth Circuit said?

"Willful, Egregious, and Reckless Indifference"

The assistant store manager knew, the court said, that what she did was "wrongful and subject to punishment," especially since she had received training and a handbook that explained "that discrimination based on pregnancy is illegal."[7] Pay the plaintiff punitive damages.

At the same time, the Eleventh Circuit Court (Missouri) ruled, in 1999, that under the PDA, a pregnant woman has no more right to light duty than any other employee as long as she has not been treated less favorably because of her pregnancy;[8] therefore, special accommodations when hiring a pregnant woman may not be required of you.

No one should suppose that all confusion created by court decisions and counter decisions renders discrimination-in-employment laws null and void. The laws still stand; and as a manager, you must act within the laws. However, just as the law creates limits that constrain your hiring decisions, it also allows you to take action to satisfy reasonable business demands.

Cases

1. 757 F.2d 1504, 37 F.E.P. Cases (BNA) 633 (4th Cir. 1985).
2. No. 87-1945 (1989); see also No. 94 C 5341 (7th Cir., March 12, 1998); No. 96–17342 (9th Cir. Ct. of Appeals, May 26, 1998).
3. No. 84-C-472 (D. Wisc. 1988); *rev'd* no. 89-1215 S. Ct. (1991).
4. 458 U.S. 219, 29 F.E.P. Cases (BNA) 121 (1982).
5. 703 F.2d 276, 31 F.E.P. Cases 621 (8th Cir. 1983).
6. No. 82-7296 (11th Cir. March 16, 1984).
7. No. 97-16108 and 97-16602 (9th Cir. 1998).
8. No. 99-6166 (11th Cir. 1999); see, also "Pregnancy Discrimination: No right to light duty for pregnant employee," *Missouri Law Letter* (M. Lee Smith Publishers, LLC, February 2000), pp. 7–8.

4

Preventing Sex Discrimination in Hiring

Economic necessity has driven many traditional homemakers into the workforce. Today, more working women are divorced or never married; the number of single working mothers has doubled since the late 1950s and early 1960s. According to the U.S. Census Bureau, women will dominate the workforce in the twenty-first century; 85 percent of all new workers will be women and minorities. Women will have fewer children on average, but they will also have fewer dollars with which to take care of them, mainly because the shift to a service economy will keep incomes lower.

Whereas equal opportunity for blacks dominated the 1960s, equal opportunity for women, in addition to equal treatment for older employees, dominates our times. That domination will probably continue, fueled by both economic necessity and personal aspirations.

The complexity and subtlety that mark sex discrimination issues necessitate this separate chapter and Chapter 9 (on sexual harassment). Legal confrontations ebb and flow in a seething whirlpool created when fast-moving change surges against a sluggish but forceful stream of long-held values, attitudes, and practices, forcing women as well as men to flounder and cast about for some lifesaving set of rules to grab on to. But, with the rules changing daily, no one has a secure lifeline to throw as yet.

Our so-called lifeline comes down to the overriding theme of this book. Safe management is effective management: data-driven, objectively administered, and constituency oriented. Let's look at specific barriers that have blocked women from pursuing opportunities available to men, or that have placed women in inferior positions, or that have made sex a part of the hiring process.

What You Cannot Do

It does not take much effort to prevent sex discrimination in the workplace. Mostly it requires not doing many of the things that male employers have done for many years. In other words, avoid doing any of the following:

> *Don't apply irrelevant criteria.* You cannot evaluate a woman's skills or abilities differently from the way you do a man's solely on the basis of gender differences unless a BFOQ or other sound business reason is involved. But then, criteria you might suppose are bona fide could turn out, upon careful examination, not to be important, for example, height requirements or strength tests. You should examine job criteria for anything that might be construed as a subterfuge to prohibit women from filling specific jobs.

> *Don't give unequal treatment.* During interviews, you cannot treat women differently from the way you do men by asking questions you would not ask men or by dwelling on sex-oriented or sexually loaded subjects. An example is a woman's physical appearance. Childbearing or child care questions, such as those discussed in Chapter 2, are irrelevant unless they are asked of men as well as of women.

Predicating the hiring of an applicant on his or her willingness to be your bed partner should be obviously taboo. Yet women (more often than men) still find "jobs for sex" a part of the marketplace. We discuss sexual harassment in more detail in Chapter 9.

> *Don't publish sexist recruitment materials.* You cannot communicate with or recruit only from a male-dominated segment of society. Good old boy networks, male social clubs, male friends, or male relatives of male employees have often been a source for maintaining an all-male elite clique, barriers that the courts break down. Organizations now have begun to resort to mixed-message communications, such as brochures with photographs of men in professional positions and women in secretarial or other line positions.

Brochures with only men in top management or in the sales force tell women, "No future for you here, sister." Conveying the mixed message, whether directly or indirectly, is as illegal as the blatant recruiting methods of the past, and it can be used against you in court. So, whereas in Chapter 1 I talk about nondiscriminatory publications and illustrate the topic with an allegedly "ageist" magazine article, here I point out the dangers inherent in sexist materials, which I illustrate with the second case in this chapter's Casebook.

› *Don't provide disinformation or misleading information.* You cannot use scare tactics to discourage women from applying for male-dominated jobs. Exaggerating the importance of being a man in order to do the job, exaggerating the importance of women in certain roles rather than others, or making success appear impossible for women are tactics that managers have used to keep women from seeing themselves in professional, management, or sales roles. Tell people the truth, and let them judge whether or not they can succeed in a given job.

› *Don't create an intimidating climate or environment.* You cannot decorate your facilities in a manner offensive to most women—nude centerfolds, obscene jokes, or sexually oriented graffiti on the walls—or permit male employees to greet female applicants with catcalls or wolf whistles, or invite them to dinner or to bed, or make other suggestions that would make women fearful of working in your organization. Likewise, in a female-dominated environment, male applicants should not be treated in a discriminatory manner.

› *Don't restrict convenience.* You cannot restrict a lavatory or dressing room to men only, even if you have only one. Schedules or other accommodations (for example, "occupied" posters to signal use) can easily circumvent limited resources.

› *Don't interfere with a person's right to apply.* You cannot prevent someone from applying for a job just because his or her spouse works for the organization. These policies usually have a disparate impact on women, but men can be affected as well. The courts allow anti-nepotism policies to prevent spouses from working for the same supervisor, as long as the policy is applied evenhandedly—that is, either the man or the woman could be required to transfer or leave the company—but they do not allow you to close the door on spouses altogether.

› *Don't offer unequal pay for equal work.* You cannot offer lower pay to women with skills and experience equal to those of men doing the same job. The Department of Labor says that women's salaries have risen to seventy-five cents for every dollar men earn, numbers that are tempered by many factors; however, everyone is entitled to earn the same pay for doing the same work under the same conditions, regardless of circumstances.

Do not confuse equal pay for equal work with equal pay for *comparable worth*, which has become a popular topic for debate in Congress. The argument for comparable worth attempts to remove the disparity in wages between traditional women's jobs and traditional men's jobs when such jobs require similar or equal knowledge and skills, make similar or the same mental demands, require similar or the same levels of accountability, are performed under similar or equal working conditions, and provide the employer with similar or equal value. The jobs are not equal, but they have comparable worth.

To date the courts have not accepted this theory and have said that it is an accident of history that men and women frequently do not earn equal pay for jobs that fall in the categories just described. Women find ready access only to some jobs or professions—for example, secretarial work—in which wages are usually lower than wages paid in jobs open mostly to men. Historically, employers have measured the pay in the jobs open to women not in terms of what their job performance is worth to the company, but rather in terms of what women have been willing to accept.

Until recently, women accepted lower wages on the basis of the same fallacious theory that employers use: Women in the workforce tend to be married and are not the sole or equal support of the family. In the past, most women have acquiesced and accepted those market rates for their jobs. Recently they have been battling low wages regardless of their family status, and they are beginning to win the war.*

Whereas the courts have accepted the validity of equal pay for equal work, they still rule that requiring an employer to remedy the inequities in a marketplace it did not create is asking too much of the individual employer.[1] But the ebb and flow of legal decisions could turn that position around, especially if Congress legislates equal pay for comparable worth.

*See reports by the National Committee on Pay Equity (1993).

What You Can Do

Before any of that happens, you can balance compensation between men and women, which leads us into what you can do to avoid sex discrimination in the workplace.

› *Publish policies, standards, or guidelines.* You can prevent accidental or apparent discrimination by following your organization's written procedures. If your organization has not published standards, ask that your personnel people produce the appropriate documents and disseminate them. Proactive management reduces the risk of needless time in court.

Policies, standards, or guidelines should identify what managers can do and cannot do when recruiting, interviewing, and hiring employees. Obviously, these policies should not be restricted to only the how to's with respect to women, but they are our immediate concern. The sample antiharassment policy statement shown in Chapter 9 (see Figure 9–1) will provide you with a model for writing any policy statement.

Policies and procedures should also include instructions on how to design nonsexist job descriptions, such as the examples in Chapter 1. The criteria for hiring should be objective and measurable, unless "soft" functions and performance criteria are inherent in the job. Then subjective criteria should be well defined.

› *Publish inviting, accurate recruitment materials.* You can describe your organization in terms that will invite *anyone* to apply. This practice requires that managers and other employees have an open mind concerning gender and sexual preferences (as well as racial and other differences). Women and minorities in high places in your organization should become visible to the public not only for recruiting purposes but also to improve your image among customers and the community at large.

Open traditionally male jobs to female employees. Few positions have BFOQs that make them inaccessible to women. The barriers are mostly social, not physical or mental. Social barriers can even play havoc with organizational policies on hiring husbands and wives, as described in the Casebook.

› *Treat a promotion as a new hire.* You can treat all employees fairly. Just because someone already works for you is not sufficient reason for treating him or her differently from the way you would treat a new hire. That difference in treatment has often retarded the advancement of women.

The courts recognize the mutual advantage of employees' learning and developing new skills on the job and of not expecting an employer to reclassify these employees immediately. An employer needs a reasonable amount of time to evaluate a new hire's potential in a job; the employer also needs time to evaluate a promotable person's potential before reclassifying that person, and thus can place the candidate in a temporary ("acting") capacity. The employer could also reserve the right to decide whether organizational needs require filling the higher-paid position after all.

However, once you are satisfied that the employee can perform the new duties and you become aware that a woman employee is performing work equivalent to that of a higher-paid man but with lower pay, you have two options:

1. Require the employee to restrict his or her activities to the lower-paid job.
2. If you let the person continue in the higher-graded job, pay the employee the higher salary plus any retroactive pay or seniority.

Delay or failure to give equal pay or to maintain an employee's seniority could be considered unreasonable by the courts.[2]

› *Guard against a dual compensation system.* If your organization pays men and women differently for the same jobs, encourage your personnel administrator to produce a single compensation system or call in a consultant who can do it for the organization.

To *correct* inequities in pay requires a detailed analysis of your compensation system, but if you follow these simple steps, you will be able to *identify* whether or not discriminatory wage variations exist. In most settings in which several men and one woman perform substantially the same work, you can judge the woman's wages against those paid to men employees (the plural is used in the Equal Pay Act itself) by doing *all three* of the following:

1. Holding all factors, such as seniority and skill levels, equal.
2. Taking an average of the wages paid to the men.

3. Comparing the woman's salaries against the *average*. If the woman's salary is lower than the average, you *may have to* raise it.

If this simple formula suggests that a discriminatory pay disparity exists, your organization should have a statistician perform a thorough analysis. Then call upon an attorney for advice before taking any action. Without legal counsel, you might take the wrong action.

The courts have declared that unless you have a compelling reason to raise it higher, you need to raise a lower salary only by the *difference* between it and the *average*. That is how the court might award damages, should you lose in court to a woman who believes her pay is inequitable.[3] In the Casebook I discuss several variations on the equal pay theme.

Reducing disparities between men's and women's wages is just good management. The labor market operates on principles of competition just as any other free market does. Offer good wages, and you will attract good people. Good employees work efficiently and effectively, reducing costs of operations and balancing the increased cost of labor.

› *Manage effectively.* As in other cases of civil rights legislation, you are free to manage your operation on the basis of sound judgments. Why would a manager do less?

Only ignorance and prejudice prevent fair and equal treatment in the hiring of women. Especially as more women enter the workforce at all levels and in all professions, the old social barriers will have to crumble. You can smash a hammer against those barriers by providing women with equal opportunities in your own hiring practices. In other words, you should take the following steps:

1. Use effective management practices to establish acceptable criteria for your actions.
2. Become aware of cultural attitudes and values that interfere with rational decision making.
3. Avoid irrelevant or extraneous comments related to sex or sex-related differences during interviews.

There is only one rule to follow for safe management: the rule of sound management.

————————— CASEBOOK —————————

Have you or your organization done what you can to prevent illegal discrimination, especially against women? In addition to applying the lessons of this chapter to the cases that follow, compare your organization's practices and policies with the decisions involved, and see how you might fare in similar circumstances.

Glass Door as Well as Glass Ceiling

A class-action suit against a major insurance company filed in March 2001 claimed that only a quarter of the company's entry-level posts were filled by women and only 12 of the company's 183 managing directors were women. In addition, no women filled zone and regional vice-president positions, roles that oversee field operations. One longtime employee (eighteen years) said that when she applied for a position as regional sales manager, she was told that it was "a rough position, unsuitable for women." She then suffered a retaliatory demotion to an entry-level position for complaining to the HR department.

None of that is true, the company argued. We take "very seriously the issue of equal opportunity." On the other hand, the statistics seem to stack the cards against the company.

What do you think happened in this case?

Don't Fight It

After a year of argument and counterargument, in March 2002, the company settled out of court, although it denied that it ever discriminated against women in any way. Still, the settlement cost the company $250 million in back pay and monetary damages, as well as all the expenses leading up to the settlement, including attorneys' fees, court costs, and administrative costs. It required this type of punishment before the company adopted a comprehensive, company-wide policy against sex discrimination, included antidiscrimination training in its training programs, posted opportunities for promotion, and eliminated discriminatory qualifications as a condition of employment. It also changed its procedures for reporting, documenting, and processing claims of discrimination, and created a position to handle such claims. Finally, it agreed to install a comprehensive record-keeping system with regard to employment applications and promotions. It also agreed to improve its record in hiring and promoting women.*

That women still face discrimination in hiring and promotion should come as no surprise to anyone who reads the newspapers. Consider this case: A national retail chain settled a sex discrimination case after the EEOC entered the fray on the side of the plaintiffs. While the chain denied liability, it nevertheless settled out of court for $12.25 million.

Is the Number of Women in Your Workforce Sufficient to Prevent a Charge of Deliberate Discrimination?

Sylvia Posner, a secretary, tried for many years to get at the big money earned by the sales force of Rural National Insurance of California, a subsidiary of a major property and casualty carrier. But every time she applied, she was turned down.

Supported by a national organization, Sylvia filed a class-action suit under Title VII. The plaintiffs testified as follows:

> The company applies no objective criteria or qualifications for Agent Trainees, an entry-level position. No minimal education, specific work experience, or net worth. In fact, they prefer prospective trainees not have prior insurance experience. Yet, in 1981, only 3.5 percent of the agents were females and only one held the position of agency manager. No woman had ever held a VP, RVP, or Director title.

With between 35 percent and 45 percent availability and a recruitment goal of 50 percent, the company still had not extended many agent openings to women. Compare the 3.5 percent figure for sales with 46.8 percent women in operation divisions. With so many secretaries, office managers, and solicitors in agent offices, as well as

---

*See, Associated Press, "U.S. Agency Seeks to Join Rent-A-Center Sex Bias Suit," *St. Louis Post-Dispatch* (March 14, 2001), B2; "Rent-A-Center to Settle Sex Discrimination Suit," *Dallas Business Journal* online (November 1, 2001).

in various operations areas, it seemed deliberate that few women held the coveted agent roles.

The company countered that whatever discrimination existed was not deliberate: "Females are either unqualified or do not apply for these jobs."

Look around your own organization. Are there women in the high-income or professional ranks? Do you think your own organization's personnel distribution would hold up in court?

All but the Smoking Gun

The Northern District Court of California decided that the company did not issue a policy or guideline saying, "Don't hire women to be agents," but that it might as well have done so.[3]

In this case, as in most, traditional conditions and informal policies block women from access to important positions. Compare the outline of Rural National's hiring guidelines or policies with your own or those of your organization:

› *Word-of-Mouth/Nepotism.* Instead of issuing written policies, standards, or guidelines, the company allowed its managers to exercise uncontrolled discretion and use a "talking network" to do the hiring from a pool of personal contacts, social/professional groups, business associates, and clients. Between 1965 and 1977, company policy favored "sons and sons-in-law, brothers, brothers-in-law, and other close relatives of agents." The use of the network and nepotism, well known to everyone, discouraged women from applying.

› *Advertising Image.* Recruitment brochures depicted only men agents (thirty-one men-only pictures on one brochure), used male pronouns only, and stated that an agent "must also serve as 'the friendly guy' who lives nearby." Noting that this condition discouraged women from applying, corporate management ordered changes in the brochures: "[P]ictures of females and minorities, appropriate to today's environment," were to be included.

› *Reputation.* The company's managers were notorious for not hiring women trainees. Women office employees testified that they believed the company would not hire women because they saw only men agents and heard male managers say they would not hire women.

› *Active Efforts to Discourage.* Testimony was heard that secretaries were given misleading information (for example, incorrect educational qualifications) when they applied. Their prospects were minimized. Their value as clerks or office managers was inflated. They were also told, "Just think of how lucky you are to be part of a successful agency."

› *Undefined, Subjective Criteria.* Subjective criteria are acceptable as long as they are inherent in the job and are well defined. However, Rural National applied the following undefined criteria:

› The desire and motivation to establish and manage an independent insurance business
› The stability to maintain such a business
› A pattern of success in past activities and employments
› The ability to make sensitive and subtle judgments
› The ability to cope with the demands of a career, with a drive to work hard
› The ability to meet and relate well to people
› An interest in having a high income and security as a private businessperson
› Competitiveness
› An active social life

These criteria, the court noted, were highly subjective and arbitrarily applied with no thought to fairness or consistency. No specific guidelines or policies ruled the process of the decision-making group, which until 1981—when a woman agency manager was hired—was all male. They were undefined and subjective, tradition-bound, uncontrolled, and unmanaged. The obvious moral to this story: Although actively recruiting women is a sound management practice, ensuring that you do not actively discourage them is equally important.

Compare your organization's hiring criteria and procedures with the previous list and decide how well yours stacks up. An effective, useful system should be well defined and objective. The criteria should be based on work-related skill requirements or observable personal characteristics, appropriate to the workforce available, and appropriate to the jobs being filled.

Natural male-female distinctions dominate gender-based cases, but a new side to sex discrimination based on sex preferences now emerges that has implications for society as a whole as well as for business.

What Does a Case of Firing Someone for Having a Sex Change Operation Mean to Your Hiring Practices?

Joelyn Cassidy, née Joel Cassidy, took her former employer to court under Title VII when the airline fired her after she underwent a sex change operation. According to Cassidy, "They discriminated on the basis of sex because they hired me as a man, and when I had the operation they treated my former maleness as a condition of employment."

The company answered only that "Title VII does not form a basis of the plaintiff's cause of action" and asked for a summary dismissal.

Give this situation some serious thought. What do you think would happen in your organization if an employee had a sex change operation? How would you handle such a situation? And finally, what do you think this case means to the issue of sex discrimination?

Because of Sex

The judge in the Northern District of Illinois applied Title VII while admitting that Congress probably never considered the term *sex* to include a person who had had a sex change operation. He concluded that the plaintiff was fired because, in effect, the employer demanded that she remain male as a condition of employment. That established a causal connection between the discharge and the alleged discrimination "because of sex."[4] The hiring standards changed, but only with regard to sex, when he became she.

So what does this case mean to you? After all, sex change operations are not common, and they pose few everyday problems.

This case broadens the definition of "because of sex" under Title

VII to include sexual preference with respect to one's own gender. While it may seem difficult to imagine, an attorney could use this case as a precedent to argue that sexual preference with regard to sex partners is also covered under Title VII (but not under ADA, which specifically excludes homosexual and similar behaviors).[5] Although the law today does not extend to sexual preference in this sense, you may at some time need to broaden your definition of sex discrimination to include homosexuality. Besides, what legitimate business reason *could* you have for not hiring a gay person?

No law says that you must hire women or homosexuals, but pressure is mounting to make homosexuals a protected class. In 1990, the U.S. Supreme Court upheld the military ban on homosexuals,[14] supposedly writing the last chapter on the debate, but since then the Ninth Circuit Court disagreed,[15] and the U.S. Circuit Court of Appeals in Washington is, at this writing, still debating the issue.[16] In the meantime, the state courts are also grappling with the matter of denying gays equal employment opportunities, most of them coming down on the side of employers who refuse to hire openly homosexual people.[17] Now, where does all this confusion leave you?

Social change may lower the barriers to hiring homosexuals, as many companies now are doing,* before legislatures and courts get around to making a difference. Giving all people equal opportunities to compete on the basis of their qualifications or their trainability is still the best rule to follow. Consider only the kind of work the applicant or employee is required to perform and the ability of a specific person to do the job and do it well, and fairly reward him or her for doing it.

When Does a Wage Scheme Discriminate Illegally?

In a professional job setting such as a college, some people are employed in the same job classification and perform substantially equal work although paid different wages. So it was at a state college on the West Coast, where a woman employee checked her salary against the highest pay in the classification and discovered that the recipient was a man. That another man also received lower pay than the

---

*Thomas A. Stewart, "Gay in Corporate America," *Fortune* (December 16, 1991), pp. 42–56.

highest-paid person made no difference. The woman took the school administration to court under the Equal Pay Act.

Could this happen in your organization? Why?

The Difference

The Equal Pay Act does *not* prohibit variations in wages, the court declared. It prohibits only *discriminatory* variations in wages *because of sex.* If a woman employee earns more (or no less) than men doing substantially the same work, even if a man is at the top of the salary bracket, the employer has not automatically violated the Equal Pay Act.

If you manage several men and one woman in a professional setting in which they perform substantially the same work, you can determine if wage variations among them are discriminatory by comparing the woman's wages with those paid to men in the manner previously described. If your analysis suggests that a discriminatory pay disparity exists, ask for a more thorough statistical analysis.

It was in this case that the court declared unless you have a compelling reason to raise it higher, you need raise a lower salary only by the *difference* between it and the *average.*[3]

These rules usually work for claims brought under the Equal Pay Act. Should a person bring a "but for" claim under Title VII, the situation could be quite different. Let's say the woman brings a Title VII sex discrimination case instead of an Equal Pay claim. In this new scenario, she could say:

> "I'm doing essentially the same work as the highest-paid person, who is a man. I am as qualified, I have as much experience, and I have performed as well as he. Therefore, I merit or deserve equal pay for equal work, and but for the fact that I am a woman, I would receive it."

The court in this case would have ruled that even if the woman employee were earning more than the average wage for the male employees, but for her sex was not receiving the higher wage paid to the comparable male employees, she should receive the higher wage.

If she also marshaled the proper evidence of intent to discriminate, she would receive the pay raise, plus back pay as damages.

Wage variations can exist as long as they reflect the "factors other than sex" exception of both Title VII and the Equal Pay Act. The nonsex justification must account for the *entire* wage difference between male and female employees, not just form a partial basis.

One such basis is called "red circle" wage rates, which are unusual, higher than normal wage rates maintained for legitimate business purposes, such as paying a higher rate to a temporarily reassigned employee or to an employee whose previous job was eliminated.

In one case, a male employee was temporarily transferred from a higher-paying position in a hospital to a lower one, where he performed the same work as did the woman employee who had been employed there before him. During the period they worked together, performing the same duties, the man's pay scale ranged from $472 to $671, while the woman's ranged from $268 to $430. The hospital justified the differential by saying that the man was only temporarily reassigned and was therefore paid a red circle rate.

The courts agreed with both the woman and the employer. The man employee had been temporarily reassigned and paid a red circle rate; but that accounted for *only part* of the wage differential. Because to fall within the "factor other than sex" exception, red circling must account for the entire differential and cannot form a partial basis for the differential, the woman employee received a pay award equal to the difference between her wage rate and the *un*explained discrepancy not covered by red circling.[6]

Contrast that decision with the red circling that occurred when a transferred man's job was eliminated. The position into which he transferred involved the same duties a lower-paid woman had also been performing, yet he was allowed to keep his higher salary. The court accepted the *sex-neutral* justification the employer offered: to enhance the desirability of the position and to provide job security to a valued employee.[7]

In yet another "but for" trial, a woman professor and her attorney argued that but for the fact that she was married, she would have received tenure. A thirty-year history of not granting tenure to married women in her field and related subjects sank the college's claims of unacceptable performance reviews. Being married had been equated by the school with having childrearing obligations that would interfere with a woman's work; only single women had ever been granted tenure. Basing her decision on the 1971 Supreme Court decision that hiring only single women as airline attendants was improper, the judge of the U.S. District Court of New York ruled against the college.[18]

Can Dual Compensation for Unequal Work Be Equal?

U.S. Ironworks, Inc., when modernizing its operations, set up a systematic approach to its job and pay analyses that compensated jobs in the manufacturing division on the basis of new objective criteria— detailed job descriptions, standardized performance evaluations, publicly known job classifications, pay scale adjustments based on periodic job reviews—the latest human resources technology to match its upgraded manufacturing process.

On the other hand, the company used subjective criteria for determining compensation for nonmanufacturing jobs, with none of the objective standards found in the manufacturing sections. Traditionally, no women were in manufacturing divisions, and few men were in nonmanufacturing. Therefore, the women plaintiffs contended, compensation was based on two different *and discriminatory* systems.

How does your organization set compensation? One system? Two?

Different Strokes

A lower court saw the contention as a backdoor attempt to use Title VII to litigate a comparable worth claim, an attempt to increase compensation on the basis of a comparison of the intrinsic worth or difficulty of two different kinds of work—one performed by men, the other performed by women.

The Eleventh Circuit Court, on appeal, saw the situation differently, identifying the issue as the company's attempt to maintain separate pay schemes for positions traditionally occupied by men, on the one hand, and positions traditionally occupied by women, on the other. That sort of duality, the court said, regardless of what protected class is affected, could be by itself discriminatory.

Yes, the appellate court said, a dual system can be discriminatory if the basis on which traditionally male and female jobs are evaluated results in different evaluations. If that basis forms the grounds for a Title VII compensation claim, the plaintiffs would be entitled to back pay.[8]

The Equal Pay Act requires employers to distribute compensation appropriately for work or services performed, but you need not use *identical* methods for determining pay in all cases. The ruling in this case means:

> The greater the dissimilarity between pay systems for jobs in the same organization, the greater the risk the differences can form a factual basis for a compensation discrimination claim.

When any protected group—for example, blacks or older employees—predominates in any particular job or group of jobs, similar methods should be used to determine the compensation of identical or similar job classifications occupied by white males or other nonminorities.

If you are ever involved in contract negotiations, be aware that the same principle also applies to allowing employees outside the protected groups, but not those who are members of the protected groups, to negotiate contracts or contract changes. You could be charged with discrimination if you treat similarly situated employees differently.[9] You must have legitimate, nondiscriminatory reasons for permitting men employees better contract terms than you do women, which reasons would be hard to find in most cases.

BFOQs or legitimate business reasons for differences in compensation packages can and do affect your decisions. Just make sure that your business reasons have a sound factual basis, such as a legal seniority system or significant variation in experience or skills.

Open traditionally male jobs to female employees. Few positions have BFOQs that make them inaccessible to women. The barriers are mostly social, not physical or mental. Social barriers can even play havoc with organizational policies pertaining to hiring husbands and wives.

Can You Ban Spouses from Reporting to the Same Supervisor?

Alice and Martin, sitting side by side in the same department and reporting to the same supervisor, began dating and not long afterward got married. Upon hearing of the marriage, management said that they would have thirty days for one of them to transfer to a different position; otherwise the less senior employee, Alice, would be removed from her position.

Feeling imposed on, neither transferred in the time allowed, and Alice was reassigned to a lower-level, lower-paying job, whereupon she filed suit under Title VII.

What does your organization say about nepotism? Who do you think won this case involving an antinepotism rule?

Neutrality and Evenhandedness

The employer won. This antinepotism rule treated *individual* cases fairly without adverse impact on a given sex. The court said that the rule, although unwritten, was itself facially neutral and evenhandedly applied. If the husband had been the junior employee, he would have had to accept the transfer.[11] Not separating husbands and wives working in the same department, especially if one is senior to the other, could result in a conflict of interest, and as such antinepotism policies serve a legitimate business interest.[12]

In addition, close personal relationships on the job could produce conflicts unrelated to business or generate unwarranted favoritism. Awkward situations can develop between members of the same family working closely together, and it makes good management sense to prevent problems proactively (before they occur).[13]

Yet, as the *National Business Employment Weekly* reported (without identifying the case), a federal judge in a government agency antinepotism case has ruled that "no law, regardless of intent, should have a 'chilling effect' upon marriage . . . . which is a fundamental right" protected by the Constitution. The article concluded that this case may require employers to reconsider policies that forbid marriage among coworkers.*

*February 11, 1990. p. 4.

Can You Ban Spouses from the Company as a Whole?

When the meat-packing plant in town opened, it established an anti-nepotism rule that said spouses could not work there even if they worked in separate departments and reported to different supervisors. The company soon found itself in court, charged with sex discrimination because the rule excluded a disproportionate number of women. Although their husbands could work there, they themselves could not.

How does your organization spell out its antinepotism rules?

Adverse Impact

Here is a case where the theory of adverse impact on a whole group could stand up to legal tests. Spouses working together in the same department could adversely affect production or productivity, but no business necessity justifies an exclusive rule that has an adverse impact on women, such as the defendant's. The Eighth Circuit Court said nay to the rule.[10] Other remedies for potential problems must be found.

Cases

1. 783 F.2d 716, 40 F.E.P. Cases (BNA) 244 (7th Cir. 1986); 770 F.2d 1401, 38 F.E.P. Cases (BNA) 1353 (9th Cir. 1985); *review denied,* 813 F.2d 1034 (1987).
2. 736 F.2d 126, 35 F.E.P. Cases (BNA) 234 (9th Cir. 1984).
3. 38 F.E.P. Cases (BNA) 197 (N.D. Cal. 1985).
4. 581 F. Supp. 821, 28 F.E.P. Cases (BNA) 1488 (N.D. Ill. 1982), *rev'd,* 742 F.2d 1081, CCA 7 (1984); *cert. denied,* 105 S. Ct. 2023 (1985).
5. 718 F.2d 910, 33 F.E.P. Cases (BNA) 1538 (9th Cir. 1983); No. 25480–4–1 (Wash. 1990).
6. 780 F.2d 917, 39 E.P.D. (CCH) 35,910 (11th Cir. 1986).
7. 866 F. Supp. 209, 45 F.E.P. Cases (BNA) 330 (M.D. Fla. 1987).
8. 784 F.2d 1546, 40 F.E.P. Cases (BNA) 678 (11th Cir. 1986), *cert. denied,* 107 S. Ct. 274 (1986).
9. 120 L.R.R.M. (BNA) 3203 (D.D.C. 1985).
10. 787 F.2d 318, 40 F.E.P. Cases (BNA) 580 (8th Cir. 1986).
11. 601 F. Supp. 160, 37 F.E.P. Cases (BNA) 843 (W.D. Pa. 1985); *aff'd,* 779 F.2d 42 (1985).
12. 462 F. Supp. 289 (S.D.W. Va. 1978).

13. 19 E.P.D. 91.3 (D.D.C. 1978).
14. 494 U.S. 1004, *cert. denied,* 494 U.S. 1003 (1990).
15. 932 F.2d 915 (9th Cir.).
16. No. 93–1924 (D.C. Cir. 1994).
17. 195 Cal. Rptr. 325 (147 Cal. 3d 712), *appeal dismissed,* U.S. 1205 (1991).
18. 87 Civ. 4777 (D.N.Y. 1994).

5

Preventing Negligent Hiring

"Is there anyone I *shouldn't* hire?" It may seem that you have little choice in your hiring decisions, that you must hire anyone coming through your door, but that is not true. You only need to give everyone applying for a job fair and equal opportunities to compete for it on the basis of the same work-related criteria. As an employer, you have the *right* to say no to anyone who does not satisfy bona fide occupational qualifications (BFOQs) or business necessities, or who cannot be trained to meet them.

You also have an *obligation* to say no to some people. After thoroughly screening all applicants, learning as much as you possibly can about the people, don't extend an offer unless you're certain about the applicant's personal and work-related past; you have a duty to your organization, other employees, and the public to screen out anyone whose record raises a red flag or whose past leads you to suspect that he or she could pose a potential threat to the constituencies that depend on your good judgment. To do less could open you to a charge of negligence.

Exercise due care in prehire screening, training new employees, assigning people to jobs, and supervising them—especially if the job can expose the public to a potentially dangerous or dishonest person. Unless you exercise reasonable care, you can be held liable to parties robbed or injured by a dishonest, unfit, or incompetent employee. Some employers are now using additional *attitude tests* to screen prospects. If Pizza Hut had known the racial attitudes of some of its employees, it might not have had to settle a hate crime lawsuit (for an undisclosed amount) under the Illinois Hate Crimes Act.[1] For a comprehensive study of screening methods, check out Edward Andler's *Complete Reference Checking Handbook* (New York: AMACOM, 1998), but for our purposes, you should know what some of the terms in this legal context mean and basic steps you should follow to prevent negligent hiring.

Definitions of Key Terms

negligence   The failure to exercise due care under circumstances where the legal duty to care is owed another person or other people. By not conducting adequate and proper reference or background checks, you could unknowingly hire someone whose past history indicates the possibility of endangering the property or lives of other people. You could be cited for negligence in that case. Negligence seems to be clear-cut in cases where an employer hires violent employees.

due care   All reasonable and legal steps to protect the organization, other employees, customers, and the general public. The Rhode Island Supreme Court, for example, asserts that the exercise of reasonable care means more than accepting the absence of complaints about dishonesty as evidence that the person is honest. Especially in service industries, in which honesty, trustworthiness, and reliability are the hallmarks of business, an employer is expected to include in its records affirmations of the applicant's qualifications.[1]

the doctrine of respondeat superior   When an employee acts within the scope of his or her job as agent for the employer, any wrongful act the employee commits can be attributed to the employer vicariously. But, under this doctrine, if an employee commits a wrongful act *outside the scope* of his or her employment or *not in furtherance* of the employer's business, the employer cannot be held liable by a third party. Now, under the doctrine of negligent hiring, the employer can be held liable in such a case.

What You Cannot Do

The courts expect employers to take all *reasonable* and *legal* steps to protect the organization, other employees, customers, and the general public. However, all reasonable and legal steps exclude the use of polygraph (lie detector) tests except in a limited number of cases, which will be discussed in Chapter 7. You must use other means to protect yourself from the possibility of hiring someone who might get you into serious trouble.

What You Can Do

What follows are reasonable and lawful steps that you can take:

1. *Request conviction information.* On applications and during interviews, you cannot ask applicants if they have ever been arrested, but you can ask for conviction records. You can also question an applicant about a report that he or she received a dishonorable or bad conduct discharge from military service.

You should ask the person convicted of a crime what the crime was. The nature of the crime could disqualify the applicant for a given position, not only because of the potential for repeating a crime but also because the conditions of a person's parole or probation may exclude him or her from holding certain jobs. You can refuse to hire anyone who falsifies or fails to disclose a conviction when responding to an appropriately worded question.

2. *Check out gaps in the record; probe.* If an applicant's job history includes a significant time gap between school and work, between military service and a civilian job, or between jobs, you may ask, "What did you do from this date to that one?"

3. *Check out unclear statements or answers.* If you have any reason to suspect an answer, later in the interview or during a second one, ask the same question in a different way; see if the answers jibe. Ask the applicant's references or previous employers what they know about the answer you find troublesome.

For example, you can ask, "What did [John/Joan] do from September 5 to January 1 that year?" The person may not know or may not be able to answer, but no law says you cannot ask. And have an attorney check public records about convictions for crimes if you suspect that a criminal record exists.

4. *Document all inquiries (including reference checks) in writing.* Enter your own notes into the interview record. Send preprinted

forms for references to complete that include an authorization to release information about him or her signed by the applicant. If appropriate, ask for a credit record from a credit bureau. If the budget allows, hire a professional company to check references of applicants you are seriously considering. However, in 1997, Congress passed the Fair Credit Reporting Act (FCRA) requiring that unless employers are under a *legal* obligation to check credit—for example, hiring someone with fiduciary responsibilities—they shouldn't routinely use consumer credit information, which could be inaccurate or under challenge, as a basis for making hiring decisions.

5. *If an applicant volunteers that he or she was hospitalized for mental or emotional problems, pursue the matter.* Yes, it is personal, but it is not private. However, take care *not to initiate this conversation.* If you seriously want to hire the applicant but have reason to believe that the person's problem—for example, violent behavior—could be a detriment, ask for a release of information or for the right to contact the attending physician; get the permission in writing, and get the information you need in writing, as well.

On the other hand, not hiring an applicant merely because he or she has a *history* of mental or emotional problems can lead to a lawsuit charging discrimination against a disabled person. The reason for *not* hiring someone must be that his or her mental or emotional problems would *continue* to pose a threat to the organization or to other people.

6. *Turn down applicants convicted of a crime or those with a history of injuring other people when they could possibly repeat their offense in a new job situation.* An accountant convicted of embezzlement should not handle other people's money, although he or she may become a fine (and honest) office administrator so long as direct access to cash or the books is not involved.

Hiring people with a history of violence can be risky business. Many employers refuse to hire them, which in itself becomes a social problem because the inability of convicted felons to get meaningful employment contributes to the repeat of criminal behavior. You could turn someone with the skills and abilities you need (but with a record) into a favorable employee, but you must also take care to protect your organization and other employees (while not overpolicing the individual).

7. *If a person is on probation or on parole, talk with his or her probation or parole officer.* The officer can alert you to whether or not the job you have in mind falls within the terms of the applicant's probation or parole. It may not.

If it does, a person's rehabilitation often depends on his or her ability to find and keep a meaningful job with a decent wage. You and the officer can make a difference, if you work as a team to help the applicant succeed.

Safe hiring practices are as subtle and complex as the human and social issues that influence them. Still, proactive management practices can prevent hiring problems from becoming legal crises.

CASEBOOK

Just how far and deep does your responsibility as an employer run? A review of the following cases should help you to answer that question.

How Much Background Checking Is an Employer Supposed to Do?

Wright Security had provided guard service for Ellerton Manufacturing for thirty years. In all that time, nothing untoward had happened to Ellerton's facility in which gold sunglass frames were produced. Suddenly, within a forty-five-day period, the company experienced three separate losses in excess of $200,000 at the plant, which they traced back to the new security guard assigned to it.

On two occasions, Ellerton claimed, the guard admitted the thieves into the plant. On the third occasion, after he had already quit Wright Security, the guard helped plan the break-in and cleaned out Ellerton's gold inventory. The company took Wright Security to court, suing for negligence in hiring, training, assigning, and supervising someone suspected of "having sticky fingers."

Wright Security argued that its applications required listing the names of former employers and three references from among people who had known the applicant for more than five years. In this case, Wright contacted the man's current employer and one former employer and also sent a reference form to his high-school principal.

None of these people said that the applicant was dishonest or criminally inclined, so Wright hired him.

Wright also claimed that all its employees received on-the-job training. Furthermore, low-level employees received supervision from trained, experienced officers. Ellerton's suit was misguided.

Does your organization hire people into positions of public or customer trust? What sort of background checks do you run, especially for positions involving sensitive commodities or information? What do you think the court thought of Wright Security's defense?

Negligence

Often, because employers run into policies of silence or of "name, rank, and serial number," they simply do not bother themselves or other people with reference or background checks. Or, if they do, as in this case, they do not dig sufficiently.

The Rhode Island Supreme Court ruled against the security company. An employer must exercise *reasonable care* in prehire screening, in training new employees, in assigning people to jobs, and in supervising them, especially if the job can expose the public to a potentially dangerous or dishonest person. Without the exercise of reasonable care, the employer can be held liable to parties injured (theft is a legal injury or tort) by a dishonest, unfit, or incompetent employee. Reasonable care was absent in this case.[1]

That the security company had a duty to make a more thorough check than it did and that it had a duty to train, assign, and supervise more carefully than it did constituted only the factual context of the case. What the court ruled has far greater implications than that context.

This case provided us with the expanded *doctrine of respondeat superior* defined earlier in this chapter. The court extended liability beyond the hiring of potentially violent employees and declared that the mere absence of specific evidence or claims of dishonesty is insufficient.

As I have said, negligence seems to be clear-cut in cases where an employer hires violent employees. In a case in Texas in 1987, in which the jury awarded the victim $5 million in damages, a Fort

Worth cab company hired a driver whose twenty years of crime included convictions for forgery, robbery, theft, and other crimes. The company hired him without a background check while he was under indictment for attempted murder in the mistaken belief that the police department would not issue a taxi permit to anyone not qualified.

Wrong. The police never refuse a taxi permit. One month later, the driver raped a woman passenger. Although the Texas Supreme Court thought the damages might be excessive, it agreed that the cab company was clearly liable.[2]

The same verdict was handed down when a trucking company was sued for negligently hiring an over-the-road driver with a history of convictions for violent sex-related crimes, including an arrest only the year before for aggravated sodomy on two teenagers he picked up while on the road for another trucker. This time, he picked up a teenage hitchhiker he repeatedly raped and beat, for which crime he received a fifty-year sentence without parole.[3]

The Rhode Island case is different from cases in which the potential for violence exists, yet the principle is the same: The employer has a duty to its other employees, to the public, and to its customers to inquire into the employee's background. The court, applying the doctrine of negligent hiring, held the employer liable when it asserted that the exercise of *reasonable care* means more than accepting the absence of complaints about dishonesty as evidence that the person is honest. But, as you can see, the court's demand for detailed background checks runs up against reference policies of silence or name, rank, and serial number (about which I will have more to say in Chapter 7).

On the other hand, an employer can defend itself against liability even if a preemployment background check discloses various forms of unacceptable behavior. Although the employee was found guilty of a "misdemeanor offense of abusive sexual conduct," the Missouri Court of Appeals decided in favor of the company when the plaintiff charged it with negligent hiring, negligent retention, and negligent supervision. She charged that the company failed to take into account two prior physical assaults: slapping his wife in one case, and fighting with a coworker in the second. According to the plaintiff, those prior assaults should have signaled that he could commit the sexual offenses for which he had been found guilty.

The court ruled:

1. The employee's prior misconduct was not consistent with the behavior with which he was charged; to establish negligent hiring or retention requires that during the background check, the employer found nothing consistent with sexual misconduct. Therefore, there was "no probable cause" to believe he would sexually contact other employees or customers.
2. The employer could not be charged with negligent supervision because the employer could not have reasonably foreseen that the employee would act in this manner.[4]

How Far Does Your Liability Extend if an Employee Commits Murder?

On paper, Rhoda Smith looked like the ideal candidate to provide weekday care for seventy-two-year-old Margie Johnson, an invalid, and her granddaughter, a thirty-year-old quadriplegic. Well-groomed and a graduate of a nursing certificate program in another state (or so she said), Smith had worked for two months at a local nursing home.

Nursing Resources, Inc. (NRI), the contractor, farmed out its jobs to Health Worker Suppliers (HWS), which at that time didn't have enough staff to provide care for Ms. Johnson. Therefore, when Ms. Smith applied for a job, HWS's HR manager called Ms. Smith's immediate past employer, who gave the common name, rank, and dates answer. As a trial, HWS sent her to work with Ms. Johnson; if she didn't work out, HWS could always fire her.

Two weeks later, Ms. Johnson and her granddaughter were found brutally murdered and their jewelry, cash, and other belongings stolen. The police arrested Ms. Smith, who they discovered had six previous felony convictions, including robbery and assault and battery. To add insult to injury, the police investigation revealed that she had never had nursing training.

When the family sued for negligent hiring, NRI's attorneys argued that (1) HWS was the actual employer, and (2) background checks, including checks with regard to criminal convictions, were not standard practice in the industry at that time and the cost of doing them would be too prohibitive.

How sound were the arguments of the company's attorney?

Outsourcing Is No Defense

In the actual case on which this one is based, a Massachusetts jury awarded the family $26.5 million ($8.5 in compensatory damages and $18 million in punitive damages). The jury ruled that outsourcing is no defense to liability when the employer exercises control over the contractor's hiring practices, which was the situation in this case. Likewise, the defendant's claim that the cost of background checks was burdensome fell on deaf ears. When an employer hires or retains a person, it should know if that person is potentially dangerous to other employees or to customers, regardless of whether that danger lurks on or off the job. Rather than appeal, the company identified here as Nursing Resources, Inc., settled with the family. The company identified as Health Worker Suppliers filed for bankruptcy.[5]

Another side to this issue concerns negligent *references* for ex-employees—that is, not disclosing threatening traits or behaviors. If the company had checked references, and if the previous employer knew of but didn't warn the company of Rhoda Smith's dangerous tendencies, the previous employer might be found negligent as well.[*]

Where does your organization stand with regard to background checks, both making them and giving out information, especially for people whose records seem shaky?

Cases

1. 474 A.2d 436 (R.I. Sup. Ct. 1984). See also Richard Gibson, "Pizza Hut Settles Suit After Judge Finds Firms Liable for Employee Hate Crimes," *The Wall Street Journal* (12/29/98, p. B9).
2. 725 S.W.2d, 701 (Tex. Sup. Ct. 1987), *rev'd on remand,* 735 S.W.2d 303.

[*]See Andler, pp. 69–81.

3. 146 Ill. App. 3d 265, 100 Ill. Dec. 21, 496 N.E.2d 1086 (1st Dist. 1986).
4. 2000 WL 1741770 (Mo. App. ED 2000).
5. Suffolk Superior Court (Mass.), No. 94–4297H; settled, 1998; see also similar negligent hiring cases, No. 145PA97 (N.C. Supreme Ct. May 8, 1998); and 655 S.W.2d 568 (Mo. Ct. App. 1983).

Section II
Safe Management Practices

"Scrap the procedures manual," personnel managers have been known to lament. "If someone doesn't follow the procedures to the letter, we wind up in court because the rules form a contract."

It's a case of damned if you do (have a manual), damned if you don't (have one) that depends on (1) how policies are worded, (2) how well managers are trained in implementing the policies, and (3) how well managers apply the policies in which they are trained.

Published policies are often successfully challenged for disparate treatment or for having adverse impact; but if you fail to publish rules, you expose yourself and other managers to lawsuits arising from subjective decision making, from mistreatment of employees, and from employees taking advantage of the absence of rules. Fail to follow published rules when evaluating an employee's performance, and you can produce the same results. Finally, not fulfilling your obligations to protect employees' privacy and reputation or to accommodate women employees or disabled people can cause lawsuits against you as well.

An Overview of Safe Management

When I talk about specific management practices, I must use a fine-tipped brush for painting a portrait of personnel decisions managers legally cannot make, decisions they should not make, and decisions they can make at the risk of winding up in court. Few universal rules govern the demands employees can legally make on employers, and they only loosely apply to specific practices. The courts usually take each case separately and often disagree with each other on the meanings of legal terminology and coverage. Definitions and perceptions, in the vast majority of cases, determine how the courts interpret words or phrases such as *employee, because of sex,* or *disability*.

Management Practices

This section covers those management practices, often governed by organizational policy statements, that most frequently come before the courts:

> Performance evaluation and corrective action
> Invasion of employees' privacy
> Abuse of privileged information
> Defamation
> Sexual discrimination and harassment
> Mismanaging people with disabilities
> Interference with employees' rights to take collective action
> Interference with employees' rights to take time off to care for their families

A manager is exposed to possible legal action on each of those counts unless he or she follows the handful of safe management guidelines spelled out in each chapter. While few universal legal rules apply, four general management rules fit most cases:

1. Respect each employee as an individual having the same rights and privileges to which you believe you are entitled.
2. Treat each employee as a colleague; the organization functions well only to the extent that each person contributes to its success.
3. Recognize that "we" are all in this together; the only "they" are competitors who would prefer that your "we" did not exist.

Golden rules such as these three distinguish safe from unsafe management, but one more rule makes your personnel decisions just a little bit safer:

4. Document all important interactions with employees because not all employees will follow the first three rules, even if you do.

Employee?

It is helpful to first know who an *employee* is. In some cases, you have obligations to employees you do not have to other people; in some cases, you have obligations to all those you engage to work for you, whether or not they are employees.

Several different approaches provide legal definitions of employee versus contractor. Under common law, a person is an employee if he or she "performs services subject to the will and control of an employer, as to both *what* must be done, *how* it must be done," *where, and when;* "the employer has the *legal right* to control both the method and the result of the services." According to the Treasury Department,* an "individual is an independent contractor if . . . the employer [has] the right to control or direct only the result of the work and the means and methods of accomplishing the result" (unless specific agreements dictate special terms); that is, an independent contractor is one with whom the employer makes special arrangements to have a specific job done, usually by a specific deadline, and the contractor then determines the how and where the job is done. However, a *specific agreement* does not make an employee out of a contractor because it affects only the basic contractual relationship itself. To be an employee means to contradict most of the features that characterize a contractor relationship.

Although there is no scientific test, three sets of criteria distinguish between independent contractors and employees: the IRS Checklist, Common Law, and the Economic Test based on federal wage and hour laws. If all or most of the conditions listed are present, the person is classified as an employee, which under the tests of Common Law, includes some temporary employees and most telecommuter workers. If not all the conditions are present, the person is not classified as an employee but rather as an independent contractor. The chart shown here, extrapolated from an Indiana case,[1] and

*Internal Revenue Service No. 937 *Business Reporting: Employment Taxes, Information Returns, 1989.*

borrowed from my self-study,* helps distinguish between employees
and independent contractors.

CHARACTERISTICS OF EMPLOYEES AND CONTRACTORS

Condition A person is an employee if . . .	IRS Checklist	Common Law	Economic Test
He or she complies with employer's rules as to where, when, and how the job is done.	•		•
Employer provides training for work to be done in a specific way.	•		•
Job is integrated into the employer's business and business success depends significantly on job performance.	•		•
The person must render the services personally.	•		
Employer hires, supervises, and pays the person directly.	•		
Employer and person have a continuing relationship even if in irregular intervals.	•	•	•
Employer sets hours of work and person is required to do the job during those hours.	•	•	
The person is expected to devote full-time to the employer and is usually restricted to providing services only to that employer.	•	•	
The work is performed on the employer's premises.	•		
The employer sets schedules and routines to follow.	•		

*See Donald H. Weiss, *Fair, Square, and Legal,* 2nd Edition (New York: American
Management Association, 2004).

The person must submit written or oral reports or other documents (for example, time sheets) on a regular basis.	•		
The person is paid by the hour, the week, or the month.	•	•	
The employer uses the person for tax purposes.		•	
The employer pays the person benefits—for example, health insurance.		•	
The person's business/travel expenses are usually paid by the employer.	•	•	
Tools and materials for doing the job are supplied by the employer.	•		•
The person does not have to invest in the employer's business.	•		
Profit or loss is not solely the direct result of the person's performance.	•		•
Performs services solely for the employer or the employer's agent.	•		
The person's services are available to only one employer at a time and not to the general public.	•		
The employer has the right to terminate the person's services and controls performance under the threat of termination.	•		
The person has the right to terminate the relationship with the employer at any time without incurring liability.	•		

Those distinctions make a difference to a variety of contractual relationships even though they make little or no difference with respect to civil rights legislation, including Title VII of the Civil Rights Act of 1964. These laws blur the distinction between employee and independent contractor; Title VII, for example, uses the phrase *aggrieved person* rather than *employee.* Whether we are talking about race, sex, age, or disability, Title VII is not limited to a situation in which an employee or job applicant is directly tied to the employer.

Until 1983, employers had generally been free under Title VII to choose with whom they contracted, as long as a true independent contractor relationship existed. Now, interfering *in any way* with someone's employment opportunity, whether the person works for the defendant organization *or for anyone else,* violates Title VII.[2]

Changes in the landscape of the workplace are blurring these definitions even more. Temporary employees flood the market, personnel suppliers rent out employees in ever-increasing numbers, and virtual companies employ more and more home-based (or telecommuting) employees.* Under these conditions, where do employer rights and responsibilities begin and end?

The courts will have to make the final determinations, but in December 1997 the EEOC gave us some help. Temporaries, even if they're not directly on the company's payroll under an agency contract, qualify as employees rather than as independent contractors and are therefore protected under federal antidiscrimination laws.†

Fuzzy edges to definitions and distinctions permeate all the cases I cover, which proves that you can take nothing for granted. If you have the mildest doubt about the legality of a personnel decision or if you are under threat of a suit for discrimination, breach of contract, or anything else, consult an attorney.

Cases

1. 593 F. Supp. 6, 32 F.E.P. Cases (BNA) 1107 (N.D. Ind. 1983), *aff'd,* 742 F.2d 1459 (1984).
2. No. 80–431 (9th Cir. Feb. 9, 1983). No. 00–763. June 4, 2001.

---

*See, for example, Carolyn Bower, "Tomorrow's Jobs May Compute, Not Commute," *St. Louis Post-Dispatch* (November 30, 1992), pp. 2A and 12A; see also, Thompson, Brenda B., in *HR Executive Special Reports: Telecommuting, Pluses and Pitfalls* (Brentwood, TN: M. Lee Smith, Publishers LLC, 1999).
†Department of Labor, *Enforcement Guidance on Application of EEO Laws to Contingent Workers Placed by Temporary Employment Agencies and Other Staffing Firms* (December 9, 1997). Available by writing to EEOC's Office of Communications and Legislative Affairs, 1801 L St., N. W. Washington, D.C. 20507. See also Linda Micco, "EEOC Issues Guidance on Temps and Discrimination," *HR News* (January 1998), p. 21.

6

Safe Evaluations and Promotions

No law says you must give employees performance evaluations. If you do not publish a promise of performance evaluations, you do not have a contractual obligation. In the absence of a contract, you may or may not evaluate employee performance at your discretion. In the words of more than one court, an employee does not have an inherent right to a performance appraisal.[1, 2]

On the other hand, if you do not have officially sanctioned and written procedures, your appraisal and promotion systems are open to challenge because they will probably be subjectively administered. Your organization's published policies and procedures with regard to performance appraisal and the execution of a system based on those policies can, in some cases, constitute an implied contract. Because a court could narrowly construe that the policy manual contains a promise to conduct performance appraisals in a prescribed manner and at prescribed times, the organization could be held accountable should you or some other manager not follow the prescriptions or not follow them properly; and they, in and of themselves, could have a disparate impact. Therefore, you should assess your organization's published evaluation procedures or promotion-from-within policy on the basis of what I say about those procedures.

In the sections that follow, I will concentrate on four ways that performance evaluations can be used to discriminate against employees and on ways to prevent a court challenge or to defend yourself if challenged.

What You Cannot Do

Among the many managerial abuses of performance evaluations, five have important legal implications: (1) using subjective criteria to produce a disparate impact on minorities and other protected groups; (2) using a promotion-from-within policy to discriminate against minorities and other protected groups; (3) misusing objective records to discriminate; (4) "building a file," that is, writing up your documentation after the fact; and (5) using a performance appraisal to retaliate for some perceived harm, such as filing an EEOC complaint.

Using Subjective Criteria

Subjective rating systems in themselves are not illegal. The EEOC and the courts recognize subjective job standards (such as communication and leadership skills) and that the words *good, satisfactory, poor,* and *unsatisfactory* carry within themselves subjective elements. So where do they draw the line?

1. When standards are unequally applied or do not exist at all; and
2. When someone shows that the standards or their absence produces disparate treatment in promotion and compensation policies and practices, as, for example:
   › When sex stereotyping tainted the process by which a woman was denied a partnership in a Big Eight accounting firm[3, 4]
   › When subjective decision making torpedoed promotion policies that have disparate impact on minorities[5]

EEOC and court rulings encourage objective performance appraisals, but they discourage using them as a subterfuge for discrimination.

Especially since 9/11/01, supervisors should not have sole discretion over rating decisions inasmuch as management biases against people with specific, usually Middle Eastern, backgrounds have increased significantly, according to the EEOC. Failing to set objective rating standards and to provide adequate training on how to interpret those standards can diminish the fairness of the appraisal system. Inadequate application of evaluations can produce a system that is in and of itself discriminatory and has disparate impact on minorities and other groups.[6-8]

Promotion from Within

Internal promotion systems, although not necessarily in themselves discriminatory, can be misapplied, as in the case of "tracking" employees by hiring minorities or women into certain jobs—for example, janitorial or secretarial—that prevent them from succeeding into higher-level positions. Safeguards built into a system, such as open posting and career planning, can prevent it from being used to discriminate. At the same time, lessons learned from the well-known Texaco racial bias settlements should send a strong message to all companies. Policies and actions should match; it is not sufficient to say merely that "we promote from within regardless of race, gender, age, disabilities, etc."; this must be followed by positive action. In the Texaco case, executives' negative biases against African Americans (whom they called "black jelly beans"), discussed and recorded on audiotape, undermined policies and diversity training, with repercussions spilling out for nearly a year.*

You can help your organization assess the health of its promotion policies by suggesting that a statistician check the organization's *internal* labor market; by yourself, you can do little to identify situations such as these we are describing. Even if the number of minorities or other protected group members in your workforce matches the available and qualified people in the population at large, if your internal market exhibits a disproportionate number of white males in high-level positions or in promotable roles relative to non-majority employees, the system could be blocking protected group members from advancing. That blockage is in itself inherently discriminatory.[8]

Misusing Objective Records

The EEOC and the courts approve the proper use of objective records. Conversely, they frown upon the misuse or selective use of those records.

---

*Among the multitude of articles, op-ed pieces, and Internet reports after the stories began making major headlines in November, 1996, I recommend *The New York Times* and *The Wall Street Journal* for comprehensive and easy-to-comprehend background (for example, "Texaco to Pay $17.1 Million in Bias Suit" and "Texaco's Board Takes Limited Role in Handling Race-Discrimination Case," *The Wall Street Journal* (No-

Attendance records, wasted materials reports, and disciplinary action reports make for good documentation in an appraisal system. If those records document unacceptable behavior or performance on the part of both white and minority groups, then tolerating it from one group of employees but not accepting the same or similar behavior or performance from the other could constitute discrimination, especially if you rate down or discharge protected group members and not majority group employees with equally abhorrent records.[9]

Retroactive Documentation

Producing documentation *after* making the decision to demote or to fire someone is in itself illegal. In addition, entering into a file every trivial thing that happens after a charge of discrimination has been brought against you can be seen as retaliation and harassment.[10] Documentation of poor performance or misconduct must be filed at the time the alleged events occurred, and the employee should be notified of that action, or you face the potential of being charged with "building a file."

Retaliation

What do you think a court might think if a previously highly rated employee files a complaint against a supervisor and is subsequently given a bad performance review? Courts have little patience with that form of retaliation. You need to be prepared to protect yourself if an employee has engaged in a protected activity, such as opposing discrimination or objecting to actions contrary to public policy. Any management decision or management behavior, some form of punishment, that can be reasonably construed as an adverse action will probably land you in court. All a court needs to see is a *possible* causal link between the employee's protected activity and the adverse action, and the burden of proof shifts from the employee to you.[15]

vember 18, 1996), p. A3; see also Allanna Sullivan, "Three Law Firms Are Awarded Fees for Texaco Case" *The Wall Street Journal* (August 4, 1997), p. 2; Bloomberg News Service, "Ex-Exec Sues Texaco for Libel" (August 13, 1997).

What You Can Do

Insofar as performance appraisals are essential management tools, steps should be taken to protect them from court challenges.

Utilizing Legally Defensible Performance Appraisal Systems

Performance appraisal systems make good management sense, and a well-designed and judiciously implemented system does not impose a hardship on employees; it is often seen by employees as a tool that helps them to succeed. Courts have ruled that criticizing an employee's job performance does not constitute the infliction of emotional distress as long as the criticism meets the following four legal standards:

1. The criticism is not extreme and outrageous.
2. The criticism is not intentionally reckless.
3. The criticism is not intended to cause emotional distress.
4. The distress the criticized employee feels is not severe.

"Extreme and outrageous conduct" refers to conduct any reasonable person would say exceeds the limits of socially acceptable employer practices. The complaint of severe mental and emotional harm often accompanies this charge and, in some cases, actually defines the outrageous conduct.[11]

Because any system, no matter how well designed or implemented, is always open to challenge, you should consider whether or not your organization's approach is legally defensible. AMACOM has published a number of good books that you can use as research materials. Here I look only at characteristics of a good system to help you evaluate your own system.

Defining Performance Appraisal

The goal or purpose of the appraisal determines the system's value, so that you can:

> Evaluate an employee's performance at a given moment—for example, at this time
> Evaluate an employee's performance over a given and identifiable period of time—for example, during the past year

A performance evaluation at a given moment should correct a performance problem or consist of the kinds of judgments supervisors most frequently make on a daily basis. It might also commend the employee for an accomplishment. The appraisal, usually unwritten and informal, is the kind of evaluation that can get a supervisor into the greatest amount of trouble because it is often undocumented.

An employee's performance should be well documented throughout the rating period. The lack of documentation weakens a system because formal appraisals, the annual kind that many companies require, live or die on the basis of the documentation that supports them. Subjective judgments infiltrate the system when supervisors rely on their memory for rating a performance or writing the narrative about the employee's behavior on the job, frequently producing one of two possible scenarios that can make a shambles of the evaluation process: the "halo effect" (responding to the best employee behavior or performance, which often shows up just before evaluation time) or "demon's jaws" (being bitten by the worst employee behavior or performance, which might only occur once in a while or shortly before evaluation time but which leaves a lasting negative impression).

The annual appraisal is sometimes used to correct specific shortcomings, but by the end of the year it is too late, and so it probably should not be used that way. It should be used, first of all, to point out how well employees met their job standards during the rating period. Second, it should be used to help employees identify the areas still in need of correction. Overall, it should be used to further employees' career opportunities. To do that, the evaluation should be based on objective or measurable or achievable goals and standards.

Measuring Against Goals and Standards

A job description should drive the appraisal process or you have nothing against which to measure performance. A meaningful job description should begin by identifying the purpose for the job's existence: for example, "to generate so much income," "to process so many applications," or "to make this many pieces." If an activity's goal does not contribute to the organization's business goals, the activity should not exist.

The job's criteria—experience or skills needed to do the job—should be related to the goal. The job's standards should be the measures by which an employee's performance relative to the goals is judged. Written, clearly stated, job-related standards, communicated to the employee at the start of the rating period, should be the *only* basis on which performance is judged. If an employee does not know or understand what the goals and standards of the job are, he or she cannot be held accountable for the job's outcomes.

Most project-oriented or management positions are described by objectives, making management by objectives more or less a necessity. In a project-oriented job, the employee performs a series of tasks that have a clear beginning and a clear end. A computer programmer, for example, works on a series of projects, often several different projects at the same time. The job standards usually include something like "Completes Assigned Projects on Time" rather than "Quantity of Work." Completing assigned projects is the objective by which performance is judged.

Managers are often responsible for their work group's success, for example, at meeting production goals, as well as for a quantity of work they personally produce. If the group meets its production goals, we say the manager did well. If it exceeds the goals, we say the manager did very well, unless, of course, the group met or exceeded its goals in spite of the manager's lack of leadership or some other downgrading factor.

One value of a written job description that includes performance standards as well as duties and responsibilities is that it prevents hidden (implicit), often subjective standards that infect evaluations. Companies that have *successfully* defended themselves against charges of illegal performance appraisal systems or abuse of those systems have had, among other things, clearly stated, job-related performance standards on which appraisals were based, and performance problems related to those standards were clearly *docu-*

mented on appraisal forms.* Standards and documentation are the two legal protections of appraisal systems.

Documentation

No one style of appraisal works in all cases. Whatever the style, there should be a direct link between the job's criteria and standards and the tools used to measure performance. The items evaluated either should contribute to successful performance or should not be included; for example, the category "Quantity of Work" applies to a production-oriented job but not well to a job that is project-oriented. And how do you evaluate a computer operator working alone on the night shift on the category "Works Well with Others"?

Several methods of evaluation contribute to the documentation of a person's job performance:

› *Rating Scales.* The most familiar and widely used system rates factors such as quality and quantity of work, attendance, leadership abilities, and so forth on the basis of a scoring system, usually 1 to 5 (where 5 is the highest score possible). Some systems double-weight production activities in order to fairly evaluate job-related factors (for example, quantity of work) against behavior (for example, attendance). Some employees can be absent for one valid reason or another more frequently than others can and still produce better than employees who never miss a day.

Rating scales, by themselves no more than report cards fraught with subjective considerations and personal biases, have little merit. A short narrative based on critical or significant incidents that you record in a performance file strengthens a rating scale system.

› *Narratives.* Describe what a person did and how well or poorly he or she did it and explain the reason why he or she received the rating. As long as the narrative is not on its face pretextual, it will almost always hold up in court.

Under "Quantity," for example, you could write: "The standard for this job is fifty widgets a year, with less than 5 percent waste.

*See David C. Martin, et al, "The Legal Ramifications of Performance Appraisal," *Employee Relations Law Journal*, Vol. 12, cited in Edmund J. Metz, "Designing Legally Defensible Performance Appraisal Systems," *Training and Development Journal* (July, 1988), p. 48.

Josephine produced forty-eight widgets with 4.5 percent waste. That is why I rated her performance 3.5."

› *Performance Files.* One way to guarantee that your narrative is objective, unbiased, accurate, and comprehensive is to keep a file of critical or significant incidents, a file into which you enter records or memos that reflect important events during the whole of the rating period. These reports describe positive or commendable incidents as well as incidents involving corrective measures.

A short memo may be all you need.

> "Yesterday Josephine realized that she was wasting time and effort by moving from her workstation to the supply closet every time she began making a new widget. Therefore, when she arrived this morning, she decided to move all the supplies she needed for the day to her workstation."

You might need a longer memo for something more important.

> "Today Josephine broke the third bit on her machine since beginning her new job. She has been shown repeatedly how to apply the proper amount of pressure, but she has not gotten it right yet. Since one important criterion of the job is the ability to use that equipment properly, she is not showing that she can do the job. I told her that unless she stops breaking the bit on the machine, she will have to return to her old job if it is still available. Otherwise, we may have to find another, lower-paying job for her or discharge her."

The incident in the example was serious enough to warrant a warning. Any incident that serious should be recognized not only with the supervisor's signature but with the employee's as well.

> I acknowledge reading this warning and understanding the consequences of not meeting the standards of the job.

That signed acknowledgment, as important as the documentation itself, could save you grief later because an employee cannot say he or she never had the problem brought to his or her attention.

The performance file ensures that you rate the employee's performance for the entire period, not just for the last few days of it. The accuracy and completeness of the appraisal depend on your ability to recall what the person did in the beginning of the period, how well he or she performed in the middle of it, and what happened as the period neared its end. Improvements in performance can affect a rating. Deterioration can be spotted early and corrective measures taken before things get out of hand. There should be no surprises during a year-end evaluation interview, and the performance file prevents surprises from happening.

Your organization has to keep other employee personnel files also, but they can be used against you even if they were put together by other supervisors several years prior to the present circumstances. Federal courts have found that supervisors can deliberately place an inaccurate, discriminatory evaluation in an employee's file with the intent to harm the employee. That record then follows the employee and adversely affects his or her future opportunities or conditions of employment or compensation.[10]

Therefore, you should give employees the opportunity to review their evaluation files and rebut them, if they believe rebuttal is necessary. They then should be required to sign a statement indicating they have reviewed their files, a procedure that by itself can prevent many frivolous lawsuits.

› *Performance Evaluation Interview.* You should have a written appraisal to share with your employees, but you should set aside ample time to discuss appraisals with the employees as well. It will not do to give an employee a document and say, "Read this, and if you have any questions or complaints, come see me." The employee may go see an attorney instead.

› *Audit systems.* A defensible appraisal program should have a built-in method of checking out an evaluation's validity. Working closely with your boss when evaluating another person's performance and having him or her review your appraisals to prevent your personal biases or some unusually bad or good feelings from coloring your appraisals could save you a great deal of embarrassment later. However, only you and other people who have worked closely with the employee being appraised can accurately assess the employee's performance; do not let your boss push you into decisions that you cannot support or that could land you in court.

Some companies use other forms of checks and balances: peer reviews, reciprocal reviews, or a grievance system.

In a peer review, employees contribute to one another's assessments. This could give you insights into employee performance to which you may not have access.

A reciprocal review provides employees with an opportunity to give feedback to their supervisors about how *they* perform *their* jobs, thereby balancing the review process. It is very difficult for an employee to charge an employer with discrimination or unfair business practices when he or she is given a chance to answer any complaints you make with complaints about you. On the other hand, you must be on guard against resenting an employee's review and retaliating.

None of these alternatives is required, especially not a grievance procedure, but check the law in your state. Some states' courts construe a published procedure as an enforceable employment contract (for example, Nebraska),[12] while others do not (for example, Florida).[13]

Personnel Decisions Based on Evaluations

You should make your personnel decisions—pay raises, bonuses, job assignments, and promotions—on the basis of your evaluations. Any other method could cause you to wind up in court for bias or discrimination or for breach of contract. In fact, if your organization permits it, major decisions such as pay raises, bonuses, and promotions should be made by a review board that uses your performance evaluations as one of several tools by which the decisions are made. If your organization does not have such a system, you might suggest taking a look at one.

One way to protect your promotion-from-within policy is to adopt a work measurement system that you can demonstrate is unbiased: standards that any well-trained, experienced employee can meet without undue fatigue. Promotion policies based on the same objective standards that govern evaluation and appraisal procedures protect against disparate treatment or adverse impact. The Eleventh Circuit Court, in 1985, accepted a process similar to the one that follows, which can help prevent subjectivity from tainting your pro-motion process.[14]

1. Establish objective or measurable job criteria (minimum ex-perience or skill requirements) for each position available.
2. Decide which applicants for a promotion satisfy the job crite-ria by reviewing the applicants' files—for example, written applications or performance appraisals. Set aside as unquali-fied applications that do not meet those minimum require-ments.
3. Under the supervision of a personnel officer, have a panel of employees familiar with the job's technical criteria examine qualified applicants' files, interview each applicant, and rate each one on a numerical scale of 1 to 4, with 4 denoting the best qualified and 1 the least.
4. Ask the panel to reconcile the differences in the ratings until a consensus is reached.
5. Have the panel issue a written report on why they rated the applicants the way they did.
6. Have the personnel officer identify applicants with ratings of 3.0 or better for further consideration.
7. Have the manager who must make the final decision or his or her advisory committee interview the certified applicants (who do not know, yet, how they were ranked).
8. Make and implement the final decision.

This process may seem complicated or cumbersome (especially for a small organization), but it or some variation of it could prevent a more complicated or cumbersome and expensive day in court.

Any management procedure is open to challenge, even the eval-uation process I just outlined. However, some systems, or the man-ner in which they are applied, are more defensible than others.

Conclusion

Every organization should satisfy a minimum level of sophistication in its performance system. It should have:

› Up-to-date, written, clear job or position descriptions that have been given to each employee at the start of the employee's tenure in a given job or position
› Job standards communicated clearly to each employee at the start of each rating period, with a written acknowledgment by the employees that they understand their own job standards[16]
› Training for supervisors on how to evaluate employee performance and how to administer the organization's appraisal system
› Performance feedback, both informally on a daily basis and during a formal appraisal interview at least once a year
› A review audit system to prevent bias or feelings from infiltrating the system
› Performance coaching and counseling systems administered by managers trained to give effective feedback and coaching or counseling
› Documentation through performance files, job-related testing, rating systems, appraisal forms, signed memoranda, and so on
› Written policy statements approving only a specified procedure for conducting appraisals

If any one of these components is missing from your organization's performance appraisal system, you and the organization could be asking for trouble.

CASEBOOK

The recommendations in this chapter follow from numerous actual cases, only a few of which can be covered in this Casebook. Use these cases to test your ability to recognize the legal problems in them and to compare the situations with possible problems in your own workplace.

Can Your Performance Evaluation System Be Illegal?

Jorge Gonzales, an installer, had worked for Independent Electric for four years, during which time he had never received a reprimand or complaint about his work. Yet, in several performance reviews, one or another factor was rated as "needs improvement," which was defined as "performance somewhat below the supervisor's expectations." The ratings were given without comment.

Because the promotion system hinged on the performance appraisal, which in this case meant that an employee's promotion depended on the supervisor's personal evaluation of the installer's work, Jorge felt that his Anglo supervisor was intentionally discriminating against him, holding Jorge back from promotion by his evaluations. An attorney for Jorge and several other Hispanic and black employees argued that the company's promotion system, in and of itself, had a disparate impact on minorities.

The company's attorney, in turn, defended Independent Electric's affirmative action program and minority representation. The company had hired and trained minorities in proportion to the workforce available in the community.

What is the principal method of evaluating employees in your organization? Objective standards based on goals and objectives, a rating scale, a supervisor's narrative? Judge your system with an eye to the district court's decision in this case.

Supervisor's Discretion Not Enough

The district court in Texas found that the supervisors had sole discretion over rating decisions. The company failed to set objective rating standards, and the criteria varied from supervisor to supervisor, none of whom had sufficient training for setting standards. In effect, the court concluded, supervisor evaluations were based entirely on subjective perceptions of skills. Those inadequacies made the utility's promotion system, in and of itself, discriminatory because it had a disparate impact on minorities.[6, 7] The U.S. Supreme Court, in 1988, reinforced the disparate impact analysis of subjective criteria.[5] As I cautioned earlier, take care to protect your own system or the appraisals you produce by creating a set of objective standards by which anyone performing a specific job can be evaluated.

Can Your Promotion-From-Within Policy Be Discriminatory?

When First National Bank defended itself against a class-action suit challenging its promotion policies, it argued that it had hired black people in proportion to their representation in the general population within the particular geographic area. Blacks, the bank showed, were hired at all levels within its organization on balance with their representation in similar skill levels in the community.

The challengers showed, on the other hand, that more than 75 percent of the above-entry-level positions and 50 percent of the highest-level managerial and technical positions were filled through a promotion-from-within policy. Even though the bank hired some minorities into higher-level positions, they did not promote them from entry-level positions with the same or similar frequency with which they promoted white males.

How does your organization operate with respect to promotions? Do you hire from without, promote from within, or use a different procedure? Are minorities or women hired into positions that block them from the promotion-from-within system itself? For example, hiring black people into only maintenance positions is tantamount to blocking them from the succession into technical, professional, or management positions.

Legitimate Business Interests

A promotion-from-within policy can foster legitimate business interests by creating a stable workforce, the Eighth Circuit Court declared. The policy usually encourages loyalty and productivity when employees can expect to move up within an organization and not constantly have to compete against outside hires. Therefore, the policy is not in itself discriminatory.

However, an examination of this organization's *internal* labor market and the statistical evidence indicated that black employees had not been promoted sufficiently in comparison to whites; the evidence created an inference of discrimination. The relationship between employees and external populations, the bank's defense, was misleading.[8]

This case demonstrates that the best defense is to ensure that minorities and women have equal access to the system and are well distributed throughout the technical, professional, and management

ranks of the organization via both the external and the internal promotion processes.

When Can Diversity Policies Create Problems?

Sally Sax, white, and Ranita Brown, African American, had been hired
at the same time by the same school district. They had comparable
credentials, taught in the same school, and had earned essentially
the same high regard from administrators, peers, and students (as
reflected in their performance evaluations). When it came time to
downsize, the school district decided to promote its diversity policies
by retaining Ranita Brown and letting Sally Sax go.

After several years and three appeals, Sally Sax's reverse discrimination case finally made its way to the Supreme Court. Sax argued
that the school district illegally gave Brown preferential treatment and
discriminated against her, Sax, in order to promote its diversity policies. She claimed that the retention or promotion decisions should
be made only on the basis of merit, and the lower courts (including
the Third U.S. Circuit Court of Appeals) agreed with her, saying that
Title VII of the Civil Rights Act of 1964 prohibits any race-conscious
decision making if it is not taken to remedy past discrimination.

The U.S. Justice Department became involved along the way.

If you were in charge of this case for the Justice Department,
how would you decide? Support Brown or support Sax?

Whom to Support? It's Up to You to
Decide for Yourself

In the actual case on which this story is based, known as *Piscataway
v. Taxman* [No. 94-5090/5112 (3rd Cir. Ct. August 8, 1996)], the Justice Department wavered back and forth between supporting Taxman (the white teacher) and not supporting her. Contrary to the
common wisdom, the U.S. government doesn't always back minorities in a confrontation. The Justice Department wanted the Supreme
Court to decide the issue, but, unfortunately for us all, the parties

settled before the Supreme Court could rule, leaving us with no clear resolution of the matter called *reverse discrimination.**

When Is Affirmative Action Illegal?

Too few African Americans had been promoted from the ranks of the city's police department. In 1993, only two of the twenty black sergeants taking the test for promotion to lieutenant were among the thirty-seven who made the upper 50 percent of the test scores. Only two of the twenty-five black lieutenants taking the captain's test finished in the top 50 percent. To rectify the situation, the department's administration discarded the 50 percent cutoff rule—much to the dismay of the leaders of several police organizations and the chief of police (himself an African American). Ten white officers immediately filed complaints with the EEOC (and five more joined them later).

"What could be wrong with this?" the police department administration wanted to know. It promoted the department's affirmative action program, and besides, written exams may discriminate against black officers who "do better in other areas of the [promotion] process."

How do you answer these officials? Is this procedure wrong?

"Race Norming"

Before 1991, the EEOC would have agreed with the police department administration, but now it sided with the white officers and told the police department to settle or be sued for civil rights violations. Eliminating the cutoff violated the "race norming" provisions of the Civil Rights Act of 1991. The police department rescinded

*See Associated Press, "High Court to Hear Reverse-Bias Case," *St. Louis Post-Dispatch,* June 5, 1997, 1A, and the Associated Press Online, "High Court to Hear Reverse Bias Case," June 28, 1997, p. B8; the Associated Press, "Administration May Join Affirmative Action Case," *St. Louis Post-Dispatch,* October 4, 1997, p. A4; the Associated Press, "Civil Rights Groups Help Fund Settlement for Reverse Discrimination Case," *St. Louis Post-Dispatch,* November 22, 1997, p. 3A; Eva Rodriguez, "Rights Group's Settlement Settles Little," *The Wall Street Journal,* November 24, 1997, p. A3.

its policy almost immediately and is now looking for new ways of sustaining its affirmative action pledges.

The whole issue of affirmative action has come into question, from the workplace to the schoolroom, and the Supreme Court has ruled on yet another university admissions policy in which it decided that considering race as a factor in admissions is acceptable as long as it is only one factor among many others; numerically weighting applications on the basis of race, however, is wrong.[17] "Many whites are resentful and blacks feel affirmative action has stalled," said a 1991 article in *Business Week.** Where you stand on the matter may depend, after all, on what you have to gain from creating or sustaining a culturally diverse workforce. From a general management point of view, it still makes good, safe business sense to promote the diversity that will make your business successful in years to come.

How Can Objective Records Be the Source of Discrimination?

Fred Jackson had an abysmal attendance record: 101 unexcused absences and one suspension in 1977, 114 unexcused absences and three suspensions in 1978, and 32 additional unexcused absences in the year he was fired (1979). The brewery management was therefore dumbstruck when they had to defend themselves in court against a charge of discrimination, under Section 1981 of the Civil Rights Act of 1866, for firing the black man on account of his race.

Jackson argued that he was fired even though white employees with comparably bad absentee records at the time of his termination were not. For example, one white employee had 98 unexcused absences and one suspension in 1977, 44 unexcused absences and one suspension in 1978, 43 unexcused absences in 1979 (the year Jackson was fired), and 51 unexcused absences in 1980, after which the white employee was suspended and subsequently fired. The evidence, Jackson claimed, pointed to discrimination on the basis of race.

For how long would you or your organization tolerate unexcused absences or tardiness? Among several delinquent employees, whom would you fire first, and why?

*Howard Gleckman, et al., "Race in the Workplace: Is Affirmative Action Working," *Business Week*, July 8, 1991, pp. 50–63.

Sheer Numbers

Excessive absenteeism and tardiness create scheduling problems, damage employee morale, and affect productivity. No court would challenge that claim. What the Eighth Circuit Court in this old (1984) but relevant case did challenge was the lack of evenhandedness in the manner in which the firing decisions were made.

Although the black employee had the worst possible record and more total unexcused absences than did the most comparable white employee, the court, in a two-to-one decision, held that the plaintiff was indeed fired because of his race. The jury's award of $125,000 in damages (including damages for mental and emotional distress) was affirmed against the employer.[9]

Why? Because firing the worst offender may not necessarily be the best course of action. Tolerating flagrantly bad behavior (the unexcused absences) was in itself poor management. Firing the black employee but not firing white employees with comparably bad records *at the same time* indicated that management was more tolerant of white employees with bad attendance records than it was of black employees: evidence of disparate treatment.

To avoid or to be prepared for litigation, your organization should publish written standards of conduct and procedures for taking disciplinary action. Supervisors should be trained in how to apply disciplinary procedures equally. All complaints of misconduct should be handled the same way for anyone against whom a complaint is raised. Incidents and any corrective or disciplinary actions should be documented *at the time they occur,* and the employees should acknowledge by their signatures that they understand the action taken.

When Is Documentation Not Legal?

Cynthia Katz believed that the only reason she had not been promoted during the years she worked for the company was that she was a woman. Less-qualified male employees received all the great assignments and subsequently all the great promotions, too, she believed. So she filed a sex discrimination suit with the EEOC, after which a manager ordered her supervisor to document in her personnel file all unusual incidents involving Cynthia.

Before she brought the unlawful sex discrimination charge against the company, Cynthia's file contained only a few complimentary letters. Within two years after she brought the charge, the file contained approximately one hundred discipline slips, including reports of trivial, petty, and insignificant incidents that were never written up against other employees. For this, Cynthia filed suit in federal court for unlawful sexual harassment.

How do you document employee misdeeds? Do you wait until you have reason to discharge him or her before writing up your case? Or do you keep an ongoing record of all reports, good or bad? Would you build a file after an employee registered a complaint with the EEOC?

Building a File

Whether discrimination charges are brought against you or not, building a file after a decision to take corrective action or to fire someone has been made is in itself an illegal act. When discrimination charges are involved, building a file, such as the one built against Cynthia, can be judged retaliatory and harassing.[14] This case should underscore the need for giving careful thought to writing up an employee's misdeeds.

Whether the issue is performance deficiencies or behavior problems, an employee evaluation should be based on the employee's actual performance or behavioral history, which is the only fair and evenhanded basis on which an evaluation system can work to your and your employees' benefit. The courts will also probably rule on your behalf if the files you keep are current rather than after the fact.

Cases

1. 502 F. Supp. 876, 116 L.R.R.M. (BNA) 2047 (N.D. Ill. 1984), *aff'd,* 795 F.2d 39 (1986).
2. 65 N.Y. 2d 724, 492 N.Y.S.2d 9, 119 L.R.R.M. (BNA) 3415 (N.Y. Ct. App. 1985).
3. 825 F.2d 458, 263, 44 F.E.P. Cases 825 (D.C. Cir. 1987).
4. No. 87–1167 (1989).
5. 56 U.S.L.W. 4922 (1988).

6. 30 F.P.D. (CCH) 33,078 (D.C. Tex. 1982).
7. 694 F.2d 1146, 30 F.E.P. Cases (BNA) 703 (9th Cir. 1982).
8. 688 F.2d 552, 29 F.E.P. Cases (BNA) 1233 (8th Cir. 1982), *cert. denied,* 103 S. Ct. 1772 (1983).
9. 728 F.2d 989, 34 F.E.P. Cases (BNA) 93 (8th Cir. 1984).
10. 682 F.2d 971, 20 F.E.P. Cases (BNA) 85 (D.C. Cir. 1982), *cert. denied,* 103 S. Ct. 1427 (1983).
11. 330 N.W.2d 428, 31 F.E.P. Cases (BNA) 139 (Minn. Sup. Ct., 1983), superseded by statute, 392 N.W.2d 670 (Minn. Ct. App. 1986).
12. 215 Neb. 677, 340 N.W.2d 388 (1983).
13. 727 F.2d 1075, 115 L.R.R.M. (BNA) 3452 (11th Cir. 1984).
14. 764 F.2d 1539, 38 F.E.P. Cases (BNA) (11th Cir. 1985).
15. See, for example, NJ App Ct, No. A-856–56–96T2, 1998.
16. See how a company can protect itself in 8th Cir. Crt, No. 97–3340, 1998.
17. U.S. Supreme Court No. 02–241 (June 23, 2003).

7

Safe Management, the Right to Privacy, and Defamation

The U.S. Constitution clearly protects everyone from government invasions into their private lives. In addition, various statutes and case laws regarding defamation protect a person's right to defend his or her personal and professional reputations as well as his or her right to privacy. Let's look at some relevant laws and key definitions before considering what you can and cannot do.

Privacy and Constitutional Guarantees

Because privacy cases involve mainly constitutional issues, and the Constitution is written to limit the powers of government, our examples deal largely with government agencies that have appeared in federal courts. Nevertheless, these cases help to identify what *any* manager should consider with respect to employees' privacy, especially because several federal and state laws limit the rights of all employers, as in the cases of polygraph and drug testing. Such laws could become forerunners of statutes that protect employees' rights against private employer invasion of privacy.

What the Laws Say

First, let's look at brief summaries of the five amendments to the Constitution that form the basis for most privacy claims:

First Amendment:	Governments are prohibited from interfering with the free exercise of religion or speech.
Fourth Amendment:	Governments are prohibited from unreasonable search and seizure of a person, or of his or her home, papers, and effects; prohibitions against illegal search and seizure include prying into a person's personal and intimate life.
Fifth Amendment:	The due process of law shall be applied to any attempt to deprive a person of life, liberty, or property, and no person may be required to incriminate or to be a witness against him- or herself.
Ninth Amendment:	Listing only specific rights in the Constitution: It is not to be construed as denying other rights reserved to the people.
Fourteenth Amendment:	Section 1 of the amendment gives equal rights to all natural or naturalized citizens.

The First, Fourth, and Fifth Amendments are most frequently invoked in privacy cases. First Amendment rights have been extended to cover the off-duty sexual activities of a police department clerk who was turned down as a cadet in the police academy.[1] Fifth and Fourteenth Amendment rights were used to prevent a city in Michigan from "arbitrarily and capriciously" discharging a married male police officer who was having relations with a married woman other than his wife.[2] The Ninth and Fourteenth Amendments sometimes show up in privacy cases, but they are invoked more frequently in civil rights cases than in privacy cases.

The safe management questions raised here concern balancing an employer's *right to know* against the employees' *right to privacy*. For example:

› Can you test for the HIV antibody associated with AIDS?
› Can you test for drugs?
› Can you test for honesty with a polygraph test?

The answers? Well, it depends. It depends on the circumstances or on the conditions dictated by law or by court decisions.

Privileged Information and Defamation

Most people consider their personnel files (including credit or background checks), medical records, and performance evaluations to be private and confidential. Employer rights and employee rights often clash over how that information is used or how it is published. And, at times, in the effort to protect certain employee information, an employer's obligation to preserve employee privacy clashes with the public's right to know, or other employees' or employers' right or duty to know. Reference checks, reports to a workers' compensation commission, performance evaluations, medical records, explaining to other employees why someone was fired—all can give rise to allegations of defamation. So managers are confronted with another legal maze through which they must find their way. Here are more definitions of key terms and a brief review of other relevant laws:

privilege   The right or need to know certain types of information. That right is usually qualified or conditional, limited to the immediate and legitimate concerns or interests of the parties involved. Not everyone has a right or need to know everything about anyone.

    However, some government agencies, such as the Internal Revenue Service, possess *absolute* privilege. They cannot be sued for publishing or soliciting information about people. This application of privilege, coupled with the Freedom of Information Act (discussed later in this list), could possibly make a person's financial life an open book.

defamation   Communicating to anyone who does *not* have the right or need to know private information that *could* cause injury to the person's personal or professional reputation. A person could feel injured—slandered or libeled—even if what you say or write is true.

slander   Oral publication of a defamatory statement.

libel   Written publication of a defamatory statement.

with malice   Deliberately publishing information that you know will harm the person in some way, especially if the information is false or if you recklessly disregard the truth.

access laws   State statutes that require employers to allow employees access to their personnel files. Connecticut, for example, requires access at least twice a year and allows employees to copy the files.

Some states' courts have construed published policies regarding access to personnel records as contracts; employers with published policies are obligated to allow employees access to their files. In states without right-of-access laws, employers may deny employees the right to inspect their own personnel records.

The Privacy Act of 1983   The law requiring federal employers everywhere to maintain a system of records and permit employees access to their own files on request, regardless of the legal status of records in the agency's locale. On the other hand, the Act restricts disclosure of information to anyone without the employee's consent.

The Freedom of Information Act   This law, its privacy provisions notwithstanding, allows third parties access to federal government information that might otherwise be considered confidential, which includes employee job performance.[3]

The issue here comes down to how to maintain and safeguard private personnel information. Your perception of what you need to know from within a personnel file can come into conflict with the right of employees to maintain the privacy of personal information.

What You Cannot Do

Let's look at invasion of privacy before discussing defamation.

Invasion of Privacy

If you manage a government agency or government-funded agency or a work unit within such an agency, you cannot take your perceived prerogatives for granted. Testing for the HIV virus associated with AIDS or testing for drug use, searching the office of an employee you suspect of *on-the-job* misconduct or disciplining an employee for what you think is misconduct outside the workplace, or using a lie detector for screening applicants for their honesty would seem to be legal. But in each of these matters, the courts have expressed serious reservations about employers' rights relative to the Fourth Amendment's protections against unreasonable search.

What a person does in his or her home is a private matter; when it comes to medical or drug screening, a person's body and body fluids are at least as private as his or her home. How you investigate a wrongdoing is governed by laws protecting due process and privacy, and lie detector testing, in most cases, is just flatly illegal. Let's take the issues one at a time.

> *Mandatory Medical Screenings.* The federal and some state courts have accepted the available medical evidence that transmitting the AIDS virus through casual contact in a workplace is, statistically, hardly possible. *Fear* of transmission is insufficient grounds for violating the Constitution. They have rejected *mandatory* medical screenings unless strong business reasons exist to require them—for example, testing restaurant employees who authorities suspect may have been the source of typhoid.[4]

> *Testing for Drugs.* Unless an employee is involved in an accident or has given someone sufficient cause to suspect him or her of wrongdoing, you have slim grounds for testing. The U.S. Department of Transportation and the courts, although restricting legal mandatory, random testing to jobs involving public safety, such as air traffic control or driving a train, or involving great hazards or government secrets, have widened the scope of permissible testing.[5] As a general rule, sufficient and reasonable suspicion of wrongdoing is the legal standard recognized by the courts. The same principle supports prohibitions against firing someone for failing a drug test. Overzealousness in applying a law is not uncommon in society.[6]

At the same time, the rules for drug testing keep getting tighter. On February 3, 1994, Transportation Secretary Federico Peña outlined regulations that expanded drug testing in the transportation industry and added alcohol testing to the list. The rules went into effect January 1, 1995, for large employers and January 1, 1996, for employers of fifty or fewer safety-sensitive workers; they cover workers responsible for public safety, including 6.6 million holders of commercial driver's licenses. Early results indicate the regulations will survive court challenges. (See Figure 7-1.)*

That's due in part to the rising popularity and acceptability of drug testing.† In a Gallup poll conducted on behalf of Accountants on Call in 1991, 75 percent of 714 respondents said that they would take a preemployment drug test "without reservation." Fewer job applicants have tested positive‡ for controlled substances, according to SmithKline Beecham Clinical Laboratories; their labs report a 50 percent drop in the percentage of workers testing positive. And more courts are upholding random testing, not only for truck drivers, bus drivers, and rail workers,§ but also for such unlikely professions as racehorse jockeys and other track workers whose actions could affect state revenues.¶

In each case, the courts have ruled that the Fourth Amendment does not prohibit drug testing when the public interest is involved.

› *Written and Other Screening Tests.* In an out-of-court settlement, a major retail chain agreed to pay 2,500 job seekers $1.3 million for subjecting them to the Rodgers Condensed CPI-MMPI, or "psych-screen," which the plaintiffs' attorney says contains many bizarre questions that invaded the applicants' privacy or violated sexual, religious, or racial discrimination laws. Even though the company says it did nothing wrong, and no court decision was handed down, the lesson is clear: Make sure that any test you use for screening applicants is job-related and validated.

› *Office Searches.* Unless your organization has published a broad policy that authorizes blanket surveillance or searches of offices, and

---

*"Drug Rules Tightened for Transport Workers," *St. Louis Post-Dispatch* (February 4, 1994); see also "Labor Letter," *The Wall Street Journal* (February 8, 1994), p. A1.

†"Drug Tests Up 300% in 6 Years," (according to the American Management Association study, January 1993), *St. Louis Post-Dispatch* (April 2, 1993), p. 1C.

‡"Fewer Job Applicants Found on Drugs," *St. Louis Post-Dispatch* (February 11, 1992), p. 10A.

§"Random Drug Tests for Rail Workers Upheld by Federal Appeals Court," *The Wall Street Journal* (June 8, 1991), p. B7; "Drug Tests for Transportation Workers Upheld by Appeals Court," *The Wall Street Journal* (April 29, 1991), p. B6.

¶"Jockeys Must Submit to Random Drug Tests in Illinois, Court Rules," *The Wall Street Journal* (August 15, 1991), p. B2.

Figure 7-1 Basic drug testing guidelines.

If this list of rules governs what you can and cannot do, failure to do what is required could hurt you as well as the company. Also, check to see if the specific agency to which your industry or company reports has targeted regulations not included in this generalized DOT list.

1. Publish in an accessible manner (for example, handbook or permanent bulletin board) all regulations related to alcohol and other drug use.
2. Define who is in a safety-sensitive position covered by applicable regulations.
3. Define all terms, including unfamiliar ones: for example, Breath Alcohol Technician (BAT), Substance Abuse Professional (SAP), and evidentiary breath testing device (EBT).
4. Identify the specific types of tests that will be required of safety-sensitive employees.
5. Specifically state what is prohibited by the applicable DOT regulations, for example, the use of alcohol within four hours before performing the duties of a covered position or reporting for duty or remaining on duty with an alcohol concentration of 0.04 percent or more.
6. Appoint key personnel to take responsibility for keeping all reference materials current, maintaining all records, and ensuring confidentiality.
7. Identify types of testing categories, for example, post-accident or reasonable cause.
8. Identify to whom and how test results will be transmitted.
9. Identify procedures that support employees who self-disclose an alcohol or drug abuse problem before you direct them to take a screening test.
10. Establish guidelines for processing and handling inpatient or outpatient care and how records will be handled to ensure confidentiality.
11. Advise employees of resources available to them, for example, through an Employee Assistance Program (EAP), for evaluating and resolving problems with substance abuse.
12. Provide supervisory training; any supervisor involved in a DOT reasonable-suspicion or reasonable-cause situation must have had this kind of training.

---

13. Describe procedures for hiring and auditing contractors who will administer a drug abuse testing and monitoring program.
14. Develop an information system (IS) that includes the address of the DOT agency to which the IS reports have to be sent and identifies the deadline date; lists required procedures used in the program, number of covered employees, types of tests performed and their results, types of actions taken for substance abuse or violations of other provisions or prohibitions, and information about employees who refuse to submit to testing.

---

the employees have acknowledged it and willingly submit to it, chances are the courts will say that you cannot violate the Fourth Amendment by searching an employee's office or locker. Precedents for applying this principle to the private as well as to the public sector already exist.[7]*

› *Off-Duty Privacy.* If your organization has a published policy ensuring employees the right to privacy outside the workplace, as long as their activities do not interfere with doing their jobs, you can expect to face, and probably lose, a court challenge if you meddle in their private lives.[8] In the absence of such a policy, even if the person committed a crime, you could be challenged in court; however, you would stand a better chance of winning if in some way the person's conduct created a burden on your ability to conduct business.[9]†

› *Polygraph Tests.* You cannot use lie detector tests to prescreen applicants for employment except under circumstances spelled out by law. (See later in list, "What You Can Do.")

› *Defamation.* You cannot always tell the truth about someone, unless the person to whom you are telling has a right to know it. In fact, speculating in public without facts to back up your opinions could be safer, although not wise, than talking about actual facts.‡

*"[Major Retail Chain] to Pay $1.3 Million Over Test for Applicants," *St. Louis Post-Dispatch* (July 11, 1993), p. C1; Jack Naudi, "Building a Safer Way," *op. cit.,* July 9, 2003, pp. C1 and C2.
†Steve Bergsman, "Employee Conduct Outside the Workplace," *HR Magazine* (March 1991), pp. 62–64.
‡Gabriella Stern, "Companies Discover That Some Firings Backfire into Costly Defamation Suits," *The Wall Street Journal* (May 5, 1993), p. F1.

You do not have to lie; you can just refuse to discuss the matter with anyone. In short, you cannot divulge private information that *could* cause injury to the person's personal or professional reputation to anyone who does *not* have the right or need to know that information. If you communicate the information with the *intent* to harm the person, even if the information is true, you could easily lose in court.

You should not offer explanations for why an employee was fired without carefully considering why anyone else has a right or need to know. You should not offer more information to a former employee's prospective employer than is absolutely necessary. You cannot discuss any information in an employee's personnel file without making yourself vulnerable, and this is especially true of an employee's medical or psychiatric reports, reports to the workers' compensation commission, performance evaluations, or salaries.

Tuck this away as a rule of thumb: Only people with a right or need to know have at least conditional (qualified or partial) privilege to that kind of information. Identify for yourself who in your organization, in any specific situation, should have information about your employees. Check to see if you are right.

Here is another wrinkle in the things you cannot do: You cannot expect a person to communicate reasons why you discharged him or her to a third party, especially if you could have or should have reasonably foreseen that the defamed person would be *required* to disclose the statement.[11]* That statement could turn out to be defamatory. Indeed, the key to understanding what you cannot do is the idea that if you, as the former employer, can predict that the employee will be under a strong compulsion to disclose the defamatory statement to someone else, as in the case of applying to a new employer, then you are making yourself vulnerable.[12-14] Self-publication under these circumstances can cause a person professional injury or harm, especially if the alleged defamatory statement is not true. If a court decides that the statement—that is, the reason for being discharged—is false, the organization can be held liable for

*Junda Woo, "Quirky Slander Actions Threaten Employers," *The Wall Street Journal* (November 16, 1993), p. B1; Mary E. Reid, "Words That May Later Haunt You," *The Wall Street Journal* (December 20, 1993), p. 10.

making the statement with actual malice for the purpose of injuring the plaintiff.

Other employers adopt the policy of silence. Statements such as "Did not perform up to standards," or, safer, "Not eligible for re-hire," offer some protection. However, termination for cause provisions of union contracts or of personnel policy manuals can clash with this policy of silence. Yet silence is difficult to enforce under the rules of unemployment compensation procedures, the 180- or 300-day filing period rules of Title VII, and other federal or state civil rights statutes. These agencies have absolute privilege.

The self-publication rule requires that the employer guarantee the truth of the stated reason for termination. Juries can now be called upon to decide on the truth or falsity of the statement and on the intent to defame with or without malice. Again, simply refusing to discuss a situation with someone could turn out to be the safest management policy.

Consider the implications of what I just described. Candid, forthright reference letters and letters of service have lost the war in court often.[15, 16] Even saying that an employee was discharged "for cause" can cost an employer a great sum.[17] So many employers, to reduce the possibility of being sued for defamation, will not give references for former employees. Others have adopted "name, rank, and serial number only" policies. A survey published by the Robert Holt personnel firm in February 1993 reveals that more than two thirds of companies responding have difficulty checking references because companies fear lawsuits from former employees.* Now comes this self-publication rule.

If you feel a need to talk about an employee's physical or mental health, or about his or her job performance, or anything at all that is truly of no concern to anyone else, you should question your motives. Do you bear ill feelings toward the person for some reason—because of an argument? Do you dislike the person for some reason—for the person's lifestyle or work habits or race or religion? Do you *want* to injure the person's personal and professional reputation? If you do, be extra careful. Defamation with malice can be very costly.

*"Labor Letter," *The Wall Street Journal* (February 23, 1993), p. A1.

What You Can Do

Difficult as it may be to see them, employers do have rights, too. How you execute them makes the difference between unsafe and safe management. Let's take the same issues in the same order in which I just discussed them.

Mandatory Medical Screening

Government employees have the constitutional protections of the Fourth Amendment, and some states (for example, California) have made these tests illegal in the private sector as well, unless strong or compelling business reasons exist to require them. Where good physical health is a prerequisite for successful performance of a job, as in certain physically taxing or hazardous jobs, requiring a medical exam as a precondition of employment is usually acceptable, as long as you ask it of everyone (male and female alike) to whom you have a job offer "pending passing a physical examination." Some insurance policies require such screenings also, where a previously existing condition could make a person uninsurable under your group plan. Mandatory testing of current employees is much more difficult to justify, unless, as in the case of airline pilots, in the public interest, physical fitness on the job must be recertified regularly.

Drug Testing

Mandatory, random screening of *current* employees for drug use is legal under the following circumstances:

> › Where the suspicion exists that the employee has been using drugs or was under the influence of them while on the job
> › When an employee has been involved in an accident or had given someone sufficient cause to suspect him or her of wrongdoing
> › For members of the armed forces or for government personnel in top-secret or other sensitive jobs
> › For prisoners
> › For persons engaged in a hazardous occupation, or one involving public safety, such as air traffic control, or for other em-

ployees falling under the public safety mandates imposed under the U.S. Department of Transportation's regulation (53 Federal Register 47,002) requiring public- or private-sector employers to conduct random urine tests

In other circumstances, you would struggle to justify such screenings in the absence of some *reasonable suspicion* that widespread drug (including alcohol) abuse exists that could interfere with your organization's ability to conduct its business.[18] In 1989, and often afterward, the Supreme Court Ruled that governments may conduct drug tests without reasonable suspicion when a special need exists; this is known as the Skinner/Van Raab Standards.[30]* Then you must be careful to administer the tests properly. (See the Casebook, this chapter.)

Careful administration of drug tests can support your decision to fire someone for drug abuse, if one of the conditions cited earlier also exists, for example, to ensure the "safe operation and maintenance of a railroad."[19] On the other hand, random testing of current employees may be a costly waste of time and resources. As reported in *Resource,*† a Bureau of Labor Statistics survey of 7,500 businesses, involving 950,000 employees (excluding applicants and new hires) tested within a twelve-month period, shows that only 9 percent were found positive for drug use.

Now comes radioimmunoassay of hair (RIAH) into the debate over the validity (not the legality) of drug testing. Depending on whom you ask, RIAH appears to be a more dependable test, inasmuch as the procedure can identify drug use far past the seventy-two hours urine analysis is capable of discovering. Cases reaching as far back as 1987 have been used by both sides of the argument to advance their causes. Recently (1999), the company called Psychemedics Corporation claims that while urine tests detect fewer drug users, hair testing reveals a far greater usage among employees.‡ Al-

*See, "Public Employee Drug Testing: A Legal Guide," The National Workrights Institute, www.workrights.org.
†The publication of the American Society of Personnel Administrators, January 1989.
‡Al Stamborski, "Why Your Boss Wants a Piece of Your Hair," and "Hair Analysis Company Draws Big-Name Clients and Vocal Critics," *St. Louis Post-Dispatch,* May 2, 1999, pp. E1 and E8.

though the courts have frequently accepted hair-testing results, the federal government and many other employers seem reluctant to use it.

If you think drug testing serves your organization's or the public's best interests, test *all* applicants for initial hire or for promotion. The courts will probably uphold this testing, as did the U.S. Supreme Court in 1989.[29, 30]*

Genetic Testing

The Health Insurance Portability and Accountability Act of 1996 (HIPAA, see later in chapter) now protects employees' medical history and possible future illnesses, but employees still fear that any tests they take to predict the likelihood of future illnesses will be used against them in employment, insurance, and injury claims. In February 2001, the EEOC filed a claim in federal court against a railroad company for requiring genetic testing of employees when they filed claims for work-related hand injuries, such as carpal tunnel syndrome. Employment decisions based on such tests, according to the EEOC's chairwoman, Ida L. Castro, violates the Americans with Disabilities Act. Unfortunately for case law, no legal decision was ever entered when the railroad company agreed to settle out of court, agreeing to stop genetic testing, destroying the results of previous tests, and purging the results from employees' records.†

Search Policies

If your organization has not published a broad surveillance and search policy, encourage it to do so, *if you think such a policy would serve the organization's, its employees', or its customers' best interests.* Publishing one just to have it on the books could alienate your employees beyond the value of the policy; therefore, be sure that a

---

*Drug testing occurs in about 20 percent of the private workforce. Cited in David O. Stewart, "Slouching Toward Orwell" (Supreme Court Report), *ABA Journal* (June 1989), p. 48; see also Eric Rolfe Greenberg "Workplace Testing: Who's Testing Whom?" *Personnel* (May 1989), pp. 39–45.
†Associated Press, "U.S. Suit Says Railroad Violated Workers' Right," and "Railroad Settles Lawsuit Over Secret Genetic Testing of Employees," *St. Louis Post-Dispatch*, February 11, 2001, p. B7 and April 8, 2001, p. A2; see also, "Genetics, Banning Discrimination," *St. Louis Post-Dispatch,* February 17, 2001.

compelling business reason, combined with due process, protects you. At the same time, you should also look at other published policies with which this search mandate could clash.

For example, if the employee works with confidential information concerning other employees, as would a human resources director, or if he or she works with sensitive information that investigators have not been cleared to see or hear, an invasion of the employee's privacy could lead to serious consequences. Finally, check to see if your organization reserves the right to inventory, in the employee's presence, an office when an employee voluntarily or involuntarily leaves your employ. Such a reserved right could preclude a lawsuit.

Off-Duty Privacy

An organization need not publish a right-to-privacy policy that incorporates conduct outside the workplace. However, if yours has published one, you should observe and uphold it. Still, you can hold a person accountable for off-duty conduct if it interferes with his or her work or is sufficiently outrageous as to interfere with your organization's ability to conduct its business—as long as you handle these situations under the umbrella of "a compelling business necessity."

Lie Detector Testing

Yes, you can use polygraph tests, *but only under special circumstances.* The federal government, in 1988, legislated a limited ban on the use of polygraphs as preemployment screening devices, the Federal Employee Polygraph Protection Act (December 27, 1988), which prohibits *private*-sector employers from using polygraph tests on applicants and employees, except:

> › For national defense or security reasons
> › When applicants or employees have direct access to controlled substances
> › If applicants or employees are security guards
> › In connection with investigations into theft or other incidents causing work-related losses, as long as there exists a "reason-

able suspicion" that a current employee (or employees) has access to the property in question and if the employer gives the employee (or employees) a written statement outlining the reasons for testing

This law does *not* apply to federal, state, or local governments—a good reason for not letting the public-agency issue blind you to legal realities. The federal law and statutes in forty-two of the fifty states restrict or prohibit polygraph examinations of applicants and employees. Many courts have extended contract laws to cover constitutional rights of private-sector employees as well as those of government employees, especially where the employer's action constitutes "outrageous conduct" in the absence or violation of a policy respecting an employee's right to privacy.

E-Mail, Voice Mail, and the Issue of Privacy

Privacy has smacked right up against a high-tech world in which people have yet to define what they mean by the word. As for the courts, they've ruled both ways on electronic invasion issues and haven't settled the issue of the right to privacy versus the right to monitor, especially with regard to voice mail messages. The only federal case of the latter type was settled out of court, although some state courts have taken a stand on the question: Do recorded conversations in voice mail or e-mail have the same confidentiality protections as live telephone calls or letters, or does eavesdropping on those messages without the permission of at least one of the parties involved constitute illegal wire tapping? The answer is still a matter of controversy that your management must decide as a matter of policy.*

At the heart of the controversy is The Electronic Communica-

---

*The following articles attempt to sort out the issues concerning control and privacy in messaging systems. "Business-Only E-Policy Under Attack by NLRB," in *Missouri Employment Law Letter* (Brentwood, TN: M. Lee Smith LLC, February 1999), pp. 5–6; "E-Mail and the Internet: Employment Law Liability," and "Practical Steps to Avoid E-Mail and Internet-Related Liability," *EEO Review* (Panel Publishers, August 1999), pp. 3–6 and pp. 6–8; see also, Dana Hawkins, "Privacy Is Under Siege at Work, at Home, and Online," *US News and World Report*, October 2, 2000, pp. 62–63; Deborah Peterson, "No More Secrets: Electronic Arsenal Erodes Our Privacy," *St. Louis Post-Dispatch,* November 26, 2000, pp. EV1 and EV7.

tions Privacy Act (ECPA) of 1986 that updated Title III of the 1968 Omnibus Crime Control and Safe Streets Act, which critics attack as poorly worded and not properly pursued through the courts. The older law (also known as the Wiretap Act) prohibits the intentional, unauthorized *interception* of oral and wire communications through recording or wiretapping. The ECPA covers all employers engaged in interstate commerce, which includes just about everyone, and includes wire communication (for example, telephones and voice mail), oral communications (that is, the expectation that oral communications not be intercepted by surreptitious means), and electronic communications (both internal and external systems). As in the case of any law, there are exceptions, including the following:*

> *In the Ordinary Course of Doing Business.* Employers have been exempted when they provide electronic, mechanical, or other devices that are used by employees in the ordinary course of doing business.[27]
> *Provider Exemption.* Interception is allowed either in the ordinary course of employment or if the interception is necessary for the use of the communication service, or if it is necessary to protect the service provider's rights or property.[28]
> *Consent (Express or Implied).* Communications can be intercepted if the employee has agreed to such interception. This exception is clearly stated in Figure 7-2.

Still, common sense should reign. Companies have a moral obligation to keep their systems free of messages that could offend or harm employees in some way. Employees have the same obligation; they also have to recognize that the company's equipment and systems belong to the company and that ownership rights open the door to other rights as well. Commonsense decisions are often related to protections that are:

> Related to quality control
> Against defamatory remarks made by employees

*For a detailed analysis of the ECPA, see Susan E. Culbreath, "The Electronic Communications Privacy Act," in *New Employment Issues in the Electronic Workplace* (Brentwood, TN: M. Lee Smith Publishers, LLC, 1998), pp. 9–20.

Figure 7-2. Sample technology policy.

[Company Name] has, at its own expense, made available e-mail, voice mail, and access to the Internet to be used only as tools for business transactions and business communication. By signing this document, I understand and acknowledge the following conditions.

What I Cannot Do

1. I agree not to use those electronic business tools for my own personal, private, or nonbusiness matters.
2. I agree not to communicate personal, private, or nonbusiness matters to any person(s) either inside or outside of [Company's name].
3. I agree not to communicate written or visual materials that could be construed as harassment or as giving offense to anyone based on race, sex, disability, age, religion, or national origin.
4. I agree not to use any of these electronic tools to solicit business for a non-work-related activity or cause, including political, nonprofit, or religious matters or organizations.
5. I agree not to clog the systems with excessive, noninformative messages and agree to talk with my supervisor if a question arises concerning the appropriate use of the equipment.
6. I agree not to send or receive, print, display, download, or send any sexually explicit images, messages, cartoons, or jokes, and should I receive such materials from another person, I agree to advise the sender of this prohibition and tell the sender not to continue this practice.
7. I agree that I have no right of privacy with respect to [Company Name's] software, e-mail, voice mail, or Internet access and waive my right to privacy in any and all of these forms of communication. I also acknowledge that e-mail messages can be traced to the sender even if "deleted." I also acknowledge that the company may be required to produce e-mail messages if suffering litigation.
8. I agree I will share any password I use with management and not use any "secret" passwords inaccessible to management without express, written consent or requirement of the company.

[Company Name's] Rights

9. E-mail, voice mail, and access to the Internet are extensions of [Company's Name], owned in whole and in their parts by the company. Therefore, the company will regularly review, audit, or download e-mail messages, and may monitor voice mail and Internet access. If the company finds that I have in any way abused these communications tools or have violated this agreement in whole or in part in any way, the company will have the right to take disciplinary action, up to and including immediate dismissal.

Acknowledgment

10. With my signature I attest that I have read and understand this company policy and rules. If I have any questions concerning the appropriate use of electronic equipment or of these policies, I will contact my supervisor. I further acknowledge that by signing this document, I waive all rights to privacy in the use of these forms of communication and that the company has the right to enforce the provisions of this document through disciplinary procedures, up to and including immediate termination.

11. Signed _____ Date _____

› Of trade secrets and confidential information
› Against copyright infringements when an employee downloads information from the Internet
› Against discriminatory or harassing comments or the downloading of offensive pornography from the Internet.

The statute's exceptions conform to the Fourth Amendment's standard of "legitimate business needs," especially in the case of an employer previously publishing rules to that effect.

As illustrated in many cases of corporate wrongdoing, such as Enron, electronic technology can be used as evidence against the company and individuals, so-called smoking guns.*

*See also, Culbreath, "The Case for Employee Monitoring," in *op. cit.,* pp. 3–5.

Defamation

It seems as if you cannot say anything to anyone about anything, but you do have more rights than that. In fact, in some cases, you have an obligation to disclose information in situations where other people have a right or a need to know all the facts.[21] The key issue hangs on the definition of defamation: the communication, disclosure, or publication of private information with malice or to someone who does not have the right to know.

You can express your personal opinion, judiciously (you have First Amendment rights, too), but when it comes to matters of fact, you should restrict your talk to the following circumstances:

> *When the third party has qualified or conditional privilege.* For example, supervisors considering employees for transfer to their work units have the right to review employee personnel records, including performance evaluations, as long as the reviewer intends no harm and limits the review to the immediate and legitimate contents.

> *When the third party has absolute privilege.* For example, if the IRS requests financial information about an employee being audited.

> *When you do not abuse privileged information.* You should base your decision to disclose information on reasonable grounds and make a reasonable effort to verify or corroborate the information on which you base the decision; an anonymous letter alleging misconduct, for example, would not provide you with reasonable grounds.

Discuss the situation with the person about whom you will disclose the information before taking action, especially if evidence contradicts an accusation of misconduct. Be certain of the factors and avoid personal opinions.

Be selective about what you publish and to whom you publish any potentially defamatory information about a personnel decision. Not every employee needs to know every detail of a situation. Don't make an example of a fired employee, unless you choose your words very carefully (and then, only if absolutely necessary). Limit the size of your audience to support the claim that people in your organization had a right or need to know whatever you decide to disclose.[22]

Conclusion

Employees sue if they believe their right to privacy has been violated in some way. The concept of privacy extends to employees' desks or lockers; these are places where they keep their personal things. It covers activities away from work on their own time ("It's my life, isn't it?"). Constitutional guarantees in the First, Fourth, Fifth, Ninth, and Fourteenth Amendments, and federal or state statutes, make most of the issues pretty clear. A person's life belongs to him or her, and only under special conditions can anyone intrude on that life.

Now, what about the matter of privacy rights that pertain to information about an employee, including freedom of information, access to medical records, and other business-related issues? Here we turn back to the concept of defamation.

Privacy rights extend beyond the constitutional guarantees against unreasonable search and seizure, self-incrimination, and so on. They include mundane matters such as the reason for firing someone or the nature of an illness. Medical records have become a major area of concern, especially since science has made genetic testing for genetic disorders an issue; medical information should *not* be included in personnel jackets but, rather, be kept separate and available only to people with proper clearance.* In 1996, the Health Insurance Portability and Accountability Act (HIPAA), Title I, not only protected the portability of health insurance coverage but also protected employees' identifiable health information as it relates to:

> ▸ Past, present, or future physical or mental health condition of an individual, of the provision of health services, and of payment
> ▸ Information maintained or transmitted that is or has been in electronic form
> ▸ Information used or disclosed by employees†

---

*See also "Employees Can Request Confidentiality of Their Medical Files," a Reuters News Service release reprinted in *St. Louis Post-Dispatch* (January 25, 1999), p. BP4.

†Made effective in April, 2003. See also, Michael D. Sorkin, "New Medical Privacy Law Spawns Piles of Paper," *St. Louis Post-Dispatch* (June 29, 2003), pp. A1 and A13; "Privacy Law Has Unforseen Implications," *op. cit.,* p. 12.

However chaotic the regulations may appear, the simple, commonsense rule is: Disclosure of medical/genetic information to the wrong person at the wrong time or with the wrong motive could land you and your organization on the wrong side of the court. Care must be taken to avoid making defamatory statements.

Defamation arises from intentionally and maliciously publishing in writing or orally providing information harmful to a person and could include such things as honestly reporting a person's misconduct in a reference when that information could prevent the person from finding employment. Defamation also arises from giving out confidential information to parties who have neither absolute privilege nor qualified privilege to receive that information.

Fear of becoming a party to a defamation lawsuit has led many employers to avoid asking for or giving references. But, then, policies of silence or of "name, rank, and serial number" are not necessarily protection, either. Sometimes, the *failure* to ask for or give references also causes an employer to wind up in court, as when an employer is sued for negligently putting someone with a suspect history into a position where he or she can injure or otherwise endanger other people. That employer could then turn around to sue you for failing to notify him or her that your former employee had been found guilty of a work-related or violent crime that he or she could or did repeat.

——————————— CASEBOOK ———————————

All the information you just read comes from a large collection of actual cases. Here is a small sampling of them. Test your knowledge of what you have read, and use the cases as a basis for deciding how vulnerable you or your organization might be to charges of invasion of privacy or of defamation.

How Far Is Too Far in Trying to Keep the Workplace Safe?

Employers have a responsibility to their employees to maintain a safe and healthy work environment. At the same time, the Fourth Amendment protects Americans from unreasonable search and seizure and assures them the right to privacy. The spread of AIDS has frightened some managers into believing that the disease threatens the safety of their employees, and they have therefore instituted mandatory AIDS testing. These managers sometimes also threaten employees with disciplinary action, including discharge, if they refuse to be tested.

When that happened at the State Office of Mental Health in a midcontinent state, the government employees went to court. Their attorney argued that the testing policy violated Fourth Amendment rights guaranteed all government employees, to have a reasonable expectation of privacy in the personal data that their blood and other body fluids carry. Mandatory testing amounts to an involuntary intrusion into their bodies: an unreasonable, warrantless search and seizure. The attorney concluded that this invasion of privacy was not counterbalanced by any significant government interest.

The issue here is: Does a government employer have a right, in the interest of the larger group's health, as the Office of Mental Health countered, to force employees to test for AIDS? Does your organization require, or is it contemplating requiring, employees to be so tested? If so, check out the court's answer in this case.

My Blood

The court agreed with the employees and their attorney, that government employees have the constitutional protections of the Fourth Amendment. The government, the court declared, has an interest in providing safe working conditions for all its employees, but, given the medical evidence available, risk of transmitting the AIDS virus through casual contact in a workplace is statistically hardly possible. In addition, the agency produced no evidence that its clients were at any more risk than were its employees. Only the *fear* of transmission dictated the agency's decisions.[4] You *can* go too far in trying to keep the workplace safe.

Because several states have antitesting statutes also, it is to your advantage to find out what the legal constraints in your state are. Do you or your personnel manager know?

Can You Fire Someone for Having a Positive Urine Test?

"Wait a minute," Karen Martin protested when her supervisor told her that the random drug test she took came back positive. "I don't do drugs." To make her case, the school bus driver submitted voluntarily to two additional tests, both of which came back negative.

"Too bad," she was then informed. "You're fired anyway."

So Karen went to court, where she argued that her Fourth Amendment rights were violated. It was a case of unreasonable search and seizure, an invasion of privacy, she protested. The bus company under contract to the school district had no basis for testing her urine by taking a random sample of it and testing it for drugs *in the absence* of any suspicion that she had ever used drugs or was under the influence of them while on the job. Had she been involved in an accident or given someone sufficient cause to suspect her of wrongdoing, the court could possibly uphold testing in this case, other courts have ruled.

Because Karen was not in the armed forces, she was not a secret service agent, she was not in prison, and she was not engaged in a hazardous occupation or one involving the safety of the general public—cases in which the courts have upheld random testing—she was not required to submit to testing.

The employer argued that random testing falls under the public safety mandate it carries under a regulation of the Department of Transportation (DOT) requiring public- or private-sector employers to conduct random urine tests on nearly 4 million transportation employees whose jobs have safety or security implications; the testing is legal because school bus drivers are responsible for the safety of the children on the bus. Although the decision does not factor into this case, in 1989 the Supreme Court sustained the DOT's regulation.

How do you feel about this case? Whose rights should the courts protect, the employee's or the employer's?

Not Without Reason

Although not an easy case to decide, the court agreed with the plaintiff's entire case, defending the employee's right to protection from unreasonable search. Although the safety of the children on the bus was a legitimate issue, some standard of *reasonable suspicion* must protect employees to prevent many abuses of drug testing in both the public and private sector.[6]

In addition, a federal court in California enjoined random testing among employees of a federal agency on the grounds that the agency did not demonstrate that it suffered a drug problem significant enough to warrant an invasion of privacy. The random testing seemed more like a pretext for uncovering off-duty illegal drug use. The "reasonable suspicion" test did not exist.[18]

Can You Fire Someone for Refusing to Submit to Drug Testing?

In California, as in other states, random testing of railroad employees for drugs is lawful, serving a compelling interest in protecting public safety. However, when a West Coast railroad company announced random drug testing for all employees, a computer programmer refused to provide a urine sample, asserting, "I sit at a computer terminal all day, and my job does not affect public safety in any way." The company fired her.

In court, charging wrongful discharge that intentionally inflicted emotional distress and the invasion of privacy, the programmer claimed that she was the only one who objected to the testing program on the basis of personal principle. She was therefore singled out for retaliation. She then sought both compensatory and punitive damages.

The employer, on the other hand, felt justified in requiring her to submit to the same drug tests other employees agreed to take because she worked for an organization responsible for public safety and covered by DOT regulations. The company had just cause to fire her.

Do you think they did? Or do you think the programmer was justified in refusing?

Drawing Lines

If you agreed with the programmer, you would have awarded her the same $485,000 the jury awarded her in both compensatory and punitive damages.[19] The company, the jury said, failed to show that a computer programmer is involved in the "safe operation and maintenance of the railroad." Therefore, it did indeed violate the woman's right to privacy.

Let's linger on this case awhile because it helps make an essential distinction. The fact that the woman was awarded punitive damages indicates that *tort law* was applied in this situation.

A *tort* is a civil wrong, a breach of duty other than a breach of contract under which compensatory damages are awarded. The victim of a tort action is entitled to a remedy from the person or group responsible for the wrongdoing. Some states, such as California, have codified various torts, but most states rely on the common traditions of case law in which judges or juries define torts. All tort cases fall into two categories: intentional and unintentional.

Intentional torts can result in heavy penalties, especially punitive damages. Although the burden of proof is on the plaintiff to show the defendant's state of mind, usually he or she only has to show that the defendant intended to commit the act and *should have foreseen* the consequences, or intended to produce the outcome in question. In some states, the willful or reckless disregard for the consequences of an action is sufficient to show intentional torts. These versions of "intent" are not difficult to prove.

Because unintentional torts, such as simple negligence, usually do not result in punitive damages, the plaintiff is usually not required to show intent. Often, the only criterion on which the tort is judged is the exercise of *reasonable care* under the circumstances, as implied in the notion of reasonable suspicion.

When punitive damages are available, they are almost always sought, especially if aggravating circumstances, such as sexual harassment or wrongful discharge, exist. Punitive damages can be very costly if you lose the case. And some states also recognize "negligently inflicting emotional distress" as a tort, but workers' compensation laws usually protect employers from liability in these cases.

These definitions explain the jury's decision in the case we cited. When the railroad discharged the programmer in retaliation for refusing to submit to the drug testing, it thereby *intentionally* inflicted emotional distress. That intent was the measure of the jury's award of punitive damages.

Let's turn now to another form of privacy. Does your organization require polygraph tests? Thinking about ordering them? First, consider the following situation.

Can You Use Lie Detector Tests to Screen Applicants?

A city in California thought it prudent to test employees for honesty. The city's employees, on the other hand, argued that the pretest and the control questions included invasive probes into arrests, heart trouble or epilepsy, present medical care, and experimentation with drugs such as LSD, heroin, or cocaine. One control question asked, "Did you ever steal anything?" The alleged purpose of that sort of question was to set a baseline for judging the subject's answers to other questions. The employees claimed, however, that the questions invaded their right to privacy under California law.

"No," the city countered. "The tests are essential for protecting the citizens of the community from emotionally disturbed employees, from liars, thieves, or physically impaired public servants."

What do you think? Did the employer have the right to require the polygraph test and to ask those questions? Would your organization ever require them? For what reasons?

Lie Detector Tests Undone

The California Supreme Court said that the pretest and control questions intrude into private matters of no consequence to the job.[23] The testers probed a person's emotions, repressed beliefs and feelings, guilt level, and fantasies. In addition, many questions coerced the subjects into self-incrimination, a violation of the U.S. Constitution's Fifth Amendment. Nothing, the court concluded, justified the city's unfortunate intrusion.

California courts are often ahead of others when it comes to employee rights. In this case, it was ahead of the federal legislation described earlier in this chapter that limits the use of polygraphs (the Federal Employee Polygraph Protection Act).

Can You Discipline or Fire Someone for Conduct Outside the Workplace?

A *Fortune* 100 company found itself in court in 1984, sued by a management employee claiming that the company's own policies protected her private life. The employee sued after she was fired for refusing to stop seeing a competitor's employee socially. When, in court, the company argued that the liaison compromised its ability to conduct business, she stated the following grounds for reinstatement and compensatory damages:

1. The Fourth Amendment guaranteed her the right to privacy with respect to her personal life.
2. The company's privacy policy ensured her the right to privacy as long as her activities did not interfere with her work.
3. Her private relationship did not interfere with her work because nothing she did related to the other person's work.

Does your organization restrict after-hours conduct? How and why? Does it publish a privacy policy? If so, how is it enforced?

Off Duty: My Time

The size and power of the employer notwithstanding, the court sided with the plaintiff. Said the California Appeals Court, even though Fourth Amendment rights do not apply here, the company's own privacy policies set a standard by which its contractual obligations under California's covenant of good faith and fair dealing can be judged; the company's failure to follow its own policies therefore provided sufficient evidence that the good-faith covenant had been violated.[8]

Not having a published policy does not protect you either. In a different case, in which a public policy violation was cited when a manager was fired for dating a coworker, the court ruled *against* the plaintiff but added that *had* he charged the company with "outrageous conduct" in violation of good faith, he might have made his case.[24]

Can You Tell Someone's Coworkers About His Psychiatric Treatment?

Eddy Brown suffered a series of emotional crises for which he sought psychiatric treatment before he did himself or others harm. He told his supervisor about it, and the supervisor in turn told Eddy's coworkers, with the good intent of enlisting everyone's aid in helping the man. Eddy did not see the situation in the same light, and he took the supervisor and the company to court.

"My medical history is confidential," Eddy charged. "My supervisor invaded my privacy by telling my coworkers about my problems. They had no legitimate interest in this information."

"But," the employer countered, "what would have happened if Eddy became violent and harmed someone, as he himself worried? Wouldn't we have been guilty of negligence?"

How would you have handled this situation? Would you have discussed the employee's problems with his coworkers? Why or why not?

A Need or Right to Know

The Oklahoma Supreme Court said the disclosure was *not* unreasonable; however, other courts will not always agree with it.[21] The court did not answer the question of possible negligence for failing to communicate the information, but it did say that the absence of "disclosure to the public" determined the absence of defamation. *Disclosure "to the public,"* to a person or persons *without a right or a need to know*, is the criterion upon which this privacy judgment hung for the Oklahoma Supreme Court. Today, under HIPAA, the situation would be entirely different. We now need to watch for court decisions that spell out HIPAA standards.

This controversial decision helps spell out various aspects of the privacy of information issue and the whole matter of defamation. Because defamation occurs only if private information that *could* cause injury to the person's personal or professional reputation is communicated with malice or to anyone who does *not* have the right or need to know that information, the court disagreed with the plaintiff. It held that the supervisor used reasonable discretion to give the information about the psychiatric treatment to the plaintiff's coworkers, to people who have the right or need to know. If the story had been told to anyone else, that would have been unreasonable, and the plaintiff would have had a case.

Or if the supervisor had communicated the information with the *intent* to harm the plaintiff, that clearly would have constituted defamation, even though the information was true.

When Do Your Statements About Someone Become Slander?

Coastal Airlines defended itself against a pilot's complaint that it slandered him by saying that any statements made about him were merely opinions, not fact, and therefore not defamatory. "Anyone is entitled to an opinion." That is not how the pilot, Bob Gillette, saw it.

He argued that when management personnel called him paranoid during an interview with a reporter, they impugned his mental state and his ability to do his job responsibly. Oral remarks to a third party, said with malice, fell short of calling him insane, but implied he was not fit to exercise his job duties properly and were therefore libel per se.

"Gillette had been complaining for years. I think you ought to know he wrote some very odd letters to the FBI. . . . He said Coastal was out to get him, that we tried to crash a plane in order to kill him. He's paranoid."

In other cases, the argument continued, remarks similar to the airline's agent's statements to a reporter—"some mental problems," "mean, demented old man," and "decided complex"—have been held defamatory per se. Further, when the reporter asked why Gillette was allowed to fly, the airline representative said:

> "It's awfully hard to fire anyone these days. Anyway, we have three of them in the cockpit. Know what I mean?"

What would stop a spokesperson for your organization from saying something possibly defamatory to a reporter? How would he or she be empowered to do that? Why? Or why would your organization not so empower someone?

With Malice

The Florida Court of Appeals agreed that the statements appeared to be a matter of opinion, but appearances in this case are not deceiving. If the remarks had been nothing more than conjecture on the part of the spokesperson, they would not have formed the basis of a lawsuit. But, the court said, the statements implied undisclosed defamatory facts and therefore could form a cause of action.

The last statement, that if it were not "awfully hard to fire anyone these days," the airline would fire him, clinched the issue by making the pilot's sanity a question of fact, not a matter of opinion, that could be confirmed (or not). That statement contained the smoking gun. The airline was guilty of defamation with malice.[10]

Can an Employee Sue if a Performance Evaluation Contains Potentially Defamatory Statements?

"The written performance appraisal," Harry Prince complained to the court, "contains statements about my competence with which I take issue. I feel the appraisal impugns my competence and is therefore defamatory. The situation is made worse insofar as my performance appraisal has been placed in my personnel file, to which any manager has access. Therefore, defamatory statements are being published. I want my employer enjoined from publishing that information."

The company responded that everyone's performance appraisal has comments about performance in need of improvement; that is part of the appraisal process. It is in the interests of both the employer and employee that evaluations be completed and used to make promotion and other personnel decisions.

Do you think the court should order the company to remove the defamatory information from the file? Does your company remove less than complimentary reviews from personnel files? Why or why not?

The Importance of Privilege

The court agreed with the plaintiff that the evaluation contained statements impugning his competence; therefore, in that regard, the evaluation was defamatory. On the other hand, the court also agreed with the company that because it intended no malice it had a right, in its interests and those of the employee, to place the evaluation in the personnel file. Unlike the airline company in the previous case, the company and its managers in this case have "qualified privilege" that they had not abused with the intent to harm the employee.[25]

What Are the Limits of Privilege?

During the more than one year that Doris Petrie had worked for Dr. Franklin and several other physicians sharing the practice, no one, including Dr. Franklin, had said anything negative about her. She was called a good, hardworking nurse: honest, generous, and well liked by everyone, including Dr. Franklin.

In fact, Dr. Franklin liked her more than did the other doctors and made his interest in Nurse Petrie well known—asking her out, sending her flowers, calling her at home, and writing notes to her— but to no avail. She did not want an office romance, and she made her wishes equally well known. That angered the doctor, and he assigned her extra and more difficult duties.

One afternoon Nurse Petrie mistakenly asked a patient to take a blood test, and when Dr. Franklin heard about it he accused her of changing laboratory slip orders on the patient's chart. Although she admitted making the mistake, the nurse denied altering the orders.

Not satisfied, the doctor demanded that Petrie name the person who altered the orders, and later, when she still had not found out who changed them, he threatened her: "If you decide to stay, I'm going to ride your ass like you have never been ridden before. I'm going to watch over you, and I'm going to make it difficult for you, if you decide to stay."

The next day, when the nurse was still unable to explain how the orders came to be changed, Dr. Franklin fired her and assembled the five-person staff to explain the events. During the meeting he referred to Nurse Petrie and said that he could not work with a liar, with someone who was not trustworthy.

Although the nurse might have sued the doctor for sexual harassment and retaliatory discharge, she instead took him to court for defamation. Speaking as he did impugned her character and opened up her life to people who had no need or right to know these things.

Nonsense, the doctor retorted. The so-called defamation took place in the course of employer-employee relations. He and the office staff had qualified privilege.

What do you think? Did Petrie's coworkers have privilege?

The Presence of Malice

The doctor paid full price for his indiscretion: a total of $125,000 in various kinds of damages. Why? Even if the office staff shared in qualified privilege, the alleged defamatory statements were motivated by what the court called "actual malice."[26] Here are the three important sources of evidence that guided this decision:

1. Until the nurse spurned the doctor's advances, she had been considered an exemplary, trustworthy employee.
2. The doctor had let it be known that he was angry about being rejected.
3. Whatever the mix-up in the laboratory orders, the situation was too insignificant to be anything other than a ruse for retaliating against the nurse for denying him.

Given those three conditions, the court concluded, the doctor had called the nurse a liar and untrustworthy either because *he knew the charges were false or because he recklessly disregarded the truth.* In either case his intent was malicious. Such malice overcomes any claim to privilege.

Can the Absence of Malice Protect an Employer from a Lawsuit?

Bob Pershing, a general manager for Cross Country Transportation, never shrank from an invitation to have a nightcap with "the boys" when he went out of town on business. This trip was no exception. Several days later his employer received an anonymous letter complaining that Bob had become drunk, argumentative, and profanely abusive, making nasty remarks about the company.

In spite of eyewitness testimony that Bob had not become drunk or made such remarks about his employer, the company fired him without talking it over with him. The anonymous letter was the only justification.

What really angered Bob the most, however, was that the man who replaced him called a meeting of 120 employees and declared:

> "I gathered you all here to tell you why Mr. Pershing is no longer with the company. The man was drunk and misbehaving in a bar. The man has a drinking problem. Cross Country Transportation looks unkindly on this kind of conduct. It was not the first time. He had been warned."

As soon as he heard about the speech, Bob sued for defamation. In response, the company argued that both Bob's successor and the employees had qualified privilege; the company had the right to inform the employees and the employees had a right to know.

What do you think? What takes priority, Bob's right to privacy or the company's and employee's rights?

The Abuse of Privilege Even in the Absence of Malice

Pay the complainant $350,000 in damages, said both the trial and the appeals courts. Yes, the employer had a qualified privilege to make statements about why someone was fired, but Cross Country Transportation crossed the line by doing two things:

1. It based its decision to disclose information about Pershing on unreasonable grounds: the anonymous letter.
2. It engaged too large an audience to support the claim that people in the company had a right or need to know.[22] Although malice was absent, those two considerations gave rise to the judgment against the company.

This is the case that provided us with the guidelines listed earlier. Before making a personnel decision that you may publish, take care to base that decision on evidence stronger than an anonymous letter or some equally unreliable source. Make a reasonable effort to verify or corroborate the information on which you base the decision, and confront the accused before taking action, especially if evidence contradicts the accusation.

And be selective about what you publish and to whom you publish any potentially defamatory information about a personnel decision. Not every employee needs to know every detail of a situation. In the case cited, rank-and-file employees two levels below Pershing heard the gruesome allegations. That dissemination, the courts ruled, abused the privilege the company would otherwise have enjoyed.

But what about people outside your organization? What are the limits here?

Could You Be Held Liable for What Former Employees Say About Themselves?

Worldwide Life and Health Insurance, as a matter of corporate policy, gives only the dates of employment and the final job title of a former employee, unless specifically authorized in writing to release additional information in response to reference checks. The company adhered to that policy after it discharged four claims representatives for gross insubordination, a charge stemming from their refusal to revise expense reports they had submitted. Yet several years later, Worldwide found itself defending itself before the Minnesota Supreme Court against charges of defamation.

According to the plaintiffs, when they sought out new jobs, they were compelled to explain why they left their last place of employment. To avoid being charged with fraud, they all had to say they had been terminated for gross insubordination, which left them still unemployed. Thus began the long journey through the courts.

What do you think? Did the fact that Worldwide had not published the defamatory information—that, indeed, the plaintiffs themselves had—get the company off the hook? What are your organization's policies with respect to terminating someone, showing cause, and providing reference information? How, if at all, would these results apply locally? Why or why not?

Implicit Defamation in Self-Publication

Ordinarily, Worldwide, because it did not give out reasons for terminating employees, might not have been liable. In general, the employer does not publish information when it gives the information to the employee, who, in turn, discloses it to someone else, such as a prospective employer. But, in matters of law, the exception frequently becomes the rule.

The Minnesota Supreme Court declared an exception to the publication rule when it said that if a defamed person is *in some way compelled* to communicate the defamatory statement to a third party, and if the defendant could reasonably foresee that the defamed person would be required to disclose the statement, then the defendant could be held liable for the publication.[11] Self-publication under these circumstances can cause a person professional injury or harm. The question then becomes whether or not the alleged defamatory statement is true; if the statement turns out to be false, then the company loses any privilege in telling the employees the reason for their discharge.

The Minnesota Supreme Court supported the trial jury's decision that evidence indicated that the fired employees had not engaged in gross insubordination. The statement was false, and therefore Worldwide made the statement with actual malice for the purpose of injuring the plaintiffs.

The court did hold out in favor of the employer in one phase of the case, however: damages. Punitive damages, awarded by the trial jury ($600,000) are not available in defamation suits involving compelled self-publication. That denial of punitive damages, the court reasoned, should deter people from *wanton* self-publication. Compensatory damages, on the other hand, are available (in this case, $300,000), and this could lead more and more employers to adopt the policy of silence.

Cases

1. 726 F.2d 459 (9th Cir. 1983), *cert. denied*, 469 U.S. 979 (1984).
2. 563 F. Supp. 585 (W.D. Mich. 1983), *aff'd*, 746 F.2d 1475 (6th Cir. 1984).
3. 788 F.2d 1223 (6th Cir. 1986).
4. No. 87-0-830 (D. Neb. Mar. 29, 1988).

5. S. Ct. No. 87-1555.
6. 628 F. Supp. 1500, 121 L.R.R.M. (BNA) 2901 (D.D.C. 1986).
7. 392 U.S. 364, 368–369 (1968). See also 23.817F.2d 1408, 1 I.E.R. Cases 831 (9th Cir. 1985), *aff'd,* 1 I.E.R. Cases 1617 (March 31, 1987); 579 F.2d 825, 829 (3d Cir. 1978); 557 F.2d 362, 363 (3d Cir. 1977); 521 F.2d 1217 (9th Cir. 1975); 479 F. Supp. 207 (S.D.N.Y. 1979).
8. 162 Cal. App. 3d 241 (1984).
9. 4256 F. Supp. (W.D. Pa.) 1328.
10. 438 So. 2d 923 (Fla. Dist. Ct. App. 1983); see also 101st Dist. Ct. (Dallas 1993).
11. 389 N.W.2d 876 (Minn. Sup. Ct. 1986).
12. 73 Ga. App. 839, 38 S.E.2d 306 (1946).
13. 16 Mich. App. 452, 168 N.W.2d 289 (1969).
14. 110 Cal. App. 3d 787, 168 Cal. Rptr. 89 (1980).
15. 506 A.2d 901 (Pa. Super. Ct. 1986).
16. 694 S.W. 822 (Mo. Ct. App. 1985).
17. 64 N.Y.2d 770, 475 N.E.2d 451 (1985).
18. No. 6-88-20729-WAI (N.D. Cal. Jan. 6, 1989).
19. No. 843,230 (S.F. Sup. Ct. 1987).
20. 816 F.2d 170 (5th Cir. 1987).
21. No. 62,086 (1986).
22. 662 P.2d 760 (Or. Ct. App. 1983).
23. 227 Cal. Rptr. 90 (Cal. Sup. Ct. 1986) (en banc).
24. 75 Or. App. 638, 708 P.2d 1256 (1985).
25. 748 P.2d 349 (Colo. Ct. App. 1987).
26. 671 S.W.2d 559 (Tex. Ct. App. 1984).
27. (1987) 24 MJ246.
28. 630 F.2d 414 (5th Cir. 1980); 704 F.2d 577 (11th Cir., 1983).
29. 992 F.2d (9th Cir., 1992).
30. 489 F.2d 602 (1989) and 489 F.2d 656 (1989).

8

Safe Management of Family and Medical Leave

Do you know if your company or any (or all) of your employees are covered under the Family and Medical Leave Act (FMLA) of 1993? How well trained are your managers in handling requests for leave and for generally complying with this Act? If you have trouble answering these questions, you and your company could be in for even more trouble—and expense—down the road. According to the Labor Department, as reported in *The Wall Street Journal,** of the 3,795 cases closed in 1998, "in about 60 percent investigators found employers had acted improperly."

The FMLA, a complex piece of employee protection, has significant implications for managers. Because of its many definitions and exclusions, it is difficult for most people to fully digest and commit to memory. This chapter attempts to break out all the main points and state them as simply as possible; however, when in doubt, shout for your attorney.

Purpose

Deriving its powers from both the Commerce Clause and the Fourteenth Amendment, the FMLA fills gaps that, by its nature, the Pregnancy Discrimination Act of 1978 cannot fill—namely, to:

> ' Balance workplace demands with the needs of families
> ' Promote the stability and security of families
> ' Promote the national interest in preserving family integrity

*The Wall Street Journal (January 26, 1999), p. A1.

The Act is to accomplish those goals by:

> › Entitling employees to take reasonable unpaid leave of up to twelve weeks in a twelve-month period for medical reasons, for the birth or adoption or care of a son or daughter, and for the care of a son or daughter, spouse, or parent who has a serious health condition
> › Accommodating the legitimate interests of employers
> › Minimizing the potential for employment discrimination on the basis of sex by generally ensuring a gender-neutral basis for making leave time available for eligible medical reasons (including maternity-related disability) and for compelling family reasons
> › Promoting the goal of equal employment opportunity for women and men*

The FMLA was designed to establish minimum standards for employment. In Paragraph 403, Congress encourages employers to adopt or retain more-generous leave policies than the law requires, and many companies go beyond the requirements of the law. For example, Johnson & Johnson accommodates children's camp schedules during the summer. Mattel, Inc., gives employees more time to spend with their children by closing down every Friday afternoon, and the company accommodates elder care as well.† Most companies have responded positively to the FMLA by hiring temporaries to fill in for clerical workers on leave. Others are cross-training employees to pick up the slack.

Thirty-five states enacted some type of family leave legislation *before* the FMLA was passed, and California has adopted legislation that provides for paid leave.‡ Others are adopting their own legislation now. You would be wise to check the status of local law with your state's department of labor.

---

*Associated Press, "Father Is First Man to Win Damages on Family Leave Issue," *St. Louis Post-Dispatch* (February 4, 1999), p. A2. An appeal was expected, but we have lost track of the case.
†"Labor Letter," *The Wall Street Journal* (January 11, 1994), p. 1.
‡"Sure 'Unpaid Leave' Sounds Simple, But. . .," *Business Week* (August 9, 1993), p. 32; see also Timothy L. O'Brien and Udayan Gupta, "Most Small Businesses Appear Prepared to Cope with New Family-Leave Rules," *The Wall Street Journal* (February 8, 1993), pp. B1 and B2.

But the question is: Do work-family programs help the bottom line? Even before the FMLA was passed, the answer, according to a Boston University report, was yes. Assuming that reduced employee absenteeism and stress, and improved morale, signal increased productivity, family-friendly policies work to the benefit of the company.* Still, many companies can be expected to skirt the law, according to other studies conducted in states that had family leave legislation in years prior to FMLA's passage in 1993. Most fail to comply because they don't know enough about the law and their obligations; poor enforcement in those states and lax penalties contribute to the absence of a strong effort to comply.†

On the other hand, with the enactment of the FMLA, many companies with fewer than fifty employees have elected to stay small, using temporary workers or limiting expansion. Some discriminate against younger women, refusing to hire them if they suspect the applicants might become pregnant or take family leave to care for a sick child.‡ The latter action only endangers the company from a different direction: a charge of discrimination on the basis of sex.

Whom the Act Protects

Employees are eligible to seek unpaid leave for medical or family care reasons if they satisfy the following criteria:

> › They work for an employer with fifty or more workers within seventy-five miles of the employee's work site. When employees have no fixed work site—for example, construction and transportation workers, salespersons—"work site" means the "home base" to which they are assigned, from which their work is assigned, or to which they report.
> › They have been working for that employer for at least twelve months before the leave request; the twelve months need not be consecutive.

*Sue Shellenbarger, "Work & Family," *The Wall Street Journal* (January 20, 1992), p. B1.
†Sue Shellenbarger, "Work & Family," *The Wall Street Journal* (September 18, 1992), p. B1.
‡Sue Shellenbarger, "Work & Family," *The Wall Street Journal* (August 5, 1993), p. B1.

> They have worked at least 1,250 hours during that twelve-month period. Hours of service are defined by Section 7 of the Fair Labor Standards Act and include idle time and incidental activities as long as the time is integrated with principal job duties.
> The full intent of these protections is clarified by definitions that can and do affect what managers can and cannot do:

employer   Any person engaged in commerce or in any industry or activity affecting fifty or more employees for each working day during each of twenty or more calendar workweeks in the current or preceding calendar year; this definition includes public and governmental agencies.

employ   To maintain fifty or more people on the payroll, whether or not every employee is "employed for each working day,"—for example, weekend security guards.

son or daughter   Any person under eighteen years of age or any person eighteen years old or older who is incapable of self-care because of mental or physical disability if that person is a:

> Biological, adopted, or foster child
> Stepchild
> Legal ward
> Child of a person standing in the place of a parent

parent   The biological parent of an employee or a person who stood in the place of a parent when the employee was a son or daughter.

spouse   A husband or a wife (which excludes an unmarried domestic partner).

serious health condition   According to the DOL, any illness, injury, impairment, or physical or mental condition—for example heart attack, most cancers, severe back condition, childbirth, and recovery from childbirth—that involves any of the following:

> Any period of incapacity or treatment in connection with or consequent to inpatient care in a hospital, hospice, or residential health care facility
> Any period of incapacity requiring absence from work, school,

or other regular duty activities, or more than three calendar days, that also involves continuing treatment by a health care provider

› Continuing treatment by a health care provider for a chronic or long-term health condition that is incurable or so serious that, if not treated, would likely result in a period of incapacity of more than three calendar days; or for prenatal care*

The DOL regulations also state that a diagnosis of an illness doesn't determine if the condition meets this definition; rather, the question concerns the fit of the condition to the criteria in the regulations. Therefore, a chronic serious health condition, such as asthma, might not fit the criteria unless it produces a period of incapacitation. Even if the condition is ultimately found to fit the definition of "minor," if it fits the previously mentioned criteria, it falls under FMLA.[1] In addition, an incapacitating "serious health condition" can result from more than a single illness or impairment. The Seventh Circuit Court of Appeals ruled in 1997 that an employee's multiple health problems—hypertension, hyperthyroidism, back pain, headaches, sinusitis, an infected cyst, a sore and swollen throat, coughing, feelings of stress and depression—no one of which taken by itself meets the criteria—did constitute a "serious health condition under the criteria of FMLA.[2] In the case of bereavement, whereas the death of an immediate family member doesn't, in and of itself, fall under the criteria of FMLA leave, leave following the death of a family member could be protected if the employee's health care provider certifies that the employee suffers from a stress-related illness as a reaction to the death.† In May of 2003, the Supreme Court, in a 6–3 decision, extended these rights to all state employees as well as to most private sector employees.[5]

---

*See "What Constitutes a FMLA 'Serious Health Condition'?" *Missouri Employment Law Letter* (Brentwood, TN: M. Lee Smith, Publishers LLC, August, 1999), pp. 4–6. In spite of challenges from the Society of Human Resources Managers (*Gemini Inc. v. Katherine A. Thorson,* Nos. 99–1656, 99–1708, and 99–2059, 1999), and others, the DOL adopted these criteria almost verbatim; see "SHRM Challenges DOL Definition of 'Serious' FMLA Health Condition" *HR News* (July 1999), p. 13.
†"Courts' FMLA Interpretations Provide Guidance to Employers," *EEO Review* (January 1999), p. 4.

health care provider   A licensed doctor of medicine or osteopathy, or other person identified by the Secretary of Labor as capable of providing health-care services.

employment benefits   All benefits provided or made available to employees by an employer, to include group life, health, and disability insurance; sick leave and annual leave; educational benefits; and pensions.

reduced leave schedule   A leave schedule that reduces an employee's usual number of hours per workweek or hours per workday.

intermittent leave   Over one week of leave, but less than twelve weeks (as defined by Department of Labor standards rather than by law). FMLA leave may be taken on a reduced work schedule basis or on an intermittent or periodic basis—for example, during recovery treatment from chemotherapy—providing care or comfort to an immediate family member suffering from a serious health condition, or when suffering from a chronic serious condition that prevents the person from periodically performing the essential functions of the position.

What You Cannot Do

Managers cannot "interfere with, restrain, or deny the exercise or the attempt to exercise, any right" under the Act. Specifically, employers cannot:

1. Deny eligible employees a total of twelve workweeks of leave during any twelve-month period when leave is taken for one or more of the following reasons:
   › The birth of a son or daughter and to care for the child
   › The placement of a son or daughter for adoption or foster care
   › To care for the employee's spouse, son, daughter, or parent, if the family member has a serious physical or mental health condition, even if another family member is available to give needed care
   › The employee is unable to perform the functions of the

position because of his or her own serious health condition

2. Deny unmarried domestic partners working for the same employer their own twelve weeks' leave time as long as the time is requested for the care of their child or parent (but not for the care of a child or parent of the unmarried partner).

3. Deny intermittent or reduced schedule leave in cases involving a serious health condition of the employee or a family member, when such leave is medically necessary.

4. Modify an exempt employee's status under the Fair Labor Standards Act or deny such an employee an intermittent leave or a reduced leave schedule or dock such an employee's pay.

5. Deny eligible employees returning from family and medical leave the position they held when they went on leave, or an equivalent position with equivalent pay, benefits (including benefits accrued while on leave), and other terms and conditions of employment.

6. Deny, reduce, or modify group health plan coverage or any other benefits to which an eligible employee would have been entitled had he or she been working continuously during the period of leave.

7. Fail to contribute to a multiemployer health plan (one to which more than one employer is required to contribute and that is maintained through one or more collective bargaining agreements) during the leave period, unless the plan expressly provides for alternative methods of coverage for the period of the leave.

8. Deny employees of public and private elementary and secondary schools the same rights, remedies, and procedures as other eligible employees, except as specified by the Act (Paragraphs 132–135).

9. Deny federal government civil service employees equal rights under the Act, except as specified by various provisions of the Act.

10. Interfere with an employee's right to:
    › Complain to anyone—for example, management, unions,

other employees, or newspapers—about allegedly unlawful practices
> Participate in a group that opposes discrimination
> Refuse an order that the worker believes is unlawful under the act
> Oppose unlawful acts by persons other than the employer—for example, former employers, unions, and co-workers

11. Discharge or discriminate against someone for:
> Filing charges of instituting or causing to be instituted any proceeding under the Act
> Giving or deciding to give any information in connection with an inquiry or proceeding relating to any right under the Act
> Testifying or agreeing to testify in any inquiry or proceeding relating to any right under the Act

What You Can Do

The FMLA allows you considerable latitude for implementation. Employers can:

1. Take all reasonable steps to avoid the risk of discriminatory treatment with regard to meeting the family and medical needs of their employees.
2. Limit the right of employees to take leave for the birth of or placement of a son or daughter to twelve months after the birth of or placement with the employees.
3. Limit total leave time of both spouses in any twelve-month period to twelve weeks if both work for the same employer and if their leave is taken for the birth or adoption of a son or daughter or for the care of a sick parent.
4. Deny leave to employees for the care of an unmarried domestic partner.
5. Deny employees an intermittent or reduced schedule leave for the birth or placement of a son or daughter, except by a formal agreement between the employer and the specific employee.

6. Require employees seeking leave (continuous, intermittent, or reduced schedule) for planned medical treatment to provide thirty days' notice (or as much notice as is practical) and medical certification outlining the dates on which treatment is expected and the duration of the treatment. Sufficient certification would include a statement of:
   › The date the condition began
   › Its probable duration
   › Appropriate medical facts
   › The assertion that the employee is unable to perform his or her job functions, or that the employee is needed to care for a sick family member for a specified time

   If a physician's statement *does not* expressly state that the employee is unable to perform the functions of his job, supposed certification fails an essential test. Your policy statement should inform employees of this criterion. If, due to circumstances, the employee cannot produce medical or other forms of certification within the law's prescribed fifteen days, the courts encourage the employer to provide a certain amount of leniency in enforcing the rules.*

7. Require employees seeking leave (continuous, intermittent, or reduced schedule) for planned medical treatment to make a reasonable effort, with the health care provider's approval, to schedule medical treatment in a manner that will not unduly disrupt the employer's operations.

8. Require, if the employer has a reasonable doubt as to the validity of an eligible employee's certification, a second opinion from a health care provider designated or approved by the employer, provided that:
   › The employer pays for the second opinion.
   › The health care provider is not employed on a regular basis by the employer.
   › In the event of a conflict of opinion, the employer pays for a third opinion approved jointly by the employer and employee; this third opinion would be final and binding.

9. Require employees seeking leave time for a foreseeable event—for example, the birth or placement of a son or

*See "Exceptions to the FMLA Rules," *Personnel Legal Alert* (Alexander Hamilton Institute, Inc., August 2, 1999), p. 2.

daughter—to give thirty days' notice, or as much notice as is practical—for example, in the event of a premature birth or availability of a child.

10. Require anyone who has requested foreseeable intermittent or reduced schedule leave for planned medical treatment to transfer temporarily to an available alternative position if:
    › The employee is qualified for the alternative position
    › The position has equivalent pay and benefits
    › The alternative position better accommodates recurring periods of leave than the employee's regular position

11. Offer exempt employees substitute arrangements for any part of the twelve weeks of leave granted under the Act, depending on the reason for the leave, such as accrued paid vacation, personal, family, or medical or sick leave.
    › Substitution of paid leave is limited to prevent employees from offsetting leave taken for the birth or adoption of a child or the placement of a foster child with sick or disability leave.
    › If the substituted paid leave is less than twelve weeks in duration, the employer need only provide an additional period of unpaid leave to bring the total of paid and unpaid leave to twelve weeks.
    › The employer may not trade short periods of paid leave for longer periods of unpaid leave.
    › The employer is not required to provide paid sick or medical leave unless the employer normally provides it.

12. Require an employee on leave to report periodically on his or her status and intent to return to work.

13. Require each returning employee to provide certification from the health care provider that he or she is able to resume work.

14. Deny to restored employees accrued seniority or employment benefits or any other right, benefit, or position of employment to which the employees would have been entitled had they not taken the leave (although eligible employees retain all accrued benefits while on leave).

15. Deny eligible employees among the highest paid 10 percent of employees within seventy-five miles of the work site restoration to their prior equivalent position if:
    › Denial is necessary to prevent substantial and grievous

economic injury to the employer's operations—for example, the cost of losing a key employee if he or she chooses to take the leave in spite of the possibility that he or she may not have his or her position or its equivalent restored.
 › The employees have been notified that the employer intends to deny restoration, as soon as the employer determines that such injury to the operations would occur.
 › In the case of an employee already on leave, he or she elects not to return to work after being notified of the employer's decision.

16. Deny health care benefits if the employer does not already offer them; however, they must be provided for employees on leave if they are made available while those employees are on leave.

17. Recover the premium paid for maintaining employees' health plan coverage during any period of unpaid leave if:
 › Employees fail to return from leave after their entitlement has expired.
 › Employees fail to return to work for a reason other than (1) the continuation, recurrence, or onset of a serious health condition that would entitle the employee to leave; or (2) other circumstances beyond the employee's control.

18. Require employees to support their claim of inability to return to work, from a health care provider, because of the continuation, recurrence, or onset of a serious health condition that would entitled the employee to leave, or other circumstances beyond the employee's control.

19. Allow an employee to telecommute in lieu of FMLA; however, the arrangement must be mutually acceptable and voluntary on the part of the employee.*

How to Figure the Twelve-Month Period

The FMLA supplies four optional methods for determining the twelve-month period in which an employee may take twelve weeks of unpaid leave.

---

*See Brenda Thompson, "Telecommuting and the FMLA," in *HR Executive Reports: Telecommuting Pluses and Pitfall* (Brentwood, TN: Publishers LLC, 1999), p. 34.

1. Calendar Year Method
2. Fixed Year Method—that is, any fixed twelve-month period, such as a fiscal year, a year determined by a state statute, or twelve months beginning on an employee's anniversary date
3. Measuring Forward Method—that is, applying the twelve-month period measured from the day an employee's *first* FMLA leave begins
4. Rolling Backward Method—that is, the twelve-month period measured backward from the date an employee uses any FMLA leave

Since the Calendar Year and Fixed Year Methods are easiest to apply, most employers use them. However, both methods (including using the employee's anniversary date) suffer from a condition known as *stacking.* An employee could wind up taking twenty-four weeks of consecutive leave time assuming he or she has a valid reason, if the employee takes twelve weeks from October 1 to December 31 and then twelve more weeks from January 1 through March 31. That's legal. The same stacking can happen with the Measuring Forward Method.

Although federal regulations allow you to select any of the four methods to calculate the twelve-month period, many attorneys and HR professionals recommend that you use the Rolling Backward Method. If an employee takes FMLA leave, you should add up any FMLA leave taken by the employee during the *preceding* twelve months and subtract it from the twelve weeks of maximum allowable time. The balance remaining is the amount the employee may take at this time. For example, an employee wants to take FMLA leave starting June 1, 1999, but she has already taken eight weeks of leave in August and September of 1998. She is now entitled to only four more weeks.

Whichever of the four methods you choose, you must document that choice in an FMLA policy statement published in your employee handbook and apply the same method of calculating the twelve-month period to all employees. You may change your method, but only with sixty days' written notice of the change to all employees. In addition, you must allow employees to retain their full benefit of twelve weeks' unpaid leave regardless of the method.

In short, you can't adopt or change any method of calculation just to evade granting FMLA leaves to eligible employees.

Notice

When employees plan to seek leave (continuous, intermittent, or reduced schedule) for medical treatment or for a foreseeable event, such as the birth of a child, you may require that they provide at least verbal notice thirty days in advance or as much notice as is practical; and you may require certification for medical leave. You may also serve notice on the employee that a requested leave will fall under FMLA within a reasonable time of receiving notice from the employee—for example, two days—but you may not retroactively designate the leave as exhausting the twelve-week leave period. Employee leave time doesn't begin tolling until the person is notified that the unpaid leave is granted or that paid leave will be substituted.*

Penalties from Civil Action by Employees: Willful Violations

An employee's right to civil action is terminated when the Secretary of Labor files an action seeking monetary relief on that employee's behalf, unless the secretary dismisses his or her action without prejudice.

damages   An amount equal to the wages, salary, employment benefits, or other compensation denied or lost to the employee because of the violation. In the absence of losses of compensation, the employer is liable for an amount equal to the actual monetary losses sustained by the employee as a direct result of the violation, for example, the cost of providing care, up to an amount equal to twelve weeks of the employee's wages or salary.

---

*See "Speak Now or Forever Hold Your Leave: Timely Designation of FMLA Leave," originally written by attorneys at the law firm of Baker & Daniels and published in the *Indiana Law Letter* (June 1997), reprinted in *1998 Executive File: Hot Employment Issues* (Brentwood, Tenn.: M. Lee Smith Publishers, 1997), pp. 13–14.

interest To be added to the amount of damages, calculated at the prevailing rate.

liquidated damages An additional final settlement of damages, equal to the sum of the damages awarded and interest on those amounts, that can be awarded unless the employer proves to the satisfaction of the court that its conduct or omission, in violation of the Act, was done in good faith and that the employer had reasonable grounds for believing that it was not in violation of the Act.

equitable relief Other awards to the employee—for example, employment, reinstatement, promotion, etc.

fees and costs Reasonable attorneys' fees (mandatory and unconditional), reasonable expert witness fees, and other costs of the action.

———————————— **CASEBOOK** ————————————

It's simple, right? An employee takes family leave—to care for an elderly parent, to have a baby, to recover from a severe injury—and you take him or her back, but give him or her a different job because the old one went away for some reason. Same pay, same benefits. Well, maybe it's not as simple as all that.

No Sick Leave or Vacation for You

Sally Bartlett's husband became nearly totally incapacitated with a life-threatening illness, and she took six full days and three partial days of work in order to assist him at home. Threatened with forfeiture of accrued sick leave days and scheduled vacation if she wanted additional time, she quit and sued her employer under the FMLA and for constructive discharge—that is, being forced to forfeit earned time. The trial court ruled in the employer's favor, that it had the right to require employees to sacrifice sick leave and vacation (paid time) when faced with a situation like this.

What does your company do when confronted with an employee needing time off to care for a sick spouse?

Interference

When the trial court agreed with the company that it had the right to require employees to sacrifice paid time off in order to take FMLA leave, Sally appealed to the Tenth Circuit Court of Appeals. That court acknowledged that the DOL regulations don't specifically define *interference,* but they do say that discouraging an employee from applying for leave is in fact interference with her FMLA rights. The company's requirements operated "as a powerful disincentive to assertion of that employee's rights under the FMLA."[3]

Take a Lower Paid Permanent Position, Ninety Days at Equal Pay or Quit

Paul Marsh, a plant manager, had a heart attack and required open-heart surgery. When he returned to work, his employer gave him three choices: shift supervisor at half his pay, shift supervisor at full pay for ninety days before his salary was lowered, or quit immediately with two months severance. Marsh quit and sued under FMLA that employees on FMLA leave are entitled to reinstatement to the same position or to an equivalent one with equivalent pay. His employer, he argued, fired him only to avoid insurance claims against their self-funded plan.

The employer at trial said no, the decision to terminate Marsh was made four days before he suffered a heart attack because of complaints concerning the man's management style. They withheld that decision until he recovered and returned to work as a courtesy.

The trial court agreed with Marsh because the company produced no documentation that they had problems with this manager. On the other hand, Marsh demonstrated high performance ratings in his reviews, including one given just one day prior to the alleged decision to dismiss him.

The company appealed.

What would have happened if your company took an action like this?

Three Important Rules:
Document, Document, Document

In spite of its claims that they had to counsel Paul on numerous occasions concerning his brusque management style, they could not produce any documentation of those counseling sessions. In addition, although the company's own HR representative said it was policy to warn employees before they are fired, Marsh never received any such warning. Without proper documentation, the Fifth Circuit Court ruled, the employer had no case.[4]

Cases

1. 123 F.3d 1140 (8th Cir., 1997).
2. 117 F.3d 1022 (7th Cir., 1997).
3. Appellate No. 98–6056 (10th Cir. April 15, 1999); see also "Forcing Employee to Forfeit Vacation, Sick Leave Can Interfere with FMLA Rights," *Missouri Employment Law Letter* (Brentwood, TN: M. Lee Smith, Publishers LLC, May 1999), p. 5.
4. No. 98–10020 (5th Cir., 1999); see also, "Employer Must Have Documentation to Avoid Reinstatement," *HR News*, April, 1999, p. 8.
5. U.S. Supreme Court No. 01–1368 (May 27, 2003); see also, Edward Walsh, "Federal Family Leave Law Covers the States, Supreme Court Rules," *Washington Post,* reprinted in the *St. Louis Post-Dispatch*, May 28, 2003, pp. A1 and A8.

9

Preventing Sex Discrimination and Sexual Harassment on the Job

Discrimination and harassment on the basis of race, color, religion, national origin, age, disability, or military status, as well as on the basis of gender, are still extremely pervasive, and just as socially and economically pernicious as ever. I pay considerable attention to the gender issue not only because women make up more than 50 percent of the population and are entering the workforce in numbers that far exceed those of any other group but also because, according to the EEOC, it may be the fastest-growing area of claims against employers. In the agency's fall report in 1997, cited in *Legal Report,* published by the Society for Human Resource Management, sexual harassment charges filed with the EEOC more than doubled from 1991 to 1997: from 6,883 in 1991 to 15,889 in 1997. The cost to employers in just monetary relief? From $7 million in 1991 to $49 million in 1997.* *Many of those cases, settled out of court, have also raised the ante for a large number of major U.S. employers.†* As a result, sex

---

*Gilbert F. Casellas and Irene I. Hill, "Sexual Harassment: Prevention and Avoiding Liability," *Legal Report* (Arlington, VA: The Society for Human Resource Management, Fall 1998), p. 1; see also, Stacy VanDerWall, "Sexual Harassment Complaints Rising, SHRM Survey Finds," *HR News* (April 1999), pp. 19 and 30; "Glass Ceiling Persists for Women, Study [by New York Based Catalyst]" *St. Louis Post-Dispatch* (May 14, 2001), p. A8.
†Internet News Service, "Firm Will Pay to End EEOC Case: $9.85 Million Is Largest Sex Complaint Settlement, 79 Women Will Share Sum" February 6, 1998; see also Businessweek.com, "Aftershocks Are Rumbling Through Astra" February 8, 1998. It didn't take long for settlement payouts to rise to $34 million; see "EEOC and Mitsubishi Unit Settle Discrimination Case," *Wall Street Journal* (September 10, 1998), p. A 24; see also case involving racial discrimination: Reuters News Service,

discrimination and sexual harassment have become the dominant *management* issues of our times. Unless we practice safe management with respect to gender, sex-related lawsuits could overwhelm the legal system.

Because discrimination and harassment still affect all protected groups, you can use this chapter as a model of how to prevent unsafe management practices of all kinds, or as a guide to what to do about them when they happen. Mistreating protected groups is illegal, no matter how you look at it; and the definitions and prescriptions I provide apply in the main to any illegal action on the part of management. Safe management comes down to the recognition of the rights and dignity of all people regardless of race, color, religion, national origin, age, disability, or military status as well as gender.

The definitions of *sexism, sex discrimination,* and *sexual harassment* describe behaviors that affect women employees more frequently than they do men, but they do affect men and, in their broadest sense, apply to race and age as well as to sex.*

Definitions of Key Terms

sexism   A value system that holds that one person is inferior to another because of gender; for example, "Women are too emotional, especially during their periods." Sexism, takes several different forms, like every form of *-ism:*

1. *Condescension.* Refusing to take someone seriously, for example, "Leave the difficult decisions to men."

"Judge OKs Boeing Bias Settlement, $14.2 Million Will Be Split 3 Ways" in the *St. Louis Post-Dispatch* October 1, 1999, p. C1; and apparently the message didn't get through to Boeing employees because in February of 2000, twenty-eight women accused Boeing of sex bias. See, Tim Bryant, "Boeing Is Accused of Sex Bias Against Women at Plants Across the U.S." in the *St. Louis Post-Dispatch*, February 2, 2000, pp. A1 and A6. And the beat goes on: "Dial Settles Harassment Suit for $10 Million," *op. cit.,* April 30, 2003, p. A7.

*The EEOC set guidelines defining religious harassment early in 1994, a move that sent shock waves throughout the United States; the controversy led the Commission to return the guidelines to the drawing board. See Richard B. Schmitt, "EEOC Guidelines Threaten to Pit Church vs. State in the Workplace," *The Wall Street Journal* (June 8, 1994), p. B9. See also, "Racial Harassment Is Wrong, Even if Harasser Is Black, Too!" *Missouri Law Letter* (Brentwood, TN: M. Lee Smith Publishers, March 2001), pp. 4–5.

2. *Verbal Abuse.* Making negative or derogatory comments, such as "I like watching your hips sway when you walk."
3. *Exclusion.* Overlooking or denying someone access to places, people, or information, especially when opportunities for advancement are involved, for example, excluding women from community organizations.
4. *Tokenism.* Including a selected one or few members of a group for very visible positions;* also called "window dressing."

sex discrimination   Employment decisions based on gender rather than on gender-neutral considerations, or different treatment of one employee merely on the basis of his or her gender.

sexual harassment   Unwelcome behavior of a sexual nature or with sexual overtones; sexual harassment takes two legal shapes:

1. *Quid Pro Quo.* (a) Where submitting to sexual demands becomes an implicit or explicit term or condition of employment, for example, "You can have a promotion but only if you have sex with me"; (b) Making decisions affecting someone's employment or compensation on the basis of whether the person submits to or rejects sexual demands.
2. *Hostile Environment.* Sexual conduct that has the purpose or effect of unreasonably interfering with a person's job performance or that creates an intimidating or offensive work environment.[50]† Whereas *quid pro quo,* above, has a uniquely sexual context, *hostile environment* does not; it can exist for minorities, older people, disabled people, and veterans as well.

unwelcome behavior   Conduct that "the employee did not solicit or incite"[1] and, in the case of a woman plaintiff, that "a reasonable woman would regard as undesirable or offensive."[38] In the case of a male plaintiff, the "reasonable person" convention might still

---

*See Jane Gordon Chapman, "Sexual Harassment of Women in Employment, Part II: Promising Solutions," *Response* (Fall 1994).
†Common experiences that usually get dismissed as just "horseplay" can create a hostile environment; see "Cops: Miami Beach Is Talking," *Newsweek* (August 21, 1989), p. 4; see also, "8th Circuit: Hostile environment creates continuing violation," *HR News* (April 1999), p. 8.

apply. It is under this definition that had her charge against President Clinton had any legal merit, Paula Jones would have sued him.

agency and employer liability   Any employee acting or speaking on behalf of the employer and relying on his or her apparent authority at the time he or she sexually harasses an employee. An employer need not know about a manager's sexual harassment of an employee to be held liable for that harassment.[2] For Title VII purposes, "the employer" need not be the "person engaged in an industry affecting commerce," but rather "any agent of such a person" as well. As long as the supervisor or manager is an "agent" of the organization when he or she sexually harasses an employee, the employer can be held directly liable for his or her actions.

An employer may be liable for wrongs committed by its personnel even if they act outside the scope of their authority, as long as they *purport* "to act or to speak on behalf of the principal and [they rely] upon apparent authority, or [they are] aided in accomplishing [their wrongdoing by having] an agency relationship." Although a supervisor might act only to satisfy him- or herself, and not for the benefit of the employer, the liability stems from the following three key points:

1. The alleged harasser manages some aspect of the principal's business.
2. He or she threatens the person's employment status and has both actual and apparent authority to carry out the threat.
3. He or she uses that authority to harass the person.*

---

*Edward Felsenthal, "Justices' Ruling Further Defines Sex Harassment," in *The Wall Street Journal,* March 5, 1998, p. A1; *Boston Globe,* "High Court Sets Guidelines in Sexual-Harassment Cases," reprinted in the *St. Louis Post-Dispatch,* June 27, 1998, p. 23; Robert LaGow, "High Court Expands, Clarifies Employer Liability for Sex Harassment," in *HR News,* the newsletter of the Society for Human Resource Development, August 1998, p. 6; "Eighth Circuit Provides More Guidance on Sexual Harassment Liability," in the *Missouri Law Letter, op. cit.,* (August, 1999), p. 3; Timothy S. Bland, "EEOC Issues Guidance in Effort to Clarify Harassment Rulings," *HR-News, loc. cit.,* September 1999, pp. 7, 15, and 46; "EEOC Explains When You're Liable for Supervisors' Sexual Racial, Other Harassment," in *Missouri Employment Law Letter, loc. cit.,* September, 1999, pp 6–7; "Is Stopping Sexual Harassment

Given those factors, the company need not have knowledge of the situation to be held responsible. However, in two landmark cases, the U.S. Supreme Court limited employer liability if the plaintiff can establish an "affirmative defense."[3, 4]*

Affirmative Defense

By applying the two-prong criteria spelled out in the guidelines issued by the EEOC in *Enforcement Guidance: Vicarious Employer Liability for Unlawful Harassment by Supervisors* (1999) you can avoid many of the penalties suffered by other employers.[49]

What is an affirmative defense with regard to harassment? When the employee or employees did not suffer any "tangible employment action," that is, "a significant change in employment status" as opposed to "unfulfilled threats," "insignificant changes in status" such as a new job title that bruises the employee's ego. However, if you can prove that the tangible employment action was *not* the result of harassment—for example, documentation of inadequate performance—the link between the action and the harassment is severed.

A second element is proof that an acceptable reporting procedure for harassment is in place and that the employee(s) did not make use of that procedure. On the other hand, if the employee(s) had reasonable cause to fear retaliation, or found unnecessary obstacles within the procedure or believed the procedure to be ineffective, or took other steps to stop the harassment (for example, complained to the EEOC), you must demonstrate that the employee's failure to follow the procedure was based on unreasonable claims. In other words, if both the complainant and you acted reasonably, in accordance the rules and policies of the EEOC and your company, you are not liable as a "vicarious" party.

Enough to Prevent Liability?" in a monograph of the *EEO Review*, (New York: Panel Publishers/Aspen Publishers, February, 1999); "Strict Liability for Sexual Harassment? Maybe," in the *Missouri Law Letter*, pp. 14 and "Is This Sexual Harassment?," *loc. cit.*, January 2000, pp. 4–5.; see also, John Vering and Tanya White Cromwell, "Prompt, Effective Action Saves Employer," *loc. cit.,* (December 2001), pp. 1–2.
*See also, "Employer Liability of Sexual Harassment after *Faragher* and *Burlington Industries*" in *EEO Review* (Panel Publishers, February 1999), pp. 4–5.

A *Wall Street Journal* article, dated March 5, 1998,* outlines steps you can take to help your affirmative defense:

1. "Tailor a sexual-harassment policy" appropriate to your business and include "real-life examples" to illustrate situations the policy covers.
2. "Require every employee," including *all* top executives, to take "customized training on sexual-harassment awareness."
3. Explain the internal procedures for victims to follow to file complaints, and promise to employ an external investigator if required. (However, the Federal Trade Commission has warned that sexual harassment investigations conducted by external investigators may be subject to the notice and other requirements of the Fair Credit Reporting Act.)†
4. Regularly evaluate how familiar employees are with "corporate sexual-harassment policies and complaint procedures."

To this list I will add a fifth step:

5. Require all employees, including *all* top executives to sign a statement acknowledging that they understand the company's policies and procedures, and, of course, document, document, document.

An affirmative defense can be used with regard to any form of harassment if it meets the two-prong criteria in sexual harassment cases. A quick, effective response is one essential aspect of the second prong of the defense.[49]‡

EEOC guidelines (Section 1604.11e) say that Title VII also protects employees from sexual harassment by nonemployees because employers should maintain and enforce antiharassment policies.[5] While you cannot guarantee that sexual harassment in the workplace will not occur, once an incident is brought to your attention,

---

*Edward Felsenthal, "Justices' Ruling Further Defines Sex Harassment," *The Wall Street Journal* (March 5, 1998), p. A1
†"FTC Opinion Letter May Make Certain Harassment Investigations Illegal," *Missouri Employment Newsletter* (June, 1999), pp. 7–8.
‡See also Jennifer Kyner "Employer Wins Racial Harassment Case Through Effective Response," in the *Missouri Law Letter,* (Brentwood, TN: M. Lee Smith Publishers, April 2001), pp. 2–3.

you should be prompt and thorough in your investigation and take reasonable corrective action when such action is indicated. You should make it clear to customers or to vendors calling on you that you do not condone any form of harassment—sexual, racial, or what have you.

Gender-based issues take many forms: compensation discrimination, maternity, discipline, promotion, insurance policies, and many others. So let's look at some things you, as a manager, cannot do.

What You Cannot Do

The following accounting* forms only a partial list of possible forms of sex discrimination and harassment.

The Obvious

› Hire or promote a man less qualified than the women available or interviewed.
› Fire a woman when a man might be merely disciplined.
› Lay off qualified women before or in lieu of men.
› Compensate and reward women at a lower rate than men.
› Make employment or promotion contingent upon meeting sexual demands, even if the other person appears to consent.[6, 7]
› Deny training or "mentoring" opportunities on the basis of gender.

Less Obvious

› Give preferential treatment to a consenting sex partner in a way that discriminates against other female employees.[8, 9]
› Call a woman "girl," "doll," "babe" or "baby," "honey."
› Ogle; block a person's way; stare at, for example, a woman's breasts; wink; blow kisses; whistle.[10]
› Comment on the appearance of a person's body or the sexiness of his or her clothing.[10]
› Make sexually oriented jokes, comments, or innuendoes.[11]

*Drawn from EEOC guidelines of 1988 as well as from a variety of cases.

> Ask questions, for example, about one's sex life or fantasies.[11]
> "Put the make" on someone, for example, pester someone to go out who has refused.
> Tell defamatory stories about a person's sex life.
> Touch, massage, rub against, hug, kiss, stroke, or just "hang around" those to whom these actions are unwelcome.
> Treat maternity-disabled employees differently from the way you treat other people returning from disability leave.[12–14]
> Provide health insurance coverage for one gender but not for the other, for example, pregnancy-related benefits for women employees but none for spouses of men employees.[9, 15, 16]
> Discharge a pregnant employee because she plans leave to have a baby as a cost-saving device.[17]
> In any way treat an employee differently from others because she is pregnant, unless the pregnancy interferes with a BFOQ or makes it impossible for the employee to perform the duties of the work available.[17]
> Transfer or discharge a woman whose spouse works for the same supervisor without giving her husband the same options.[18, 19]
> Respond differently to a woman's requests, for example, for a particular travel associate, than you would to a man's similar request.[20]
> Use subjective criteria in promoting people or considering them for partnership (for example, in a law firm) unless the criteria are clearly inherent in the job.[21–23]
> Impose personal or social values on a person's private life unless the person's conduct clearly interferes with your organization's ability to conduct its business.[24]
> Ignore or plead ignorance of sexual harassment occurring in your organization; managers are liable for actions of their employees.[2, 20, 25, 26]
> Retaliate against employees who reject your sexual advances or who file a claim of discrimination or harassment against you or your organization. In an Illinois case, the court ruled that a favorable but *dishonest* evaluation is a form of "actionable retaliation" because it denied the plaintiff the kind of feedback he needed in order to gain promotions.[27]

> Reinstate an accused harasser without a thorough investigation.[41]

What You Can Do

At the risk of belaboring the obvious, I will say that if you reread the lists in the previous section and restate the items in their converse, you will see the essence but not the detail of what you, as a manager, *can* do. Still, I will not deal with each point separately. Instead, I'll talk about some of the less-obvious situations that can create a manager's thornier problems.

Guidelines for Safe Maternity Leave Policies

Long before passage of the Family and Medical Leave Act of 1993, the courts ruled that Title VII, as amended in 1978, explicitly includes pregnancy-related disabilities within the scope of "sex" discrimination:

> [Women] affected by pregnancy, childbirth, or related medical conditions shall be treated the same for all employment-related purposes, including receipt of fringe benefits under fringe benefit programs, as other persons not so affected but similar in their ability or inability to work. . . .[12]

The rules for pregnant or childbearing employees should ensure the same terms for anyone experiencing a long-term medical absence.[13]* At least four states (California, Connecticut, Massachusetts, and Montana) and Puerto Rico have laws requiring *preferential* treatment for pregnancy. Other states—such as Hawaii, Kansas, Illinois, New Hampshire, Ohio, Minnesota, and Washington—have adopted regulations that have the effect of law. The U.S. Supreme Court, deciding a California case, said that Title VII merely establishes a floor beneath which pregnancy disability benefits may not drop, rather than a ceiling above which they may rise. Therefore,

*See Chapter 8, "Safe Management of Family and Medical Leave."

states, within certain limits, may require employers to provide preferential treatment.[12] You should check or have someone else find out what the laws in your state say. One major U.S. firm checked too late and wound up settling a class action suit against it for $66 million.*

Maternity Benefits for Spouses

An important collateral issue is the status of maternity benefits for spouses. According to the Supreme Court, you or your organization should provide equal coverage.[16]

In 1983 the Supreme Court heard a case that charged the employer with providing women employees hospitalization benefits for pregnancy-related conditions to the same extent as for other medical conditions, but not extending the same benefits to pregnant spouses of men employees. The married men employees complained that the company's insurance provided them less comprehensive protection than it provided married women employees, and the Supreme Court agreed with the men. The Court would not agree with a lower court's opinion that employees' spouses were not covered by the pregnancy amendment to Title VII; Congress, it said, did *not* expressly limit it to "women employees" or intend that the "basic purpose" of the amendment was to protect "women employees" only.[13]

If an employer provides complete health insurance coverage for the dependents of its female employees and no coverage at all for the dependents of men employees, it would clearly violate Title VII. Likewise, limits placed on pregnancy-related benefits for employees' wives penalizes married men *if* the plan offers more extensive coverage for employees' spouses for *all* other medical conditions requiring hospitalization. They would then receive a benefit package for their dependents that was less inclusive than the dependency coverage provided to married women employees.[16]

A few employers try to get around the high cost of equal benefits by offering men a "baby bonus" instead of comprehensive maternity benefits. The Seventh Circuit Court has nixed that idea.[28] The most creative idea is not necessarily the best.

*John J. Keller, "[Long Distance Phone Company] Will Settle EEOC Lawsuit for $6.6 Million," *The Wall Street Journal* (July 18, 1991), p. B8.

Equal benefits do not stop with benefits for current employees. A conversion health insurance policy for former employees should include pregnancy coverage for former women employees or for wives of former male employees. That the insurance policy is a matter between the former employee and the insurance company is irrelevant. The employer is ultimately responsible for a discriminatory fringe benefit plan even if third parties are involved in adopting it.[29, 30]

Equal Treatment for Pregnant Women

A pregnant woman is entitled to fair and equal treatment, and as I said before, in some states she is entitled to preferential treatment not only with respect to maternity benefits but other management decisions as well. For example, you could lay off a pregnant woman to answer a downsizing problem, but only if you can defend that reason on the basis of legitimate nondiscriminatory reasons. To lay off or discharge a pregnant employee because she plans to leave when she has her baby means treating this employee differently from others merely because of her pregnancy. To even consider the woman's plan to leave is a smoking gun.[15]

You do not have to *fire* a pregnant woman or one planning to bear children to get in trouble. Under Title VII, any decisions adversely affecting a woman employee that appear correlated with information about her intentions of raising a family could end in a lawsuit for constructive discharge, that is, creating conditions that appear intolerable to the employee and cause her to quit.[31]

Preventing Conflicts of Interest

You can ban spouses from reporting to the same superior in order to try to prevent a possible conflict of interest. Your organization can enforce written or unwritten antinepotism rules as long as they are facially neutral and evenhandedly applied in a nondiscriminatory way, for example, requiring a male spouse, if he is the junior employee, to accept a transfer or accept discharge.[18] Not separating husbands and wives working in the same department, especially if one is senior to the other, could result in a conflict of interest, and as such antinepotism policies serve a legitimate business interest.[19]

Conflict of interest is not the only legitimate reason for antinepotism rules. A close personal relationship could produce interpersonal conflicts unrelated to business or generate unwarranted favoritism. Awkward situations can develop between any members of the same family working closely together.[32]

Antinepotism rules usually apply to married couples, but cohabitating unmarried couples may as well be married as far as some organizations care. Whether or not you can take action to separate these employees on the job, to require them to marry, or to discharge them depends on the circumstances in which you conduct your business. Let's take, for example, a situation involving a public position, such as that of a librarian who as a part of her job spends a lot of time with children. If cohabitation clearly violates community standards, the librarian's conduct can serve as a compelling business necessity for requiring the couple to separate, marry, or accept discharge.[24]

Community standards such as these can become subjective if they fail to take into account that social and personal values have changed. The changes have created new conflicts between personal privacy and organizational good that have hidden in the folds of sex discrimination. Invade a woman's private life, and you invade us all.

Separating the two provinces, personal and organizational, forms the basis of effective personnel management. Personnel policies are not themselves as important as how you implement them. If you have a human resources department, it will police your policies, especially if you call some of the questions raised here to the department's attention. Still, you can manage better if you use the following tips for proactive handling of personnel matters in the following areas:

› *Privacy*. Recognize and respect employees' rights to their own private lives. As long as their personal life styles do not interfere with their job performance or with the conduct of your organization's mission, you have no business interfering in their lives.

› *Fairness*. Policies are written to benefit the organization and to guide employees in the directions that best benefit the organization with the least amount of inconvenience to the employees, where possible. But policy effectiveness depends on how managers manage.

You may not intend to discriminate against women, but the rules regarding antinepotism, unwed parents, and alternative life styles, for example, tend to work against women, racial minorities, and homosexuals. But, while the rules apply "in general," actual decisions apply "in particular."

› *Alternatives.* Thinking beyond superficial issues requires you to suspend your immediate judgment in order to consider only legitimate business necessities. Marital status is not the issue; conflict of interest or non-work-related conflicts, ability to work with and communicate with other employees or with the organization's customers are. Likewise, transferring either person, separating workstations, promotions, and so on, are possible solutions *in addition to discharging the woman.* Creative *and* lawful decision making is called for.

But can you expect equal treatment from the courts? It depends on the factors that determine the factual basis of a legitimate business reason. Appealing to "community standards" could be a subjective factor, about which I cautioned you in Chapter 4.

Rejecting Women Employees for Promotion

No law says that when men and women compete for the same job, you have to promote the women over the men. The laws say only that you should prevent subjective criteria from tainting your promotion decisions. Here are some guidelines, taken from a court case,[33] that can help:

› Do not allow a supervisor's recommendations to be the most important or only component in the selection process.
› Produce written instructions delineating appropriate criteria to apply when making promotion decisions; apply objective measures anywhere possible.
› Caution supervisors about using vague or undefined criteria; conduct proper training programs that include written instructions on the proper use of objective criteria.
› Notify all employees of the selection criteria; use an open-posting system. Produce safeguards to prevent discriminatory

practices, for example, a review committee that includes members of protected classes.

Acting on Complaints of Harassment

The courts and the EEOC recognize that "sexual attraction may often play a role in the day-to-day social exchange between employees" and distinguish among "invited, uninvited-but-welcome, offensive-but-tolerated, and flatly rejected" sexual advances.[34]* Let's revisit the idea of unwelcome advances.

Personal relationships always muddy business waters, but relationships between sexually active adults create serious issues for managers to consider. When does an innocent flirtation become sexual harassment? How serious is *one* incident? How do you determine culpability? Then, once you do, what do you do about it? Jobs, reputations, families, and lives are at stake here, and care must be taken.

Since harassment is in the eye of the beholder, mistaken intentions could result in inappropriate charges. Friendliness, thoughtless or innocent remarks, bids for attention can all be misread. To help out, the EEOC published guidelines† in early 1988 stating that "a single incident or isolated incidents of offensive sexual conduct or remarks generally do not create an abusive environment [unless] the conduct is quite severe [*Section C2*]."

The commission quotes the U.S. Supreme Court: "[The] mere utterance of an ethnic or social [or sexual] epithet [that] engenders offensive feelings in an employee would not affect the conditions of employment to a sufficiently significant degree to violate Title VII."[35]

With regard to quid pro quo, frequently a single incident offense is sufficient for action. On the other hand, in most cases, a hostile environment exists only when there is a *pattern* of unreasonable conduct. However, the Court of Appeals for the State of Michigan, applying the "reasonable woman" test to a case involving a single incident, ruled that *one incident* counts if the unwelcome action "sub-

---

*See also, Brenda Thompson, "Cupid in the Cubicles: The Perils of Workplace Romance," in *HR Spotlight*; *Missouri Employment Law Letter* (Brentwood, TN: M. Lee Smith Publishers LLC, Fall, 1999).

†"EEOC Policy Guidance on Sexual Harassment," Washington, D.C.: The Bureau of National Affairs, 1988.

stantially interfer[es] with an individual's employment . . . or creat[es] an intimidating, hostile, or offensive employment . . . environment."[42] You can be sure that this case will provide the standard for many future rulings.

The EEOC spells out how to judge the merits of a harassment complaint when, upon investigation, the alleged harasser denies that the advances were unwelcome.[33] How do you decide?

First, the victim, say, a woman, should have communicated her displeasure, asserting "her right to a workplace free from sexual harassment." For example: "Stop it. I don't like what you're doing"; "I have no wish to see you socially"; "Please stop making sexual remarks or jokes around me." These and similar statements clearly indicate that the behavior is unwelcome. Nonverbal behaviors, such as pushing away an offensive person or facial expressions of annoyance, also show that the advances are unwelcome.

Still, this type of protest is *not necessary* for creating credibility. The victim may come to you without ever telling her perceived persecutor how she feels because she may fear repercussions, such as being fired, and not confront her harasser directly. Then, you are obligated to conduct a thorough investigation (which I describe later in this chapter).

Additionally, a person complaining of sexual harassment need not also complain of or show severe psychological injury. Justice Sandra Day O'Connor has ruled that damages can be awarded even if the harassment does not lead to a nervous breakdown.[43]* A thorough and prompt investigation is still required, and could hold off the possibility of a class-action suit, the first of which was allowed by a federal court in May 1993.[46] Still, prohibition policies and prompt *remedial* action may not be enough. Deterring lawsuits requires deliberate *preventive* action, such as training and sensitivity sessions.[45]

Second, the plaintiff strengthens her case if she makes a contemporaneous complaint—that is, a complaint made at the time the harassment occurs or shortly after it stops. The EEOC calls a complaint *contemporaneous* even if it is made *after* the victim quits her job

---

*"Severe Distress Not Required for Emotional Distress Civil Rights Claims," *Missouri Employment Law Letter* (Brentwood, TN: M. Lee Smith LLC, May, 1999), pp. 2–3.

as long as "she notified her employer of the harassment at the time of . . . departure or shortly thereafter," which often happens for the same reason the victim does not confront the harasser directly: because of fear. The employer is still obligated to investigate thoroughly, to determine whether the employee quit as a result of a constructive discharge.

Third, you need to determine if the plaintiff had ever given the alleged harasser reason to believe that sexual advances were welcome. For example, in a 1983 decision, the EEOC ruled against one of three women because she responded in kind to sexual horseplay and gave her employer reason to believe that his behavior was acceptable to her.[11]

Investigating Claims of Harassment

To prevent being held liable for the acts of other people, you need to thoroughly investigate claims of harassment. The U.S. Supreme Court hedged on employer liability when it said employers are not "automatically liable" for the actions of their supervisors.[35] Each case must be taken on its own merits, but the principle of agency is consistent with the intent of Title VII and with EEOC Guidelines on Sexual Harassment (Section 1604.11c):

> An employer . . . is responsible for its acts and those of its agents and supervisory employees with respect to sexual harassment regardless of whether the specific acts complained of were authorized or even forbidden by the employer and regardless of whether the employer knew or should have known of their occurrence.

What any coworker, supervisor, or recognized third party does while doing business for or with the employer becomes the employer's responsibility.

Prompt Remedial Action

In some cases of relatively minor consequence, all that is needed to prevent employer liability for sexual harassment is prompt remedial action; no one expects "instantaneous redress" for all infractions.[25]

The law does not require an employer to fire an employee for harassment. It requires only that the employer take prompt remedial action reasonably calculated to end the harassment.

On the other hand, if the complaining employee has been coerced, propositioned, or placed in a threatening situation, or has experienced a job detriment, promising to transfer the offended party or slapping the offender's wrist may not be sufficient. An organization's remedy to a complaint should be weighted against the seriousness of the offense. A more dramatic yet *reasonable* action may be necessary after you conduct a serious investigation. The punishment should fit the crime.

Just what are reasonable standards for (1) preventing sexual harassment in the organization, and (2) taking remedial action should harassment occur?

Set aside the law for a moment. A manager's response to the threat of a hostile environment in which sexual, racial, or any other form of harassment exists must be swift and effective. You want a productive, profitable work environment, one in which your most important resource, your personnel, feels safe from harm and from unreasonable interference with work performance. This is a management concern, not merely a matter of law.

A Question of Policy

You probably do not determine policy, but you can influence it. If your organization does not have a written policy prohibiting harassment, you might produce, or ask personnel to produce, a statement that includes the main points in the suggested antiharassment policy statement shown in Figure 9–1.

A Matter of Training

Policies have little value unless training informs managers about the policies and how to administer them. If your organization does not have such a training program, encourage it to implement one simultaneously with the publication of the policies.

Effective Investigation

To determine whether or not discrimination or harassment exists in your organization, first determine if any of *your* own behavior is

Figure 9-1. Sample antiharassment policy statement.

Purpose

This policy ensures that all employees will enjoy a safe work environment free from unreasonable interference, intimidation, hostility, or offensive behavior on the part of managers, coworkers, or visitors. It also acknowledges that harassment, sexual or otherwise, is against the law and will not be tolerated by this organization.

Policy

[*Organization's name*] will maintain a workplace free of harassment of any kind and from any source, either management, co-workers, or visitors, while treating all complaints fairly and evenhandedly in order to prevent frivolous or malicious accusations.

Definitions

unreasonable conduct   Treating someone as if that person were inferior to you. This includes condescension (refusing to take someone seriously), verbal abuse (making negative or derogatory comments), exclusion (overlooking or denying someone access to places, people, or information, especially when opportunities for advancement are involved), and tokenism or "window dressing" (including selecting one or few members of a group for very visible positions).

discrimination   Employment decisions implicitly or explicitly based on factors other than job-related considerations or treating one employee differently merely on the basis of a protected characteristic, for example, sex.

harassment   Unwanted, or unwelcome, verbalisms or behaviors of a sexist, racist, or ageist nature or with overtones related to a protected characteristic—for example, sex, race, ethnicity, religion, age, disability, or military status.

hostile environment   Conduct that has the purpose or effect of unreasonably interfering with a person's job performance or that creates an intimidating or offensive work environment.

quid pro quo sexual harassment   (1) Making submission to sexual demands an implicit or explicit term or condition of employment; (2) making decisions affecting someone's employment or compensation on the basis of whether the person submits to or rejects sexual demands.

(continues)

Figure 9-1. (Continued).

unwelcome behavior   Conduct that the employee did not solicit or incite and that a reasonable woman or man regards as undesirable or offensive.

Responsibilities

Employees
1. Be sure beyond a reasonable doubt that the conduct you find offensive is discriminatory or harassing. Find witnesses or other substantiation.
2. Let the offending person(s) know that you find the conduct offensive and ask that it stop immediately.
3. If it does not stop, or if it recurs, file an official complaint with [*name of appropriate channel*].

Management
1. Refrain from all forms of discrimination or harassment at all times.
2. If observing discriminatory or unreasonable conduct, ask the offending person(s) to stop immediately, explaining what the conduct is and how it offends.
3. If the conduct continues or recurs, file an official complaint with [*name of appropriate channel*].
4. The [*title of organization's officer*] will handle the complaint by making a complete investigation and writing up the complaint and the results of the investigation within [*number of days*].
5. The investigators will make every reasonable effort to determine the facts and resolve the situation.

Sanctions

The organization has the right to apply any sanction or combination of sanctions to deal with unreasonable conduct or discrimination:

1. Counseling with the offender(s)
2. Transfer
3. Probation, with a warning of suspension or discharge for continuing or recurring offenses
4. Suspension with or without pay (depending offense)
5. Discharge for cause

discriminatory or unreasonable by asking the following questions:

› "Do I share power with the people I work with—that is, do I treat them as equals?"
› "Do I say or do things behind a protected person's back that I would *not* say or do if he or she were present?"
› "Would I accept what I say or do if the remarks or actions were directed at *me* or at something that distinguishes me from other people?"
› "Would I want what I say or do to appear in the evening newspaper or on the TV news?"

A no to any of these questions should raise a red flag for you.

Now change the pronoun I to *other managers* or *my coworkers* and answer the questions again. You might even ask the other managers and your coworkers to give themselves this little self-assessment.

If you receive a complaint of harassment, take the complaint seriously* and act professionally, even if the story appears sensational or titillating. The victim is entitled to a fair hearing, but so is the alleged harasser.

When evaluating a story of harassment, recognize that unreasonable behavior, especially sexual harassment, usually occurs in private and without witnesses. Sometimes what appears to be consenting sexual behavior often results from fear rather than agreement, and a complaining employee may have held back his or her complaint for fear of retaliation. You should therefore accept the victim's complaint at face value until you have completed a proper evaluation of the evidence. Take the following steps before reporting an incident as a bona fide complaint:

1. Ask the complaining party to be specific, asking for as objective an account as possible (for example, "Please describe what happened during your last encounter with that person"), and do not put words in his or her mouth by asking laundry-list or multiple-choice questions.

---

*A study by the American Management Association in November 1991 showed that 60 percent of sexual harassment claims end in discipline for the alleged offenders.

2. Get all the facts needed for proceeding with an investigation, including the frequency of the harassment, the length of time it has been going on, the steps the alleged victim has taken to let the other person know that he or she is offended and wants the behavior to stop, etc.
3. Ask for witnesses' names or for corroborating evidence.
4. Do *not* ask *why* the alleged victim did or did not do something, for example, complain earlier.
5. Find out what the alleged victim expects or what he or she wants you to do next, and do not ask leading questions, such as, "Do you want a transfer?"
6. Ask for permission to conduct a thorough investigation, and if he or she denies permission because he or she fears reprisal, reassure him or her that no reprisals will occur for bringing the complaint or for permitting an investigation.
7. Contact the right officer in your organization to find out how to proceed and how to apply the organization's harassment policies properly.

Some do's and don'ts for talking with the alleged harasser and with witnesses (if any) are listed in Figure 9–2.

Conclusion: Proactive Management

Use effective management practices to establish acceptable criteria for your actions, become aware of cultural attitudes and values that interfere with rational decision making, and avoid irrelevant or extraneous comments.

A slogan of the 1960s was, "If you're not part of the solution, you're part of the problem." Take a stand—not only against sexual harassment, which is probably the most common kind of harassment today, but also against *any* form of harassment. A manager abuses his or her resources only at the risk of losing his or her business. You cannot be an effective manager unless you consider your employees as your most valuable asset.

—————————— CASEBOOK ——————————

A few sample cases should help reinforce what you learned in this chapter and give you the opportunity to take a closer look at your

Figure 9-2. Dos and don'ts of looking into charges of harrassment.

Do	Don't
Talking with Alleged Harasser	

Do	Don't
Talk in private and promise confidentiality.	Don't confront or be combative, especially in public.
Take the situation seriously and come directly to the point—for example: "A sexual harassment complaint has been brought against you."	Don't make light of the situation or minimize its importance or seriousness.
Maintain objectivity and be as unbiased as possible.	Don't take sides of talk about rumors as if they were facts; also, don't preach or be judgmental.
Inquire into the history and circumstances of the complaint, asking about what the person may have done, not about what he or she intended—for example: "Did you put your arms around someone this morning?"	Don't ask about intentions until you ascertain the truth of the complaint.
Keep the discussion on track.	Don't get sidetracked.
Keep each allegation separate and ask for a response to each one separately.	Don't confuse issues, but be patient if the alleged harasser is confused.
If the person admits to the charges, insist that the behavior stop, and identify the consequences or next steps should the behavior continue or recur.	Don't be patronizing or judgmental; deal with the facts, law, and policy only.
If the person denies the allegations, explain the steps the investigation will take to determine the truth.	Don't make accusations or threaten punishment.
Document the meeting.	Don't rely on memory.
Take the appropriate next steps as spelled out by policy.	Don't let the matter die of its own accord; it won't go away.

(continues)

Figure 9-2. (Continued).

Talking with Witnesses

Talk in private and promise confidentiality.	Don't confront or be combative, especially in public.
Take the situation seriously and come directly to the point—for example: "You were identified as a witness to an incident this morning, and I'd like us to discuss the matter."	Don't make light of the situation or minimize its importance or seriousness.
Maintain objectivity and be as unbiased as possible.	Don't take sides or talk about rumors as if they were facts; also, don't preach or be judgmental.
Inquire into the history and circumstances of the complaint, asking about what the witness might have seen or heard.	Don't ask about assumptions or opinions or make judgments about the situation or the people involved.
Keep the discussion on track.	Don't get sidetracked.

---

own and your organization's management practices with respect to sex discrimination and sexual harassment.

When Does Being a "Boy" Do Harm?

Joyce Whit often complained that the boys club atmosphere—including pornographic pictures, ribald stories, sexually explicit language, and jokes—offended her and was unacceptable. When she received a barrage of love letters from one of the so-called boys, it was too much. Failing to get action from the higher-ups, she sued.

In response, the company's attorneys called the men's behavior "nothing more than harmless locker room antics or romantic advances." In the eyes of a "reasonable man," no harm was done.

How do your eyes behold this case?

"Reasonable Woman"

For more than 150 years, the legal gauge of behavior expected of both men and women had been the "reasonable man" convention, and in one of the two actual cases compressed into this story, the lower court held to the convention. However, neither a federal trial court in Jacksonville, Florida,[38] the Ninth Circuit Court in San Francisco,[40] nor the Supreme Court[44] have agreed. The Supreme Court's test, according to Justice Ruth Bader Ginsburg, was not whether the offensive behavior impairs a person's productivity, but rather whether it makes it harder for a person to perform a job.

Now the courts have held, in harassment suits brought by women, that even the gender-neutral "reasonable person" standard misses the point that women and men behold behavior differently. In the boys club case, experts testified that while 75 percent of the men polled would be flattered by sexual advances, 75 percent of the women said they would be offended.* The judge in the case then ruled that "pornography on an employer's wall or desk communicates a message about the way the employer views women, a view strikingly at odds with the way women wish to be viewed in the workplace." In another case, in which psychological damage was not at issue, the Eighth Circuit Court applied the "reasonable woman" test, even though the woman had posed nude for a national magazine. It doesn't matter what a person does outside the workplace; unwelcome sexual advances and innuendoes toward her from male coworkers constituted sexual harassment.[46]

Amorous Overtures

A love-struck (or lust-struck) supervisor, Barry Olson, wanted very much to spend off-duty time with his employee, Anna Mason. However, Anna didn't want to spend time with him and told him so. Still, Barry persisted, going so far as, in March of 1995, to touch her inappropriately and to promise to leave her alone if she would just let him "touch [her] down there."

When Mason complained to the plant manager, Mary Goodman, the manager warned Olson to stop, but made no record of the complaint. The harassment continued with staring, uninvited visits to her workstation, and frequent requests to start an affair. After complaining to other supervisors of his misbehavior, Mason was further humil-

---

*See also Arthur S. Hayes, "Courts Concede the Sexes Thinking in Unlike Ways," *The Wall Street Journal* (May 28, 1991), p. B1.

iated by Olson's public announcement to the crew that a different employee with less seniority than Mason was promoted to a higher position in the team. Mason quit and charged Olson and the company with sexual harassment and retaliation for refusing his overtures and for complaining about them.

The company argued on appeal to the Eighth Circuit Court in 1999 that, yes, the harassment took place but that it ended after the last overt act of touching Mason's breast much earlier in the situation. The three-hundred-day limitation period under Title VII had expired and acts prior to May 3, 1995, could not be admitted.

What do you think the Eighth Circuit Court thought of that argument?

Hostile Environment

Get real! No, those weren't the court's words. Rather, the court explained that, even though sexual contact ceased, the ongoing hostile environment established by Olson created a "continuing violation." Therefore, in spite of the nonsexual harassment during the later stages of Mason's employment, the complaint falls within the limitations period. All the charges stay, and a jury could easily and properly find that Olson had sexually harassed Mason.[51]

Several other issues should be noted. Olson's manager may have given him warnings, but (1) she didn't document the warnings, and (2) she did nothing else to stop him or to prevent him from harassing Mason. In addition, clearly, the case violates both prongs of the "affirmative defense": a job detriment occurred and the employer failed to take prompt remedial action. Don't make the same mistakes.

Can You Be Sued for Giving Preferential Treatment to a Lover?

In working with women colleagues, Clay Anderson would touch them sexually. When he did that often to Ellen Davis, she told him angrily and just as often to "keep your hands off" and "would you please stop this."

Eventually Clay stopped, finding a willing sexual partner elsewhere in the group. Even though the lover's job performance was deficient in a variety of ways, she was given plum assignments. Winking women tolerating the affair were also given preferences. Ellen was fired for supposedly poor job performance.

Is promoting someone who consents over someone who refuses sexual advances a form of sexual discrimination?

Adverse Working Conditions

The decision in this 1986 case reinforces one made in 1983. In the earlier case, Title VII was applied when the plaintiff was denied opportunities granted to a co-employee who had consented to sexual advances.[8] In the present case, according preferential treatment to a female employee who submits to sexual advances and other sexual conduct violates Title VII because the manager demonstrates through his conduct that job benefits are conditioned on an employee's tolerance of sexually charged conduct or advances.[9] The law clearly prohibits such behavior.

It does not matter that a female is ultimately selected for promotion or preferential treatment. Another female employee, *perceiving* that better employment opportunities are predicated on submitting to sexual conduct, *and* that had she been a man she would not have been treated that way, is free to charge the offending supervisor with sexual discrimination. The liability is fairly clear.

Need we spell out the moral? Whether you are a male or a female manager, if you feel it necessary to approach an employee sexually, take care not to deny employees opportunities merely because they refuse to submit to your sexual advances or favor employees who do. Better still, unless you are talking about a case of true love (followed by marriage or alternative arrangement), avoid intimate relationships with employees, period.

Harassment Leads to Attempted Suicide

No matter how often Jason Schmidt told his coworker, Felix Alder, to stop calling him names like "bitch," "queer," or "queen," Alder persisted. Complaining to their supervisor, Dan Collins, only made the situation worse because Collins liked Alder and believed Schmidt to be a whiner and complainer. When Alder asked Schmidt for oral sex, Jason went to Collins again, only to hear that "You gotta take care of your own problems. Handle it yourself or shut up."

After Schmidt attempted suicide, he was hospitalized with severe depression. After he returned to work with a letter from his therapist, he asked for a transfer away from Alder. Collins shrugged it off, refusing to do anyone "any special favors." Months of torment ended when Schmidt quit because Collins again refused to grant him a transfer. He then sued the company for violating state laws against harassment and discrimination on the basis of disability.

How would you have handled Schmidt's situation?

Same-Sex Harassment Is Still Harassment

In the actual case, the man I've called Jason Schmidt won at trial, receiving $45,000 in compensatory damages and $25,000 in punitive damages. The appeals court, upholding the jury's decision, added attorney's fees on top of the damages.*

Although this case involves an ADA element (depression is a disability), the same-sex harassment concerns us more. The U.S. Supreme Court, on March 4, 1998, ruled unanimously that same-sex, homosexual harassment falls under the prohibitions against discrimination because of sex: acting toward a member of one sex in ways you would not toward a member of the other sex. In this case, the plaintiff "was forcibly subjected to [public] sex-related, humiliating actions against him . . . [and was] also physically assaulted in a sexual manner, [threatening] him with rape." When his complaints failed to produce remedial action, he quit, "asking that his pink slip reflect that he 'voluntarily left due to sexual harassment and verbal abuse.'" Writing for the court, Justice Scalia cited the intent of Title VII of the Civil Rights Act of 1994, which is to provide for striking "at the entire spectrum of disparate treatment of men and women in employment." Therefore, "because of sex" protects men as well as women. In the same manner that the courts have previously ruled

*"Case Studies, 'Get Him Off My Back,'" in *The EEO Review* (Panel Publishers, December 1999), pp. 1–2.

that same-race harassment is illegal, same-sex "exposure to disadvantageous terms or conditions of employment to which members of the other sex are not exposed" is illegal as well.[36, 48]*

Title VII doesn't really single out job discrimination and harassment against gays and lesbians, but numerous states (West Coast, East Coast, and states in between) have adopted laws prohibiting mistreatment of people on the basis of sexual orientation or transsexual changes.† Your response to this matter should be no different than it is to opposite sex discrimination and harassment,‡ and should include the following:

> Clearly stated policies and procedures that prohibit discrimination against and harassment of gays and lesbians
> Training of all employees, including top executives
> Serious, objective investigations of complaints
> Prompt remedial action

When Does Consent Violate Title VII?

Everyone, including her supervisor, Bob Kraft, called Lisa Engels the prettiest employee at National Savings and Loan. Kraft often told her that he hired her mainly for that reason.

He also often told her that unless she had sex with him, he would have her job and make employment anywhere else in town just about impossible. Frightening her with his power, he forced himself on her both during and after bank hours. He fondled her in front of others, followed her into the women's rest room where he exposed himself to her, and several times raped her at work. Overpowering and intimidating, he reduced her frequent and strenuous

*"New Guidelines for Employers on Avoiding Sexual Harassment Liability," *op. cit.,* pp. 7–8

†See Linda Greenhouse, "High Court Widens Workplace Claim in Sex Harassment," *The New York Times On-Line* (March 5, 1998); see also, Tim Poor, "Same-Sex Harassment Is Illegal, Supreme Court Rules," *St. Louis Post-Dispatch* (March 5, 1998), pp. A1 and A11; Jan Crawford Greenburg, "Harassment Ruling Is Two-Sided, Workers Find, Reasoning in Same-Sex Ruling Limits Claims, Benefiting Employers," *Chicago Tribune,* reprinted in *St. Louis Post-Dispatch* and "Decision Has Had a Wide Impact on Sexual Harassment Cases," *St. Louis Post-Dispatch* (August 4, 1999), p. A8.

‡"Employment Discrimination Against Gays and Lesbians: The Law Is Changing," in *The EEO Review,* Panel Publishers, December 1999, pp. 4–6.

protests to a silent glare. Soon, he tired of her and stopped his attacks.

Fear overcoming anger, Lisa kept silent for a year. When she finally realized that she would have to submit to Kraft again if she ever wanted advancement, she filed a Title VII suit in federal court and with the EEOC against both Bob Kraft and National Savings and Loan charging sex discrimination (creating a hostile working environment) and sexual harassment. Both respondents claimed innocence.

According to Kraft, the sexual relationship was voluntary; Lisa agreed to having sex with him. Their only dispute came about when he complained about her job performance. He asked for a dismissal of the charges on the basis of mutual consent.

The management of National Savings and Loan washed their hands of the incident, pleading that they had had no knowledge of the sexual relationship and therefore were not responsible. Besides, the relationship was between two consenting adults, and they could not have reasonably known about it. They too asked for a summary dismissal.

After six years, the case worked its way up to the U.S. Supreme Court. According to the EEOC, in its Policy Guidance on Sexual Harassment, the case posed three key questions:

1. Does unwelcome sexual behavior that creates a hostile working environment constitute employment discrimination on the basis of sex?
2. Can a Title VII violation be shown when the district court found that any sexual relationship that existed between the plaintiff and her supervisor was a "voluntary one"?
3. Is an employer strictly liable for an offensive working environment created by a supervisor's sexual advances when the employer does not know of, and could not have reasonably known of, the supervisor's conduct?[35]

What do you say? Can consent and harassment coexist? Can harassment form a basis for sex discrimination? And can you, as an employer or manager, be held liable for the actions of one of your supervisors?

Involuntary Consent

Yes. Yes. Yes. The Supreme Court upheld the plaintiff's charges on all three counts. According to Justice Rehnquist: "When a supervisor sexually harasses a subordinate because of a subordinate's sex, that supervisor discriminates on the basis of sex."

Unwelcome sexual advances, requests for sexual favors, or other verbal or physical conduct of a sexual nature mark sexual harassment. The key word is *unwelcome.*

By definition, behavior harasses if it is unwelcome. It is unwelcome if the person experiencing it says it is. The person would not experience that conduct, in most cases, if he or she were of the same sex (although in 1981 and 1983, homosexual harassment came under the protection of Title VII).[6, 7] Therefore, sexual harassment creates a hostile environment predicated on sex differences and is a form of sex discrimination that violates Title VII.[1]

Even if consent is voluntary, the court responded to the second question, that the demands are unwelcome is sufficient to support the charge of harassment.

"The fact that sex-related conduct was voluntary, in the sense that the complainant was not forced to participate against her will, is not a defense to a sexual harassment suit brought under Title VII. . . . The correct inquiry is whether [the victim] by her conduct indicated that the alleged sexual advances were unwelcome, not whether her actual participation in sexual intercourse was voluntary."

Consent at gunpoint is less than *willing participation*; therefore, the complaint is enforceable under Title VII.

Is There a Title VII Violation if There Is No Job Detriment?

When Sarah Beckwith's boss in the city administration made additional job training contingent on her going to bed with him, she reached her limit of tolerance. She had been the victim of repeated sexual remarks, verbal insults, and aggressive assaults long enough. She quit and went to court, alleging that her supervisor created a hostile and offensive working environment for women, that her resignation constituted constructive discharge because her working conditions had become intolerable, and that her supervisor created a job detriment by limiting her access to training.

The employer asked for a dismissal on the grounds that Sarah voluntarily resigned without pressure from the organization. The district court dismissed the case, ruling that Sarah did not show that a tangible job detriment resulted from the manager's demands and therefore could not show that the man created a hostile and offensive working environment under Title VII. In addition, constructive discharge can give rise to a Title VII claim if a hostile environment exists, but the judge agreed that Sarah resigned for reasons other than "a sexually demeaning work environment." Finally, he said that Sarah had not shown that additional training was in fact conditioned on responding to the manager's sexual demands. Sarah then appealed to the Eleventh Circuit Court.

What would happen in your shop if an employee complained that future training appeared contingent upon sleeping with the boss?

Tangible Detriment Not Always Required

The Eleventh Circuit remanded two of the three charges back to the district court for further hearings on the facts: (1) that the manager did in fact create a hostile environment, and (2) that training was in fact contingent on submitting to having sexual relations.

The circuit court agreed that the plaintiff did not suffer constructive discharge because she did not resign under pressure from her employer.[1]

But the facts are not as important to us here as are the criteria that the court set in this case.

"Under some circumstances," the court rules, "[creating] an offensive or hostile environment due to sexual harassment can violate Title VII [even if] the complainant [does not suffer] tangible job detriment." Discriminatory working conditions can exist where a pattern of harassment subjects a person to disparate treatment regardless of whether or not the employee also proves she has lost a tangible job benefit. These are the three tests the claim must pass to qualify under Title VII:

1. That the employee is a member of a protected group
2. That the unwelcome sexual harassment based on the sex of
   the employee affects a "term, condition, or privilege" of employment
3. If the employer is to be held liable for the hostile environment created by a supervisor or coworker, that the employer
   knew or should have known of the harassment in question
   but failed to take remedial action

Concerning the first point, the court would not recognize a
Title VII liability if the supervisor's or coworker's sexual behavior
was offensive to men and women alike; the conduct created disparate treatment based on gender. But the court's use of the phrase
term, condition, or privilege of employment raises an important issue.

According to the court, an employee's psychological state may
be included in the above phrase if the sexual harassment is so *pervasive* that it creates an "abusive" work environment. Under these conditions, a tangible job detriment need not be shown.

This criterion underlies a later 1985 decision in which an appellate court upheld a female employee's claim that her male supervisor
sexually harassed her by physically grabbing her arm and preventing
her from leaving the office. The court rejected the employer's argument that although the supervisor exerted unnecessary force or violence, because there were no sexual overtones to the incident, it did
not qualify under Title VII. The use of physical force toward a
woman employee that would not have been applied in a similar circumstance to a man employee, if sufficiently pervasive, can form an
illegal condition of employment under Title VII, according to the
court.[37] How you treat someone significantly different from you—
for example, a member of the opposite sex—does matter.

A pervasive atmosphere can poison a workplace, and you, as a
manager, should be on guard to prevent it from creating a hostile
or abusive situation. Even directing sexual advances at consenting,
noncomplaining female employees or allowing fellow managers to
be crude and foul-mouthed in front of female employees could jeopardize your shop.

If you ignore promotions that co-managers give to subordinates
who are their lovers, a female employee could sue your organization
although she herself does not directly experience sexual harassment.

She might have a case if she feels forced to work in an atmosphere in which such conduct is pervasive, especially if she feels harassed by having to watch willing sex partners receive preferential treatment to her detriment.[38, 39] The EEOC, in its 1988 guidelines, made it clear that how you as a manager act with regard to your organization's overall situation can influence the outcome if push comes to shove.

Even cases of quid pro quo harassment, in which the Supreme Court *always* holds an employer liable, often come up for debate. For example, what if the employer does not know about the problem?

Cases

1. 682 F.2d 897, 29 F.E.P. Cases (BNA) 787 (11th Cir. 1982).
2. 830 F.2d 1554, 45 F.E.P. Cases (BNA) 160 (11th Cir. 1987).
3. 118 S. Ct. 2275 (1998); 118 S. Ct. 2257 (1998); see also, No. 97–9102 (11th Cir., 1998); 261 F.3d 751 (8th Cir. 2001).
4. See also No. 96–5235 (10th Cir. 1998), in which the court held the employer liable because its harassment policies and actions taken were deficient.
5. EEOC Decision No. 84–3, 34 F.E.P. Cases (BNA) 1887 (February 16, 1984).
6. 25 F.E.P. Cases (BNA) 5656 (N.D. Ill. 1981).
7. 36 F.E.P. Cases (BNA) 1644 (M.D. Alabama, 1983).
8. 570 F. Supp. 1197, 32 F.E.P. Cases (BNA) 1401 (D. Del. 1983).
9. 98 F.R.D. 775, 40 F.E.P. Cases (BNA) 208 (N.D. Cal. 1986).
10. Massachusetts Commission Against Discrimination (June 3, 1987).
11. EEOC Commission Decision No. 84–1.
12. 509 F. Supp. 6 (N.D. Ill. 1980); see also L-37088–89 (Brager Cty. Super. Ct. 1992) and 17492/91 (N.Y. Sup. Ct. 1992).
13. 807 F.2d 1536, 42 F.E.P. Cases (BNA) 1141 (11th Cir. 1987).
14. No. 85–494 (January 13, 1987).
15. 680 F.2d 1243, 29 F.E.P. Cases (BNA) (9th Cir. 1982).
16. No. 82–411 (June 20, 1983).
17. 486 A.2d 126 (Me. 1984).
18. 601 F. Supp. 160, 37 F.E.P. Cases (BNA) 843 (W.D. Pa. 1985), *aff'd* 779 F.2d 42.
19. 462 F. Supp. 289 (S.D. W. Va.).
20. 601 F. Supp. 243, 39 F.E.P. Cases (BNA) 1398 (D. Mass. 1985).
21. 41 F.E.P. Cases (BNA) 1489 (D.C. App. 1986).
22. 825 F.2d 458, 263, 44 F.E.P. Cases (BNA) 825 (D.C. Cir. 1987).
23. No. 87–1167 (1989); however, see also 836 F. Supp. 152 (S.D.N.Y.); Civil Rights Act 158.1, 387; Fed. R. Civ. P. 2121.1, 2127, 2143; no. 91 Civ. 0035 (K.M.W. 1993). Appeal dropped by plaintiff February 16, 1994.
24. 436 F. Supp. 1328 (W.D. Pa. 1977), *aff'd,* 578 F.2d. 1374 (1978), *cert. denied,* 99 S. Ct. 734 (1978).
25. 828 F.2d 307, 44 F.E.P. Cases (BNA) 1604 (5th Cir. 1987).
26. 766 F.2d 424 (8th Cir. 1984).
27. No. 84–2233 GB (May 13, 1987); 1998 WL 824501 (N.D. Ill. 1998); see also

"Overly Favorable Evaluation Constitutes Retaliation," in *Missouri Employment Law Newsletter* (February, 1999), pp. 1–2.

28. 842 F.2d 936 (7th Cir. March 16, 1988).
29. 683 F. Supp. 1302, 46 E.P.D. (CCH) 37,868 (D.S.D. 1988).
30. 463 U.S. 1073 (1983).
31. No. 83–1557 (3d Cir. 1984).
32. USDC-DC, 4.23.79.
33. 758 F.2d 1462, 37 F.E.P. Cases (BNA) 1232 (11th Cir. 1985).
34. 561 F.2d 983, 999, 14 E.P.D. (CCH) 7755 (D.C. Cir. 1977).
35. 106 S. Ct. 2399, 40 E.P.D. (CCH) (1986); see also no. 90–4030 (D.N.J. January 6, 1992, *as amended* January 30, 1992), *dismissed without prejudice;* no. 92–5074 (1992) *aff'g* 64 F.E.P. Cas. 190, 780 F. Supp. 1026.
36. 528 F. Supp. 1380, 30 F.E.P. Cases 1205 (S.D. Ohio 1982).
37. F.E.P. Cases (BNA) 364 (D.C. Cir. 1985).
38. 46 F.E.P. Cases (BNA) 1272 (D.D.C. 1988).
39. 538 F. Supp. 857, 30 F.E.P. Cases (BNA) 1212 (N.D. Ohio 1982).
40. 924 F.2d 871, 878–8779 (9th Cir. 1991); no. 86–927-Civ-5–12 (M.D.F. 1991).
41. No. 121611 (Mich. Ct. App. 1991).
42. No. 91–5261 (3d Cir. 1992).
43. 114 S. Ct. 367 (1993). 462; 92 S. Ct.
44. No. 93–7188 (2d Cir. 1994). Review denied by the Supreme Court, June 13, 1994, as reported in the *St. Louis Post-Dispatch* (June 14, 1994), p. 9A.
45. No. 5–88–163 (D. Minn. 3d Div. 1993).
46. No. 92–2059 (8th Cir. 1993).
47. U.S. S. Ct., No. 96–568 (March 4, 1998).
48. 239 F.3d 243, 245, 2nd Circuit Court, 2001; see also, 97–3678P (8th Cir., July 1998); No. 96–4155 (8th Cir., August 1998); No. 97–4245 (8th Cir., October, 1998); No. 97–9102 (11th Cir., November 13, 1998); No. 99–15895 (9th Cir., April 2001).
49. 238 F.3d 1045 (8th Cir., 2001).
50. No. 98–1275 (8th Cir. 1999).

10

Mismanaging People with Disabilities

All EEO laws and regulations ebb and flow around (1) *definitions* and (2) *perceptions;* even the words the lawmakers use change with prevailing political tides. Whereas the Rehabilitation Act of 1973 refers to handicapped people, the Americans with Disabilities Act of 1990 calls handicaps *disabilities*.* Regardless of which word you use, what constitutes a handicap or a disability has more to do with definitions and perceptions than with medical diagnoses. Again, I will define a few key terms before I look at what you cannot and can do; in the Casebook, I review a variety of unusual cases related to disability or impairment that show the complexities of equal opportunity issues.

The ADA, which took effect on July 24, 1992, reinforces the definitions spelled out in the Rehabilitation Act of 1973, and the EEOC has expanded the list of ADA-covered disabilities. According to the EEOC, disability-discrimination complaints have been declining since 1996; however, since the first ADA lawsuit filed on December 28, 1993, a total of 91,000 ADA complaints by end of fiscal year 1998 have been filed.† The most common complaints referred to were back impairments (20 percent) and mental illness (13 percent). Even though a Harvard study shows that AIDS is the most litigated disease ever (mainly in the state courts and local human relations commissions), AIDS-related problems were cited in only 2 percent of the ADA complaints.

---

*See also Julie Rovner, "Provisions: Americans with Disabilities Act of 1990," *Congressional Quarterly* (Washington, D.C.: July 28, 1990), pp. 2437–2444.
†Susan Garland, "Employers Fear the Supreme Court Will Dramatically Expand the Scope of the ADA," *Business Week* (April 26, 1999), p. 72; Diane Stafford, "Workers with Disabilities Still Have a Hard Time Finding Jobs Despite Low Unemployment Rate," *St. Louis Post-Dispatch* (August 19, 1999), p. C7.

Definitions of Key Terms

physical impairment [Any] physiological disorder or condition, cosmetic disfigurement, or anatomical loss affecting one or more . . . body systems: neurological; musculoskeletal; special sense organs; respiratory, including speech organs; cardiovascular; reproductive; digestive; genitourinary; hemic and lymphatic; skin; and endocrine.[1]*

impaired or handicapped person Any person who (1) has a physical or mental impairment [that] substantially limits one or more of such person's major life activities; (2) has a record of such an impairment; or (3) is regarded as having such an impairment.[1] A 1998 ruling by the U.S. Supreme Court, although it doesn't involve an employment situation, has practical implications for you with regard to AIDS (and other disabilities). In it, the justices denied lower court opinions that "a condition must more or less visibly interfere with the person's public life or economic life on a fairly consistent basis"; instead, they said, some conditions (for example, AIDS, epilepsy, diabetes) may affect the human biological system in ways that create inherent disabilities, whether visible or not.[2]

Between 1999 and 2002, the U.S. Supreme Court rendered four highly publicized decisions that have made a significant difference in the definition of physically impaired person.[24-27]† In one, the Court

---

*Kim Curtis, "Companies Struggle to Adapt to Mental Health Disability," *St. Louis Post-Dispatch* (May 20, 1999), p. B2. See also Kim Curtis, "Courts Reject Many Mental Disability Claims," *The Wall Street Journal* (July 22, 1997), p. B1; "Court Allows Mental-Illness Benefit Caps," *The Wall Street Journal* (August 5, 1997), p. B1.
†For the full text of referenced cases (24–26), check out LawMemo.com on the Internet or the following Cornell University web pages: http://supct.law.cornell.edu/supct/html (97–1943.ZS.htlm, 97–1992.ZS.htlm, and 98–591.ZS.htlm.). For print references to all four cases, see Susan Garland, "Protecting the Disabled Won't Cripple Business," *op. cit.*, p. 71; Lynette Clemetson, "A Sharper Image of Bias," *Newsweek* (July 5, 1999), p. 27; Associated Press, "Disabilities Act Doesn't Cover Poor Eyesight, Blood Pressure," *St. Louis Post-Dispatch* (June 23, 1999), pp. A1 and A9; "High Court Settles ADA Debate," *Personnel Legal Alert* (Ramsey, NJ: Alexander Hamilton Institute Inc., July 19, 1999), p. 1; Peter Petesch, "Supreme Court Holds That Mitigating Measures Belong in ADA's Disability Equation," in Rose Proskauer-LLP (ed.) *Legal Report* (a publication of the Society for Human Resource Management, July–August 1999), pp. 7–8; "Supreme Court: Mitigating Measures Count," *Personnel Legal Alert* (August 2, 1999), pp. 1–2; Robert Thompson, "Disability Deter-

ruled against two near-sighted pilots whose corrective lenses provided them acceptable eyesight. Sandra Day O'Connor, writing for the majority said,

> Three separate ADA provisions, read in concert, lead to the conclusion that the determination whether an individual is disabled should be made with reference to measures, such as eyeglasses and contact lenses, that mitigate the individual's impairment. . . .[24]

In the second case, the majority of the Court ruled that a truck driver suffering from hypertension had no ADA claim because medicines had corrected his condition.[25] The third case presented a different problem, one in which a person blind in one eye learned how to compensate for his loss of depth perception; therefore, the court could not consider him a disabled person under the ADA. Finally, in 2002, the Supreme Court made it more difficult to prove that a partial disability, such as carpal tunnel, falls under the definition of an impaired person. In another case, the Eighth Circuit Court defined *substantial limits* in major life activities, such as work, if a person is "significantly restricted in the ability to perform either a class of jobs or a broad range of jobs in various classes as compared to the average person [having] comparable training, skills, and abilities."[26]

major life activities   Functions such as caring for oneself, performing manual tasks, walking, seeing, hearing, speaking, breathing, learning, and working.[1]

reasonable accommodation   Making an effort to manage a disabled employee's work or workplace to meet his or her special needs or to protect him or her and other employees. Specifically, accommodation means to create a physical and social climate in which a person with special needs is capable of performing the essential functions of a job and provides the person with an "equal employment opportunity without imposing undue hardship on the employer or other employees."[3] ADA makes tax credits and other

minations Must Reflect Corrective Measures, Court Says," *HR News* (August, 1999), pp. 1, 9, and 11; "High Court Ends Term with Important Rulings on ADA, Punitive Damages," *Missouri Employment Newsletter* (Brentwood, TN: M. Lee Smith Publishers LLC, August 1999), pp. 6–7.

financial considerations available to employers. Employers have protections, as well.

In one 1997 case, for example, the Sixth Circuit Court ruled that an employee with a mental disability need not receive the same level of medical benefits as those with physical disabilities; at the same time, the EEOC recognizes mental health disabilities, and such claims have risen by 20 percent a year since the ADA was passed. In one case, settled out of court, an employee received $1.1 million when his employer failed to accommodate his clinical depression with a little extra time off.*

The Ninth Circuit has ruled, and the Supreme Court agreed, that employers don't err when they apply a collective bargaining agreement's seniority provisions to deny employees seeking accommodations for disabilities; collective bargaining rights gets precedence under the "rule of per se unreasonableness" over those of individual workers with disabilities.[4]

temporary disability "An injury or illness that is medically treatable without significant symptoms . . . [and] a major life activity is not permanently substantially limited."[1]

essential job functions Activities that are, in the employer's judgment, basic to the performance of a job or are required by a business necessity. Meeting the following criteria will protect you if you are challenged in court:†

› You have prepared job descriptions, which outline essential and marginal job functions.
› You have described the nature of the work relative to the operation of the business and its relation to the organizational structure.
› You have met the conditions of a bargaining agreement (where applicable).
› You can demonstrate the amount of time spent on the function.

*Kim Curtis, "Companies Struggle to Adapt to Mental Health Disability," *St. Louis Post-Dispatch* (May 20, 1999), p. 3C
†See also, Tim O'Reilly and Naomi Svendsen, "Job Analysis Can Help Determine Which Functions Are Essential," *HR News,* a publication of the Society for Human Resource Management (July 1999), p. 5; Carrie Schierer, "Detailed Job Descriptions Save Employer in ADA Case," *Missouri Employment Law Letter* (Brentwood, TN: M. Lee Smith Publishers LLC, March 2001), pp. 1–2.

> You have spelled out the consequences if the person can't perform or if you permit the person not to perform the functions of the job.
> You can describe other workers' experiences in the job or in similar jobs.

marginal job functions   Activities that can be assigned to other people if a reasonable accommodation is required.

Not only are those definitions very comprehensive, they are quite specific; one section also identifies the importance of perception: "Any person who . . . is regarded as having such an impairment." If you *think* someone is handicapped, you could, in fact, create the conditions whereby he or she can charge you with discrimination.

Take AIDS, for example. If you erroneously think that someone suffering from AIDS can spread the disease through casual contact on the job and, on that basis alone, treat that employee differently from the way you do others, you have admitted that the employee is impaired or disabled.[6-9] You thereby make yourself vulnerable to a legal challenge.

It is largely your responsibility as an employer to identify what constitutes a disability, and an erroneous perception has the same impact (if not more so) as a correct one. You should know just what is covered by the broad legal definitions, which is not as simple as it may seem.

Epilepsy, even if controlled by medication, has been called a disability.[10] High blood pressure (hypertension) limits a person's major life activities, too, and is therefore called a disability by the courts.[11] A cancer-induced mastectomy? Yes, according to a federal court in Missouri.[12] Obesity? In some courts, yes,[13] in other courts, no.[14] Alcoholism or other substance addictions? In some courts, yes,[15-19] in other courts, no.[20] You probably should get a copy of the EEOC's guidance on job accommodations* and seek legal advice before mak-

---

Reasonable Accommodation and Undue Hardship Under the Americans with Disabilities Act, available through EEOC Publication Center (800-800-3302) or on the Internet at www.eeoc.gov; see also, John F. Wymer, III, "Reasonable Accommodation and Undue Hardship," *Legal Report,* a publication of the Society for Human Resource Management (May–June 1999), pp. 6–9.

ing personnel decisions that could possibly adversely affect a handicapped person's job opportunities or conditions of employment.

What You Cannot Do

What are your boundaries when you manage people with physical or mental disabilities?

You cannot fail or refuse to hire any person because he or she has a disability as long as she or he is capable of successfully and safely performing the duties of the job. When you do manage someone with a disability, you cannot:

› Discriminate against him or her with respect to compensation, terms, conditions, or privileges of employment.
› Limit, segregate, or classify employees in any way that would deprive or tend to deprive a person of employment opportunities or have an adverse effect on the person's status as an employee. The EEOC has also sued a benefits provider, claiming, under ADA, that employers may not deny benefits to AIDS victims.[23] This case may work its way up to the Supreme Court before a settlement is reached.
› Fail to provide training to a person because he or she has a disability.
› Discharge any person because he or she has a disability. The Ninth Circuit Court has ruled that you bear the burden of proof, not just your *gut feeling,* if you claim that a person with a disability poses a direct threat to him- or herself or others.[28]
› Retaliate against any employees or applicants for employment because they made a charge, testified, assisted, or participated in any manner protected by the Rehabilitation Act of 1973 or the ADA.

Using Genetic Test Information to Discriminate

A dozen or so states have adopted legislation prohibiting employers from using genetic tests as a basis for discrimination. For example, Section 4 of Missouri's genetic testing law, effective January 1, 1999, states:

An employer shall not use any genetic information or genetic test results . . . of an employee or prospective employee to distinguish between, discriminate against, or
restrict any right or benefit otherwise due or available to
such [person].

Exceptions include the following:

> Underwriting in connection with health, long-term care, or
  disability insurance
> Any action termed *legal* under law or regulation
> Actions taken with the person's written permission
> Genetic information that would preclude a person from per-
  forming the essential functions of an assigned job

It's best to check with your legal counsel concerning the status of
information about genetic testing in your state.

Government Employers

In a decision strikingly different from the one the Supreme Court
made in May 2003 with regard to the Family and Medical Leave Act,
the Court ruled that state governments, by virtue of the Eleventh
Amendment of the Constitution, are immune from private suits
under ADA from state workers. First, according to Chief Justice Wil-
liam Rehnquist, the ADA was based on an inadequate legislative
record; Congress has not demonstrated to a high level of proof that
the states have been guilty of a "pattern of unconstitutional discrimination." Secondly, the majority held that Congress can't impose
obligations on the states that extend beyond Constitutional demands, which, Rehnquist said, the ADA does.[29]
    It doesn't follow, therefore, that governments can't take *volun-
tary* measures to accommodate persons with disabilities. The federal
government itself, in 2000, set up ADA accessibility guidelines to
apply to its Web sites. This will probably have effects on all federal
contractors and other employers as well.*

---

*"ADA Accessibility Guidelines to Apply to Federal Web Sites Soon," *HR News*
(June 1999), p. 24.

What You Can Do

You, too, have rights. You can deny a disabled or impaired person a job if the disability or impairment would interfere with the person's ability to successfully perform the duties of the job or would pose a direct threat to property or to the safety of other people. You cannot fire a person merely on the basis of a disability, but you can fire or otherwise discipline someone for good cause, or if the disability creates a burden on your ability to conduct business or to guarantee the employee's safety or the safety of other people.

Three general guidelines can help you to manage people with disabilities, including those suffering from alcohol or drug addiction:

1. *Be flexible.* You cannot be rigid in your approaches to employees suffering from any kind of disease, be it AIDS or alcoholism or diabetes. You need to develop new ways of perceiving a person's abilities or capabilities and new ways of thinking about disease. However, if you are too lenient with substance abusers, you could be accused of negligence.

2. *Be patient and forbearing.* Satisfying a "reasonable accommodation" standard requires patience and forbearance as well as compassion, especially if the person's ability to perform essential job functions satisfactorily has not been impaired. Give people an opportunity to perform, give them control over their work space, and evaluate their work on the basis of facts. If performance begins to slip, it is your responsibility to find out why and to do what you can to help before summarily dismissing the offending employee.

Here is the point: Even if the steps you take do not work, you need to take them before you can decide to not hire or to fire an otherwise qualified person with a disability. That this "reasonableness" rule applies to meeting religious or military obligations as well as physical or mental needs makes this point most important.

3. *Be observant.* Failing to recognize the cause of a performance or behavior problem will not exempt you from liability should you take an adverse action against a person with a disability or impairment. Erratic performance should be a red flag for a manager to investigate the cause or causes of the slippage; and should an impairment be responsible, the employer should offer the person an

opportunity to receive treatment.[19] The courts have said that you can choose the accommodations, although you should take into consideration the wishes and needs of the individual with the disability.[30] Be sure to take into account mitigating circumstances, such as eyeglasses or medications or natural adjustments, and both the positive and negative side effects of the corrections. Avoid perceiving a disability if a person's condition—for example, cancer—has been corrected by surgical or other means.

To execute these guidelines, here are some steps you can take:

> Alter a work area to allow access or permit an employee with a disability to telecommute if appropriate and under extraordinary circumstances.*
> Reorganize the person's work assignments.
> Reorganize the work distribution in the unit.
> Provide special equipment, such as enlargers for computer screens for the sight impaired or telecommunication devices for the hearing impaired (TDDs).
> Provide interpreters to the hearing impaired during meetings, performance appraisal discussions, and training programs.
> Train supervisors and coworkers to work with persons with disabilities—for example, provide sign language classes for people who will be working with the hearing impaired.
> Make reasonable allowances for absences or modify work schedules to accommodate necessary medical appointments.
> Reassign a person with a disability to a different job or workplace if safety is a concern.
> Encourage medical or psychiatric treatment; take steps to get the organization enrolled in an employee-assistance program (EAP).†

Because alcoholics and drug addicts often go through a period of psychological denial of their problems and frequently become bel-

---

*See also, Brenda B. Thompson, "Telecommuting and ADA Compliance," in *HR Executive Special Reports: Telecommuting Pluses and Pitfalls* (Brentwood, TN: M. Lee Smith Publishers LLC, 1996, 1999), pp. 15–18.
†Dianne Kiranne, "EAPS: Dawning of a New Age," *HR Magazine* (January 1990), pp. 30–34; see also "How to Recommend Psychological Help," *The Wall Street Journal* (June 13, 1991), p. B1

ligerent and rebellious when confronted directly, the steps for dealing with addictions differ in one respect: Instead of confrontation, it is best, regardless of the type or severity of the disability, to observe performance relative to objective standards. When an employee's work suffers in comparison to those standards, deal with *that fact* and do not accuse him or her of anything. Your responsibility extends only to uncovering and dealing with a performance problem. If performance does not improve or if the employee cannot perform an available alternative function in your business, then you have a basis for firing him or her. If you accuse someone of drinking or using drugs, you run the risk of being sued for defamation.

Drinking alcohol is not illegal, and only some drug usage is. Alcohol or drug use becomes your affair only if drinking alcohol or using drugs during work hours violates company policy. If you catch an employee in the act, you have a basis for challenging alcohol or drug use. Without calling the person an alcoholic or addict, refer a problem employee to two forms of counseling: performance counseling first, and, if he or she admits to drinking or drug use, substance abuse counseling second.

If counseling does not bring about a desired change, offer a leave without pay if paid leave is not available or is exhausted. As long as a disability is correctable and the person is likely to respond to treatment, as is an alcoholic, leave is reasonable if reassigning the employee to a less difficult or demanding position is not possible.

Let the employee receive disability benefits, especially if the impairment results from a work-related injury. If performance, attendance, or behavior problems stem from a health-related condition, require a medical or psychiatric evaluation. If you have to consider firing an employee, offer him or her a "last chance" or "firm choice" option between rehabilitation or discipline (including dismissal).*

I am not suggesting that managing an employee with a disability is no different from managing employees without disabilities or that it is always easy. But a wise Native American proverb gives

---

*For a thorough description of some steps an organization can take to help its addicted employees, see *HR Magazine on Human Resource Management* (April 1990), pp. 46–49, 50–54, 55–58, 61–62; see also Ron Winslow, "New Study [by the Harvard School of Public Health and Boston University] Shows In-Patient Treatment May Be Best Course for Problem Drinker," *The Wall Street Journal* (September 21, 1991), p. B1.

good counsel: "Before you judge any other man, walk in his moccasins along a pebbly shore."

EEOC Guidelines: ADA and Workers' Compensation, 1996

ADA and workers' compensation laws don't define disabilities the same way. A person may receive workers' compensation and still be covered by ADA. Employers may not ask either applicants or third parties about prior workers' compensation claims or occupational injuries; they can't require an applicant to undergo a medical exam unless and until they make a conditional offer of employment, and then only if they ask the same questions and require the same exams for all entering employees in the same job category. ADA's confidentiality provisions apply to medical information concerning an applicant's or employee's job-related injury or workers' compensation claim, with limited exceptions:

1. Employers may not refuse to hire a person with disabilities because of a supposition of increased risk of injury unless they can show that the employment would pose a direct threat, that is, if they can show a significant risk of substantial harm to workplace health or safety that can't be eliminated or minimized by reasonable accommodation.

2. An employer may not refuse to allow an employee the right to return to work if covered by an ADA-defined disability, as long as the employee can perform the essential functions of the job (as opposed to marginal functions) and the employee could return to full duty if the employer determines that the employee is ready to return to work, with or without reasonable accommodation. As long as the employee is covered by ADA, it doesn't matter if workers' comp determines that he or she is permanently disabled by its definitions.

3. Although ADA doesn't require employers to provide reasonable accommodation for employees injured on the job, if the disabilities are covered by ADA and the employee can perform the essential functions of the job, unless employers can demonstrate that holding a position open for the injured per-

son and/or providing accommodations would impose an undue hardship on the company and/or other employees, the employee would likely be covered.

——————— CASEBOOK ———————

Making safe decisions about managing people is never simple. Making safe decisions about managing people with disabilities or whose life functions are impaired is exacerbated by the fact that so much vagueness and so many ambiguities clutter up the situations in which you make your decisions. Test yourself with the cases that follow.

Excessive Absenteeism or Disability?

Billy Lowery suffered from posttraumatic stress disorder (PTSD), according to the anger management counselor to whom Ace Communications sent him. During the six years he had worked for Ace, he had suffered from headaches, insomnia (and nightmares when he did sleep), impaired judgment, concentration problems, flashbacks and bad memories, anger, hostility, and unwarranted suspicions. He fought often with other employees and had been suspended five times. Three years of outpatient counseling, seven weeks on disability to attend a VA program, workload accommodations: None seemed to help.

After reviewing Billy's record, a new manager concluded that his predecessors were too soft on Billy, and when the employee applied for a paid disability leave to stay at a residential PTSD center in California, he agreed only to unpaid leaves in thirty-day increments, and only if doctors certified the need for treatment.

The doctors complied with a written report shortly after Billy entered treatment and sent a second report six weeks later recommending four more months of inpatient treatment. In response, the manager wrote that Billy's leave had expired, that the doctors' letter provided inadequate information, and that he would be fired unless the caregivers provided additional information. However, neither Billy nor his doctors answered.

The manager's next letter offered Billy the opportunity to apply for up to twelve months of unpaid leave; when Billy failed to respond to that offer, the company sent him a pink slip for excessive absentee-ism. Billy sued under ADA: Ace had fired him without providing him the reasonable accommodation of a leave for treatment.

Ace's attorneys argued that the ADA covers only people who are able to perform a job's essential functions. Since Billy had applied for and received Social Security disability benefits, by his own admission, he was unable to work and unable to perform the essential functions of the job, which included attendance at work.

How would you or your company handle this complicated case?

Social Security and Essential Job Functions

The Tenth Circuit Court, in the case on which this story is based, said that Ace created a negative employment action with regard to a legally protected leave (a decision that applies also to FMLA leave or leave covered by company policies). The court ruled that receiving Social Security disability benefits doesn't imply that Billy was not also a "qualified individual with a disability" protected by ADA; Social Security and ADA use different definitions of disability because the statutes serve different purposes. Attendance at work as an essential function of the job doesn't apply when an employee is undergoing inpatient care; the only question would be whether Ace had shirked its own duties to reasonably accommodate the employee's request for disability leave. Ace's own written policies said that he should have received a paid leave of absence for inpatient care. Demanding additional information from Billy's caregivers only reflected a pretext; the company, the court said, had sufficient information to determine the case.[21]

Moral: Publish disability leave policies; train your managers to follow them and to make appropriate responses to specific types of requests for ADA and/or FMLA leaves.

Fired for Accommodating Employee's Disability

Frank Scheid suffered nocturnal epileptic seizures and often came to work late; on some occasions, he also missed Mondays altogether. Billie Strather, his supervisor, allowed the tardiness and absences because Frank made up his missed time during the evenings, but his coworkers complained to Strather's supervisor, Alan Banks. Although the company manual included epilepsy among its ADA policy's list of disabilities, the supervisor wrote a memo stating that employees could not make up lost time because of illness. "The heck with the ADA," he told Strather, who ignored the memo and continued to allow Scheid his flexible schedule.

Soon after, Banks fired Scheid, claiming that the man had falsified his time sheets, which clearly showed the evening hours he worked. When Strather demanded to see those time sheets and produced the company's ADA policy under which she gave Scheid his accommodation, Banks fired her, too, for colluding with Scheid to falsify the time sheets.

Strather sued under ADA, claiming that Banks fired her in retaliation for defending Scheid's rights and opposing his termination. A federal jury in Arkansas awarded her $244,500.

What do you think the Eighth Circuit Court said when the company appealed?

You Didn't Do Right

It seemed to the court that the company's ADA policy was only a bunch of words in this case. Rather than demonstrate a good-faith effort, the company helped Strather show that the policy was disregarded by her supervisor and supported by the company.[31] Not only did the company retaliate after she showed her supervisor the company's own ADA policy, the whole episode violated the law itself.

In a different case, unlike the one we described, a good-faith effort saved an employer from suffering punitive damages when its supervisor violated the ADA.[32] According to Justice Sandra Day O'Connor,

> Under the terms of the Civil Rights Act of 1991, punitive damages are available in claims under Title VII of the Civil Rights Act of 1964 (Title VII) . . . and the Americans with Disabilities Act of 1990 (ADA). . . . Punitive damages are limited, however, to cases in which the employer has en-

gaged in intentional discrimination and has done so "with malice or with reckless indifference to the federally protected rights of an aggrieved individual."

Make sure your managers understand your company's policies and the law before you and the company have to defend yourselves against lawsuits.

What Constitutes a Physical Impairment?

When Julie Daniels applied for a janitorial position, the well-trained interviewer, Fred Benjamin, never asked her any questions concerning her medical or health history. He did, however, tell her that the job required the ability to lift forty-five pounds just about every shift.

"That's okay," she said. "I can do that."

"Good," Benjamin said, and he offered her the job "contingent on passing the physical exam."

"Well, I did have some back problems, a while back, but it doesn't stop me."

The company's physician reported that Daniels had arthritis in both her lower back and knees that would interfere with her ability to lift forty-five pounds. A second opinion confirmed the first one, and Benjamin sent Daniels a letter withdrawing his offer.

Her attorney filed a suit under ADA claiming that the company discriminated against his client because they regarded her as having a disability. Daniels, he said, deserved ADA protection because she had a disability that met ADA criteria of an "impairment that substantially limited her in a major life activity of working."

The company's attorney countered that Daniel's impairment failed to meet ADA criteria; it only disqualified her from performing the essential functions of the job for which she had applied.

The case on which this story is based was tried in a state court and never reached the federal level. What do you think the court did?

What Does Having a Disability Mean?

Case dismissed.[33] The employer was correct in its argument that just having a disability doesn't qualify for protection under ADA. Each claim of disability must be taken on its own merits. In this case, unless corrective measures had been taken, the applicant failed to meet the qualifications under the essential functions of the job. On the other hand, had such measures been taken—for example, back and knee surgery that eliminated the arthritis—she might have had a case. Might have had.[22, 33]

How Important Are Your Perceptions?

After becoming ill, Dennis Kroyan sought medical attention that produced a large number of absences. In spite of a doctor's note explaining that Kroyan was under his care (which satisfied company demands), Dennis's supervisor, Ira Shankman, insisted on knowing the reasons for the medical appointments.

"I'd rather not say," Dennis replied. "It's very personal."

Ira pressed him anyway. "C'mon, Dennis. I'm your friend, not just your supervisor. You can trust me to keep a secret."

"Okay," the employee reluctantly conceded. "I think I've got AIDS and something the doctor called ARC."

Shocked and concerned about the spread of AIDS in the company, Ira went straight to his supervisors, who would have been kinder had they fired Dennis. Instead, they made his condition known to his coworkers.

Not long afterward, Dennis received life-threatening phone calls from other employees. Frightened by the calls, he did not return to work and entered the hospital, where tests confirmed the diagnoses. Distressed by the way they had treated him, Dennis took his employers to court for discrimination on the basis of disability. "My supervisors disclosed private information about my health in violation of Massachusetts General Laws, C. 151 B Section 4(16). If I suffered from any other disease, no one would have said anything to anyone."

"We had a legitimate business interest in getting and publishing the information from Kroyan," the company countered. "We must consider the other employees when a contagious disease is present. In that situation, we had to balance the individual's right to privacy against the population's right to know, and the right to know won."

How do you feel about this matter? If one of your employees were to contract AIDS, how would you or your company react?

Facts vs. Perception

If you sided with the company, you made the same mistake it did. The Superior Court of Massachusetts concluded that under Massachusetts law, AIDS is a qualifying disability. In drawing its conclusion, the court cited the statute and a publication of the AIDS policy of the Massachusetts Commission Against Discrimination. The law says that an employer may not discriminate against any person because of his or her disability where the person "[is] capable of performing the essential functions of the position involved with reasonable accommodation." Only if "the employer can demonstrate that the accommodation . . . would impose an undue hardship to the employer's business" would the employer be exempted from the law or the Commission's policy on AIDS (which says that AIDS victims are entitled to protection under this law).[5] Other decisions also have provided AIDS victims with equal protection.[6-9]

This case establishes that an AIDS victim may qualify for remedies because his or her manager *erroneously perceived* that the victim is contagious to coworkers. Under both Massachusetts Law and the Rehab Act, if an employee is not likely to spread AIDS, which medical evidence shows cannot be spread by casual contact, then the erroneous perception indicates that the employer regards the employee as impaired or disabled. Discriminating against that person—in the present case, divulging privileged information—violates the law to the same extent that discrimination on the basis of a *correct* perception violates it.

The privacy issue in this case was measured against the standard set by the Massachusetts Supreme Judicial Court in 1984[6] that requires the employer to show that a legitimate business interest is served by prying into or disclosing privileged medical information. That interest is a matter of fact, rather than a matter of law, that the company in this case could not substantiate. The company discriminated against the disabled employee and invaded his privacy as well, all on the basis of an erroneous perception that through casual contact an AIDS victim endangers the general population.

When an employer adversely affects a disabled person's job opportunities merely on the basis of a disability, he or she risks litigation. Before making a decision that affects or limits a disabled person's right to opportunity, you should become more aware of the disability itself and of local and federal laws or regulations governing accommodating disabled people. You would ensure compliance *and* reap the rewards of tapping a person's potential.

What Constitutes Reasonable Efforts to Accommodate?

When the managers of Williamson's Wood Works realized that Bob Pantella suffered from a serious illness that brought on physically uncontrollable seizures, they became quite alarmed. They encouraged him to seek medical help, and when he did he found out that he suffered from diabetes mellitus and a hyperactive thyroid. Several seizures later, management transferred him into a less-dangerous work environment in which he would not have to operate a forklift, but where he could still contribute and keep his job. After four more seizures that came without warning, the company let him go.

In court Pantella charged that, under Oregon's laws, the company discriminated against him on the basis of "a physical or mental impairment [that] with reasonable accommodation by the employer, does not preclude the performance of the work involved." He also claimed his condition was controllable and under control.

The company's attorney countered with an enumeration of the steps his client took. One, they maintained a position for the man over nine months, during which time he suffered four uncontrollable seizures. Two, they transferred him to a safer environment from a part of the warehouse where he worked close to potentially dangerous machines and posed a considerable safety hazard to himself and others. Three, they eliminated the need for him to operate a forklift, the operation of which posed a safety hazard to both the employee and others had he continued to drive one. The managers, in short, had shown their willingness to accommodate Pantella's disability, but his condition was uncontrollable and they had to let him go.

Do you think the employee had a case? How far would your company have gone to accommodate someone in this situation?

Unsuccessful but Sufficient

Score one for the managers. According to the district court in Oregon, the employer had made several efforts to accommodate the employee, including transferring him and reassigning his work in order to protect him and other employees. Although unsuccessful, the efforts sufficed to satisfy Oregon's reasonable accommodation standard.[3]

No general rules define *accommodation.* However, an employer is *not* required to exhaust *all* possible avenues to ensure meeting an employee's special needs. In the sample case, demanding that the managers move hazardous equipment or redesign the warehouse's physical layout to satisfy the employee's safety needs would have caused an unnecessary and undue burden for the employer. The court agreed that the managers took reasonable steps to accommodate the employee, and that is all that matters.

Do You Have to Accommodate Alcoholics and Drug Addicts?

The company's finance and insurance manager, Doug Frala, called in sick and remained absent for several days. The doctor's diagnosis was hepatitis complicated by drug withdrawal symptoms. He prescribed a month at a residential drug treatment facility where Doug could receive treatment for both problems. However, when Doug asked the company's president for a one-month leave of absence, he was fired. "We can't afford to be without you for that long, Doug. It'll be better if we just replace you now," his employer explained.

Would your company have let Doug go? Why or why not?

When in Ohio

Ohio statutes define the word *handicap* in broad terms:

> A medically diagnosable, abnormal condition [that] is expected to continue for a considerable length of time, whether correctable or uncorrectable by a good medical practice, which can reasonably be expected to limit the person's functional ability . . . so that he cannot perform his everyday routine living and working without significantly increased hardship and vulnerability to what are

considered the everyday obstacles and hazards encoun-
tered by the nonhandicapped.

Medical testimony in this case supported the plaintiff's contention
that addictions, including alcoholism, create a debilitating chemical
imbalance that is an abnormal physical condition. It can limit the
addict's individual functional ability, including physical endurance,
mental capacity, and judgment. Treatment can produce remission,
but the effects of a drug may remain for a significant period of time.
Alcoholism is therefore covered in Ohio law.[15]

Nevertheless, Ohio law also permits the employer to discharge
the employee if he or she cannot perform his or her duties and responsibilities or some other duties necessary for the conduct of the
employer's business (reasonable accommodation). The court in this
case ruled that the plaintiff had been a good employee, and, had
he not admitted to his alcohol addiction and requested the leave of
absence, he probably would not have been fired. The company had
granted lengthy leaves of absence to other employees, one with phle-
bitis and another who had suffered a heart attack. The only distinguishing condition here was the nature of the plaintiff's disability.
Therefore, the company was guilty of discrimination under Ohio
law.

The company would have been guilty under Iowa law, too.[16]
And the federal courts, guided in part by a 1984 Supreme Court decision, have said that unless an employer gives an alcoholic employee
a firm choice between rehabilitation and serious disciplinary action,
it has not made reasonable accommodation.[17, 18]

The laws in some states do not recognize alcoholism and drug
abuse as disabilities and do not go along with federal guidelines with
respect to reasonable accommodation. Cases that come before courts
in these states are usually decided in the employer's favor.[17] Still, you
should look into the specific laws in your own state before sighing
with relief.

Cases

1. 475 U.S. 1118, 43 F.E.P. Cases (BNA) 81 (1987); see also, 930 S.W. 2nd 43 (MO. App. E.D. 1996).
2. U.S. S. Ct., No. 97–156 (June 25, 1998).

3. 618 F. Supp. 41, 36 F.E.P Cases (BNA) 1849 (D. Or. 1985).
4. No. 97–16779 (9th Cir. Ct., 1998); No. 98–4247, 7th Cir (August, 1999); U.S. No. 00–1250 (April 2002).
5. No. 80,332 (Mass. Super. Ct., Aug. 15, 1986).
6. No. 14,940/85 (N.Y. Sup. Ct., Queens County, Feb. 11, 1986), 10 Mental and Physical Disability Law Rptr. 133–135 (1986).
7. 54 U.S.L.W. 2330 (December 11, 1985).
8. 392 Mass. 5098 (1984).
9. No. F.E.P. 83–84 (February 5, 1987); see also Missouri Commission on Human Rights (August 24, 1990).
10. No. 86–1571 (9th Cir. April 22, 1987).
11. No. C250, 870 (Cal. Sup. Ct. October 28, 1982).
12. 46 F.E.P. Cases (BNA) 971 (W.D. Mo. 1988).
13. No. 179 (N.Y. Ct. App. May 7, 1985).
14. 415 N.W.2d 793 (N.D. 1987).
15. 250 Ohio St. 3d 279 (1986).
16. 366 N.W.2d 522 (Iowa Sup. Ct. 1985).
17. 598 F. Supp. 126, 36 F.E.P. Cases (BNA) 425 (D.D.C. 1984).
18. No. 83–3160 (D.D.C. January 14, 1985).
19. U.S.D.C. Miami, Fl. (March 1, 1988).
20. 676 P.2d 602 (Alaska 1984).
21. No. 96–2194 (10th Cir. Ct. May 6, 1998); see also No. 97381P (8th Cir. Ct. July 1, 1998). However, in another case, the same court ruled that attendance does form an essential function if, for example, it involves face-to-face contact with customers: WL778329, 8th Cir. Ct. (1998).
22. 1998 WL 780345, 8th Cir Ct. (1998). See also, 772 F.2d 759, 39 F.E.P. Cases (BNA) 9 (11th Cir. 1985).
23. 93 Civ. 1154 S.D. N.Y.
24. No. 97–1943 (June 1999).
25. No. 97–1992 (June 1999).
26. No. 98–591 (June, 1999); No. 98-2071, 8th Cir. (June 1999).
27. No. 00–1089 (January 2002).
28. No. 97–17147, 9th Cir. (1999).
29. No. 99–1240 (February 2001).
30. No 97–2433, 8th Cir. (March 1999).
31. 2001 WL548561, 8th Cir. (2001).
32. (98–208) 527 U.S. 526 (1999) 139 F.3d 958, vacated and remanded.
33. 11 NDLR 304 (ND Ill. 1998) (No. 97C 3701), cited in *The EEO Review* (Panel Publishers, September 1999), pp. 1–2; see also Nos. 24–27 above.

11

Employee Action Rights and Labor Laws

So yours is a nonunion shop: no contract obligations, no shop stewards, no grievance committee. What does the National Labor Relations Act (NLRA) have to do with you? Labor laws do not affect you, right? Well, until you read what these laws say you cannot and can do even in a nonunion shop, you should not be too certain of that.

What the Laws Say

The four federal laws that affect most labor-management relations are: (1) the National Labor Relations Act; (2) the Labor Management Relations Act; (3) the Fair Labor Standards Act; and (4) the Labor-Management Reporting and Disclosure Act. Each of these laws protects nonunion employees on the job and extends employees' rights to organize on their own behalf, including the right to form unions. They therefore affect management practices with regard to pay (for example, minimum wage and overtime), concerted action, disciplinary procedures, and discharge policies.

᛫ 1. *National Labor Relations Act of 1935 (NLRA).* This law protects employees' rights to take concerted action, that is, work together, to alter work conditions by:

> ᛫ Using any bulletin boards that publish general community information
> ᛫ Holding meetings during work hours, with no loss of pay or

threat of retaliation, to discuss safety or other working conditions

It allows *all* workers to engage in other concerted activities for the purpose of collective bargaining through their own representatives—including forming, joining, or assisting labor organizations—or other mutual aid or protection. (At the same time, it prevents nonunion employees from being forced or coerced into joining a labor organization or engaging in collective bargaining except where membership in a labor organization is a condition of employment and is created by contract.) And, companies cannot have the right to interfere with any employee attempting to organize the employees for the purpose of collective action or to discriminate or take steps to discipline, discharge, or retaliate against him or her for doing it.

The NLRA, Section 8(a)(2), also prohibits establishing company-dominated labor organizations—that is, a group that meets to discuss topics such as working conditions—the so-called company unions. In 1992, the NLRB ruled that a company had violated this section by forming teams, which is fast becoming a popular employment involvement method for streamlining production, problem solving, other cost-reducing measures, quality control, and so forth. Furthermore, the NLRB has made it clear one need not show anti-union animus for the Board to hold that an employee involvement is illegal.

In 1996, Congress passed the Teamwork for Employees and Management (TEAM) Act to amend the NLRA to exempt joint labor-management committees that discuss matters of mutual interest, and President Clinton vetoed it. In 1997, the 105th Congress introduced a House bill (HR634) and Senate bill (S295) with an amendment that Senator Nancy Kassebaum offered to clarify what activities would be exempted: health and safety issues in nonunion settings and where the teams would have equitable worker-management participation. The Act would not apply to union contracts, where any and all discussions are already protected, and equitable participation would prevent an adversarial relationship from developing. Although the amendment passed, the bill itself died in the face of threats to filibuster it by Senator Edward Kennedy and other Democrats on the grounds that employee-involvement teams are nothing more than a sham. As of this writing, the bill has not been passed; therefore, before setting up work teams of any kind, check with your legal or HR counsel for a ruling as to your plan's legality.

2. *Labor Management Relations Act of 1947 (LMRA)*. The Taft-Hartley Act, as this Act is also called, amends the NLRA and provides additional support for mediation in labor disputes that affect interstate commerce, equalizes legal responsibilities of labor organizations and employers, gives the president of the United States emergency powers, and allows for other actions designed to protect the nation's general welfare.

3. *Fair Labor Standards Act of 1938 (FLSA)*. Also known as the Wage-Hour Act, this law establishes fair labor standards in employment in and affecting interstate commerce, and for other purposes. It protects all workers, including children and women, by establishing minimum hourly wages and distinguishing between nonexempt employees (those to whom you must pay overtime for hours in excess of forty hours a week) and exempt employees (those to whom you do not have to pay overtime).

4. *Labor-Management Reporting and Disclosure Act of 1959 (LMRDA)*. This law, subtitled the Labor Reform Act, forms an umbrella that covers nonsupervisory nonunion as well as unionized employees by preventing labor organizations, employers, or their officers and representatives, including labor relations consultants, from distorting and defeating the policies of the LMRA.

What You Cannot Do

Each of the four labor laws limits managers in its own specific way.

The National Labor Relations Act

This Act created the National Labor Relations Board (NLRB) and also defines "unfair labor practices by employers."

It says that you, as a manager, cannot interfere with, restrain, or coerce employees exercising their rights. You cannot dominate or interfere with the formation or administration of a labor organization or contribute financial or other aid to it; however, you are required to allow employees to meet with you during working hours without a loss of time or pay to discuss issues of collective interest. Along those lines, you cannot refuse to bargain collectively with the employees' representative, either. (However, see the section under "What You Can Do" with regard to rejecting proposals.)

You cannot discriminate in hiring or tenure on the basis of union or nonunion membership. You cannot use the terms or conditions of employment to encourage or discourage membership in a labor organization, except where an agreement exists that requires membership. And you cannot fire or otherwise discriminate against an employee for filing charges or giving testimony under this Act.

Associated with this nondiscrimination policy is protection for the practice of "salting" in which union members apply for positions in a nonunionized company that a union has targeted. According to the National Labor Relations Board (NLRB), refusing to hire union members "deprive[s] employee applicants . . . the full freedom of self-organization by the National Labor Relations Act."[*] This decision by the NLRB covers the following two forms of discrimination:

1. The employer refuses to hire a qualified applicant with union membership or sympathies.
2. The employer refuses even to consider a qualified applicant with union membership or sympathies.

No matter how tempted you may be to turn away a "salt," be advised that the decision is illegal without a solid, business-related reason that does not unfairly discriminate.

Labor Management Relations Act, 1947

Under this amendment to the NLRA, you cannot conduct unwarranted or sudden lockouts. You cannot pay, loan, or deliver money or other assets to a union, union official, union welfare fund, or em-

[*]FES (A Division of Thermo Power) and Plumbers and Pipefitters Local 520 of the United Association, 331 NLRB No. 20 (2000), cited in "NLRB Explains Approach In 'Salting' Cases," *Fair Employment Practices Guidelines* (July 15, 2000), pp. 3–4; see also, Sherwood Ross, "More Workers Are Being Punished for Union Activities, Board Says," Reuters NewsService reprinted in the *St. Louis Post-Dispatch* (December 18, 2000), p. BP4.

ployee involved in a labor dispute and, in your role as a manager of your organization, you cannot make direct contributions to political candidates.

Fair Labor Standards Act

You probably know that under this act you cannot employ children under age 16 ("oppressive labor") and certain categories of children ages 16 to 18. You may also know that this is the legislation that created the minimum hourly rate, which is increased from time to time and that is sometimes superseded by minimum wage standards mandated by state laws. And this law says you cannot work nonexempt employees for more than forty hours a week unless you pay them at least time and a half their regular rate of pay for the overtime.

Less well known is that the Act also specifies that you cannot use gender as a basis for discriminating in wages, except where wages are based on a seniority system, a merit system, a piecework or commission or bonus system, or on a factor other than sex. The law also specifies that you cannot simply lower the wage rate of any employee just to end wage disparities.

Finally, in agreement with the NLRA, you cannot discharge or otherwise discriminate against any employee for taking part in a collective action of mutual benefit with respect to wages or other working conditions. Likewise, you cannot discharge or otherwise discriminate against any employee for filing, instituting, or causing to be instituted a complaint relating to the Act, or for testifying or being about to testify in an action protected by the Act.

In 2003, Representative Judy Biggert (R-IL) introduced the Family Time Flexibility Act, which would allow private sector workers the option of negotiating with their employers to choose comp time or overtime pay. Since 1977, federal workers have been able to take advantage of this change in the law (the Fair Labor Standards Act of 1938), and state and local public workers since 1985. The bill would match public sector workers' comp time provision of time-and-a-half, meaning for every hour of overtime, the employee is entitled to an hour and a half of either pay or comp time. Choosing comp time in lieu of overtime pay can't be forced on employees.

Representative Biggert's believes that her bill amends the FLSA in a way that reflects today's workforce when most women now work outside the home. According to the Employment Policy Foundation, a business-oriented nonpartisan organization,* women embrace this belief, because 81 percent of women favor compensatory time as an option for greater workforce flexibility. As of this writing, the bill is still working its way through Congress.

Labor-Management Reporting and Disclosure Act, 1959

In language similar to that used in the NLRA, this law says that you cannot interfere with employees' rights to work, organize, choose representatives, bargain collectively, or engage in concerted action for their mutual aid or protection.

What You Can Do

Yes, managers do have rights under these acts. Again, taking them in the order presented previously, let's take a look at what you can do and in some cases must do.

National Labor Relations Act

As long as you do not interfere with your employees' right to take collective action or form a union, you can freely express your own viewpoints, arguments, or opinions in writing, print, graphics, or visuals about unions or collective bargaining. While ensuring that what you say does not threaten reprisal or force for forming or joining a collective bargaining unit or promise benefits for not forming or joining one, you can express your opinion and reject proposals or requests for concessions. These limits also apply to forming joint labor-management task forces or employee-managed teams.

In addition, you may counter aggressive union recruiting tactics as long as no "unique obstacles" bar the organizers' way. In 1992, the Supreme Court ruled 6–3 that a store owner in a shopping plaza legally barred nonemployee labor organizers from distributing hand-

---

*That the foundation is "nonpartisan" is disputed by "Knowledge Manager" David Creelman in his online evaluation, "What Is the Employment Policy Foundation?" HR.com (March 2002).

bills in the plaza's parking lot. As a general rule, Justice Clarence Thomas wrote for the majority, an employer can't be forced to allow nonemployee organizers onto its property, except in the rare case where employees are too inaccessible to be reached by "reasonable means" and "through normal channels." No "unique obstacles" prevented organizers from reaching the employees in this case.[3]

Where a union exists, you can hear employee grievances and adjust them without union representation as long as the adjustment is consistent with the terms of a contract or agreement in effect, and as long as the bargaining representative has been given an opportunity to be present. Decisions on grievances taken to the NLRB are not final; the law says you can appeal any such ruling in any appropriate U.S. circuit court of appeals.

Labor Management Relations Act, 1947

This law prohibits wildcat strikes as well as unwarranted lockouts. The law gives you the right to make every reasonable effort to reach an agreement with your employees on rates of pay, hours, and working conditions, including notice of changes, and to arrange promptly to hold a conference to settle any differences between both parties. If a conference is not successful, the law requires that you both participate fully in meetings called by the Federal Mediation Service.

The Federal Mediation Service was created to try to avoid industrial controversy by offering services either on its own initiative or by request from you or your employees. The service's main goal is to try to reach an agreement through conciliation within a reasonable time. If the service's director cannot produce an agreement, he or she will try to get you and your employees to find other means of settling the dispute without resorting to a strike, a lockout, or other coercion—for example, submitting the employer's last offer to a secret ballot of the employees.

Now you do not have to agree with the mediator's solutions, because failure to agree is not a violation of any duty or obligation imposed by the law. On the other hand, if the mediator sees the situation as posing a serious threat to the general welfare of the nation, the service will advise the president of the United States of that perceived threat. The president, in turn, is empowered to direct the attorney general to petition any appropriate district court to stop a threatened strike or lockout or to end one or the other in progress. If the court agrees that a strike or a lockout will adversely affect an entire industry or substantial part of it or would threaten the national health, safety, or security, it can stop the strike or lockout or take other appropriate measures.

Fair Labor Standards Act

Many employers see this law as unfriendly toward them. However, it allows you some freedom to decide on what you can do with regard to specific forms of compensation or benefits not covered by the law:

› Gifts, special bonuses, rewards for service
› Payments made for occasional periods in which no work is performed, for travel expenses, or other reimbursable expenses
› Recognition for service awards
› Contributions irrevocably made to a trustee or third party in a retirement, pension, or insurance plan
› Extra compensation paid on a premium rate for:
  › Overtime after a regular eight-hour day
  › Overtime on a nonwork day
  › Work outside normal hours as agreed on through collective bargaining
› Compensation through a guaranteed wage plan based on a bona fide individual contract or collective bargaining agreement

By creating a class of employees called *exempt employees*, the law allows you to *not* have to pay overtime to some people if they work beyond forty hours a week. You are a member of this class, because it covers executives, managers, and first-line supervisors, as well as employees whose jobs require making decisions and using personal judgment, creativity, or innovativeness but who are not classified as managers. Teachers and educational administrators, salespeople, and other people working on commission or for tips for service, employees of service organizations in which more than 50 percent of the organization's gross income derives from *intra*state as opposed to *inter*state commerce—these are all people to whom overtime need not be paid.

These definitions are now undergoing challenges from on-call employees and exempt employees. Nevertheless, federal courts in San Francisco, St. Louis, New Orleans, Houston, Salt Lake City, and Cincinnati have all ruled that being on call doesn't impose an excessive burden on employees as long as on-call rules do not "'prevent employees from effectively using the time for personal pursuits.'"* Those rulings, however, have no effect on docking the pay of salaried employees taking time off for, say, a medical appointment.

If you dock salaried employees for time off, you could be obligated to pay them overtime for any extra hours they may have worked. Several major companies are trying to settle out of court in situations like this, in which they could be liable for several millions of dollars in *back pay*. Even the Family and Medical Leave Act doesn't clearly decide all the issues; this law does not apply to employees in enterprises with fewer than fifty employees. Not paying salaried employees taking family or medical time off could be construed as "docking them."† Once more, when in doubt, shout for an attorney to help you make decisions.

Labor-Management Reporting and Disclosure Act, 1959

This law does not prescribe employers' rights so much as it describes what you must do to comply with them. It identifies a number of reports you must file with the secretary of labor, including several reports relevant to safe management.

Conclusion

Some managers see these laws, for example, the minimum wage law, as heavy burdens. Other managers recognize that this legislation has

---

*See Junda Woo, "More On-Call Workers Sue for Overtime," *The Wall Street Journal*, p. B1, quoting a federal appeals court in Cincinnati without identification.
†Richard B. Schmitt, "Employers' Overtime Liability Expanding," *The Wall Street Journal* (November 5, 1993), p. B1; see also, Adam Geller, "Salaried Employees Are Suing for Unpaid Overtime," Associated Press, reprinted in *St. Louis Post-Dispatch* (August 4, 2002), pp. E–E2.

been, in part, responsible for the strength of the U.S. economy and for the standard of living we all enjoy. In some respects, these laws guarantee that employers and employees alike work to meet each other's needs, while they protect the welfare of both individuals and the nation.

─────────────────── **CASEBOOK** ───────────────────

Less than 20 percent of U.S. workers belong to unions. Still, the force and power of unions have been felt in all industries and in society as a whole. And, yes, these labor laws we have been discussing have given those unions greater voice in the economy than their numbers would suggest they should have. Just how important these laws are to society is well illustrated in the following cases.

When Does Innocence Cross Over into Unlawful Interference?

Both Phyllis and Fred, low-level supervisors, had a personal interest in what was happening when a union began its organizing campaign at their food-processing plant.

"How are things?" Phyllis asked one of her line employees, referring to the union campaign.

"Okay" was the noncommittal reply.

"Think the union will come in?"

"Guess so," the employee responded. "Talk around here is that it will."

"I don't know," Phyllis replied. "What I've heard seems to indicate it could go either way."

Fred stopped another employee and raised the same issue. "Think the union will come in?" When the employee did not respond, Fred added, "I'm just curious. You know, person to person."

"I guess so," the woman answered.

"Why? Do you think you've gotten a bad shake from the company?"

"I really don't want to talk about it."

"Don't mean any harm," Fred reassured the woman. "We've known each other a long time, and I'd like to know, personally."

"Well, I think it'll make it on the first ballot."

Two innocent conversations that were independent of each

other and each a matter of curiosity, or so it seemed to the supervisors.

Not from the union's perspective. After the union lost the election, it alleged that those two conversations constituted unfair labor practices that violated the NLRA.

How about it? Does chitchat such as that constitute unlawful interrogation that has the effect of restraining or coercing employees engaged in concerted organization activities?

A Time and Place for Everything

If you answered yes to that question, you agreed with the NLRB when it said that even if the conversations had been just small talk, the law still prohibits any such discussion during an organizing campaign. The conversations were unlawful because they served "no legitimate purpose" and could have had a chilling effect on the exercise of the employees' union activities. Even an innocent and friendly conversation can be called an *interrogation,* the technical term denoting "illegal questioning of employees about their union membership, activities, and desires."[1]

When Does the Information You Disseminate Cross the Line?

The law allows managers to explain their positions about a particular union and offer their personal opinions, urging employees not to sign up. They can also explain that the organization need not agree to anything promised to employees by a union unless the union is certified and a contract is signed. So what is the big deal about innocent conversations?

How about these preelection statements? First, a question-and-answer fact sheet an employer sent to all employees with the intent to delineate the employees' legal rights under the Act claimed:

Question: Can I lose my job if the union calls me out on strike?

Answer: If the union calls you out on strike to try to force [the organization] to agree to union promises, [the organization] is free to replace economic strikers.

This means that when the strike is over, you may no longer have a job, and the law does not force [the employer] to rehire you.

In a letter to the employees, the same employer stated:

Most important of all, you could lose the right to speak and think for yourself. If a union is certified, you will have to deal through union representatives and may not be permitted to go directly to [the employer] about particular problems you may have.

The union lost and went straight to the NLRB, charging that the employer violated the NLRA by issuing a technically inaccurate statement and a second that was "implicitly threatening" to employees. The NLRB agreed.

Can you spot the two offensive statements? What disqualifies them?

Error and Overstatement

Reread these two sentences:

1. This means that when the strike is over, you may no longer have a job, and the law does not force [the employer] to rehire you.
2. Most important of all, you could lose the right to speak and think for yourself.

The first statement seems correct but is a technical misstatement. An employer may, lawfully, permanently replace economic strikers, but while the word *rehire* implies a total severance of employment, the law gives an economic striker the right to reinstatement as long as his or her position is still available.

The Board also found the second statement objectionable because, although the statement seems to be accurate, it is not technically correct and thereby forms a "retaliatory threat." The statement, the Board said, suggests that if employees form a union, the employer would sever their right to deal directly with management. That is a threat, not a piece of information.

The terms of a collective bargaining agreement could, and often do, prevent employees from taking a grievance directly to management, but in the Board's opinion this statement implies that management itself will deny employees their right to direct access if the union wins. So, although the employer won the battle at the ballot box, it lost the war in front of the NLRB.[2]

Most people do not realize that even a single, offhand comment can result in the NLRB's overturning the results of an election, if in its opinion that comment might have tainted the results because it appeared to be coercive. Because it is the Board's objective to ensure that a union election be conducted in an "atmosphere" free of coercion, the Board advises supervisors to become aware of the T.I.P.S. formula: Do not *T*hreaten, *I*nterrogate, *P*romise benefit, or engage in *S*urveillance.

Cases

1. 265 N.L.R.B. No. 182 (1982).
2. 265 N.L.R.B. No. 135 (1982).
3. U.S.M., 112 S. Ct. 841; Labor 47, 86, 386; Statute 219(8).

12

The Uniformed Services Employment and Reemployment Rights Act of 1994 (USERRA, 38 U.S.C. §§ 4301–4333)

Veterans of World War II and the Korean War came away with a meaningful Veterans Bill of Rights. Laws were passed to protect Vietnam veterans, but they didn't have sharp enough teeth. Now those who serve in the military have legal standing and protections that reservists, members of the National Guard, and veterans never had before. The new law, commonly called the Uniformed Services Employment and Reemployment Rights Act (USERRA), makes it illegal to discriminate or otherwise injure the employment, seniority, or benefits rights of those who serve in uniform at the behest of the federal government or in times of state emergencies, with double damages of back pay or lost benefits if the action is willful (intentional).

Only a few cases have gone as far as a federal appeals court (see the Casebook), but the effects of the law are being felt by employers. For example, a *St. Louis Post-Dispatch* employee told a returning Air Force Reserve sergeant that he could return to work only two days (fifteen hours) a week rather than returning to his previously held position. That position had been classified as part-time but he often worked an equivalent of a full-time position. After he complained about his treatment in the *Labor Tribune,* amends were made, and he was taken back to his former position at thirty-seven and a half hours a week with retroactive pay dating to when he had applied for reemployment.*

Purpose of USERRA

After the Persian Gulf War, Congress passed this law "to clarify, simplify, and where necessary, strengthen the existing veterans' employment and reemployment rights." The law specifies that it is designed to do the following:

> Encourage noncareer service in the uniformed services by eliminating or minimizing the disadvantages to civilian careers and employment that can result from such service
> Minimize the disruption to the lives of persons performing service in the uniformed services as well as to their employers, their fellow employees, and their communities, by providing for the prompt reemployment of such persons upon their completion of such service
> Prohibit the discrimination of anyone because of his or her service in the uniformed services
> Prohibit discrimination when the employee's military status was a "motivating factor," even if that was not the sole factor in the action[1]

As in most other cases of discrimination, the standard of proof under USERRA is the "but for" test. Once the employee establishes that his or her military status was a substantial or motivating factor

---

*Repps Hudson, *"Post-Dispatch* Brings Back Reservist at Full-Time Hours," *St. Louis Post-Dispatch,* (May 2, 2003), p. G2; see also, "Be Prepared to Navigate Military Leave Minefield," in *Missouri Law Letter,* (May 1999), pp. 7–8; Tim O'Neil, "How Laws Protect National Guardsmen While Citizen-Soldiers Are Protecting Us," *op. cit.,* (October 11, 2001), p. A14; "Your Citizen-Soldiers Need Help from HR," *Missouri HR Hero Extra,* a bonus supplement to *Missouri Employment Law Letter,* (January 2002). See also, Matt Tarasevich, "Military Leave: What Employers Need to Know" in *Hot Employment Issues,* 2002 Edition (Brentwood, TN: M. Lee Smith Publishers, LLC, 2002), pp. 10–11.

in your decisions, only you can prove that you would have taken this action whether or not the employee's military status had taken place. One court has ruled that all the employee needs to demonstrate is that his or her military status was one of the factors that "a truthful employer would list if asked for the reasons for its decision."[2] Another court stated that an employee's military status "is a motivating factor if the [employer] relied on, took into account, considered, or conditioned its decision on that consideration."[3] The Ninth Circuit Court ruled that employers must "articulate nondiscriminatory reasons for the allegedly discriminatory conduct."[4]

If you can "articulate nondiscriminatory reasons," it then becomes the employee's onus to demonstrate that the reasons given by the employer were a mere pretext for discrimination. Several courts have referred to the Congressional Record and a decision by the Supreme Court in *NLRB v. Transportation Management Corp.,* 462 U.S. at 401, as the basis for approving shifting the burden of proof.

The direct effect of the law on you as a manager is designed to prevent employment discrimination because of past, current, or future military obligations, including decisions affecting:

> Hiring
> Promotion
> Reemployment
> Termination
> Benefits

The law also protects the civilian job rights and benefits of employees during their military service, except for preservice positions that are "brief or nonrecurrent and that cannot reasonably be expected to continue indefinitely or for a significant period."

Whom the Act Protects

The law protects both full-time and part-time employees who are past members, current members, and persons who apply to be a member of the branches of uniformed services. It also covers people who have been absent from a position of employment because of "service in the uniformed services," that is, performance of duty on a voluntary or involuntary basis including:

> Active duty
> Active duty for training
> Initial active duty for training
> Inactive duty training
> Full-time National Guard duty
> Absence from work for an examination to determine a person's fitness for duty
> Funeral honors duty performed by National Guard or reserve members
> Duty performed by intermittent disaster response personnel for the Public Health Service and approved training to prepare for that service

The uniformed services include:

> Army, Navy, Marine Corps, Air Force, or Coast Guard
> The reserves of those services
> Army or Air National Guard
> Commissioned Corps of the Public Health Service
> Any other category of persons designated by the president in time of war or in an emergency

What Employees Must Do

To be protected by USERRA, employees must provide employers with advance oral or written notice that they are members of a service. Either they must provide the notice or an appropriate officer in the branch in which the employee serves may do so.

Of course, employees might not always be able to give notice to their employees because of circumstances that include:

> Military necessity prevents the giving of notice
> The giving of notice is otherwise impossible or unreasonable

What You Cannot Do

USERRA applies to all public and private employers in the United States, regardless of size. It also applies in overseas workplaces that are owned or controlled by U.S. employers. The restrictions on managers flow directly from the protections the law provides. Employers cannot:

› Fail to or refuse to reemploy any person or to otherwise discriminate against any person with respect to compensation, terms, conditions, or privileges of employment because he or she is a member of a military service or commissioned member of the Public Health Service
› Discharge any person because he or she is a member of this protected group
› Limit, segregate, or classify employees or applicants for employment in any way that would deprive or tend to deprive a person of employment opportunities or have an adverse effect on the person's status as an employee
› Fail to provide training to a person because he or she is a member of this protected group
› Retaliate against any employees or applicants for reemployment because they made a charge, testified, assisted, or participated in any manner in an action protected by this law
› Print or publish (or have someone else print or publish) any notice or advertisement relating to employment that may adversely affect members of this protected group
› Fail to post and keep posted in an obvious place a notice concerning the contents of this law
› Fail to return service members to the seniority escalator at the point the person would have occupied if the person had been continuously employed
› Fail to qualify returning service personnel for reemployment positions that they otherwise would be entitled to hold for reasons other than a disability incurred during or aggravated by military service
› Fail to make reasonable efforts to accommodate a disability that would allow the person to perform a job he or she would

have held if he or she had remained continuously employed or employ that person in a position of equivalent seniority, status, and pay

What You Can Do

While many employers take the commendable step of providing all or part of an employees' pay while they perform military service, there is no obligation under USERRA for them to do so. The law recognizes employers' rights when they make:

> › A reasonable effort to accommodate a protected person's job and job benefits
> › A reasonable effort to accommodate the demands of a protected person's duties in that person's service

It also allows employers to refuse to reemploy persons who have been separated from service with a dishonorable or bad conduct discharge or under other than honorable conditions; or the dismissal of a commissioned officer involving a court martial or by order the president of the United States during the time of war; or the dropping of a person who has been absent without leave or imprisoned by a civilian court for more than three months.

Enforcement

Unlike most other civil rights protections that are enforced by either the EEOC or the Department of Labor, this law has established a specific office in the Department of Labor: the Veteran's Employment and Training Service (VETS). If an aggrieved returning member of a uniformed service and the VETS believe that they need to take further action, they could refer the case to the attorney general of the United States. Of course, as in almost all civil tort cases, private court action always remains a possibility. In addition to all other awards, violators could be assessed reasonable attorney fees and other costs.

Conclusion

When my buddies and I came out of the service in 1957, after three years in the army, we didn't have the same worries military personnel now have. We had the G.I. Bill. Everyone loved people in uniform. Doors were thrown open to veterans. Today, we don't have citizen soldiers drafted to perform wartime services.

The men and women today are often National Guardsmen or reservists. They have families to support or to raise. They have jobs in which they've traveled a career path. They have benefits to protect. Without the protections provided by USERRA, many of these good men and women might find themselves out of a job, denied their benefits, and suffering the way so many of our Vietnam veterans have suffered. Sadly, we must protect people from discrimination of all sorts because too many managers haven't yet learned the lessons of empathy and compassion that would allow minorities, women, the disabled, and our service men and women the freedom of action promised to them by our social, legal, and political systems.

———— CASEBOOK ————

The story of what effect USERRA will have on employers and employees alike as a result of the conflict in Iraq is yet to be told. Thousands of reservists and national guard members have been uprooted and at this writing in 2003 fear for both their lives and their futures. The lack of precedents under USERRA provides few lessons they or their employers need if they must arm wrestle over the employment status the service personnel left behind.

The Job and the Reserves

Hilliard Bradford served in the army reserves, and, according to Bradford, his manager seemed to disapprove of this, although he never came right out and said so. Instead, the manager transferred him to a less-favorable job with irregular work schedules and longer workdays. Finally, the manager fired him for falsifying a timecard.

In court, the company claimed that they had transferred Bradford to a similar position to accommodate his reserve duties. If Bradford hadn't falsified his timecard, they wouldn't have fired him. The company's attorney said that the company would fire any and all employees (reservist or otherwise) who did such a thing. The company then asked for a summary judgment in its behalf.

Do you think the court granted a summary judgment? If so, why?

Good Faith Effort

If you said yes, you're right. The district court did grant a summary judgment favorable to the company. When Bradford, in the actual case, took his cause to the court of appeals, the court found that it was a question of fact whether Bradford's reserve status was a "motivating factor" in the transfer; the district court should not have summarily dismissed his claim. On the other hand, the appellate court affirmed the summary judgment on Bradford's termination. Even if his reserve status was a motivating factor in his termination, he failed to show that the company lacked good faith when it found that he had intentionally falsified his timecard.[5]

Cases

1. 240 F.3d 1009, 1012–13 (Fed. Cir. 2001). See also, Roxane N. Sokolove "A Call To Arms: Triggering Employers' Obligations Under USERRA," *The Metropolitan Corporate Counsel* (November 2001), found in a search of the Internet (August 27, 2003).
2. 37 F. Supp. 2d 47, 54 (D. Me. 1999).
3. 974 F. Supp. 571, 576 (E.D. Tex. 1997)
4. 150 F.3d 1217, 1220 (9th Cir. 1998).
5. 252 F.3d 307 (4th Cir. 2001).

Section III
Safe Firing Practices

Once upon a time, you could fire anyone you wanted, anytime you wanted, for virtually any reason or for no reason at all. Employers in the United States took their freedom to discharge employees (the doctrine of employment/termination at will) as a matter of law rather than as what it is: a labor-management philosophy that most courts recognized as an implied contract favoring the rights of employers.

The Freedom to Discharge Employees

Employment at will presumes that employers hire and fire people for and at their own convenience. The theory allows employers, in the absence of a written agreement, to hire someone for an unspecified period of time and fire him or her with or without cause, with or without notice—in short, to employ and terminate at will. Of course, the philosophy assumes that the employee has the equal right of quitting at any time, with or without cause, with or without notice.

However, times are changing. Society, through contract law and public policy, constrains managers in many new ways. Organizations themselves, by publishing employee handbooks, constrain them in still other ways. Employees constrain managers by becoming more aware of their own rights and by attacking the at-will notion of employment in many courts that are friendly to the plaintiff.

To reduce the risk of legal challenges to your personnel decisions, you need to have a clear sense of what employment (or termination) at will means and how the doctrine is being attacked. In this section, I will look at the definitions of key terms that underlie many of the issues related to disciplining and firing employees. In the chapters that follow, I will spell out what you cannot and can do with regard to safely disciplining or terminating employees, including issues related to public policy and age discrimination.

Definitions of Key Terms

contract   An agreement in which one party promises to do something or provide something for another, in return for consideration—something of value, which may or may not be tangible—for example, money. In an employment contract, the promise to pay someone for his or her labor is consideration.

explicit contract   A written or oral agreement that offers consideration and spells out the terms and conditions of employment. An employment agreement is a bilateral contract.

bilateral contract   An agreement in which *both* parties knowingly offer to participate in some endeavor and to provide something of value in return for something of value—for example, to give money in return for services.

unilateral contract   An agreement in which only *one* party offers something of value. The other party may *not know* that the contract exists or that an offer has been made. For example, if you make a specific promise (even orally)—an offer—when someone accepts a position, that offer can, in some states, bind you. Promising *not* to fire someone "unless [he or she] screws up badly" could come back to haunt you in court.[1]

implicit (implied) contract   Any statements you make, oral or written, that an ordinary, reasonable person can interpret to set specific terms and conditions of employment could possibly be construed as an implied, binding, usually unilateral contract.

Various state courts often differ as to the nature of an implied contract or how binding one is. In 1974, the Pennsylvania Supreme Court ruled that the absence of an explicit contract does *not* mean that an employee handbook or a personnel guide creates an implied contract.[2] Employment is at will.

Some courts agree with Pennsylvania's, but, in 1980, when an employee challenged his firing by saying that the company promised not to discharge anyone without just cause, the Michigan courts called the promise a contract. The company, the courts said, had to—but did not—show cause when it fired him. In so saying, the Michigan courts recognized the existence of implied contracts in employee manuals. They also held that, in the absence of explicit contracts or specific disclaimers, circumstances can dictate that an implied contract *supersedes* written policies.[3, 4] Now, some courts agree with Michigan's. Where does your state's court stand? It's hard to tell without a scorecard. It's best to check out your state's laws with an attorney.

good faith, fair dealing A special case of implied contract. The covenant of good faith and fair dealing, although poorly defined, has been adopted by several states, notably Alaska, California, Connecticut, Massachusetts, and Montana. This doctrine imposes contractual constraints on promises made in employment relations by recognizing the importance of trust in negotiated agreements. For example, discharging a salesperson to avoid paying a large commission is a bad faith action that violates the covenant because the salesperson trusts you to make good on your promise to pay what you agreed to pay.[5] Some courts have extended the covenant to include making exaggerated claims and promises when recruiting employees and the failure to follow internal grievance procedures, to employ reasonable appraisal procedures, or to keep explicit promises prior to terminating someone.[6–9, 11]

As clearly implied by the title of this book, fairness is an essential management trait. The appearance of unfairness, the failure to counsel employees before disciplining or firing them, inconsistency when dealing with employees, failure to document problems, and failure to explain to employees why you're firing them can land you in court whether you intended to injure anyone or not.

outrageous conduct Conduct that any reasonable person would consider exceeds the limits of socially acceptable employer practices. Has been added by some states to the standards for breach of contract. The complaint of severe mental and emotional harm often accompanies this charge and, in some cases, actually defines the outrageous conduct. This, among other claims, was the situation in Oregon when a company security officer denied an employee suspected of violating company rules her right to remain silent and threatened her with arrest.[10]

disclaimer An explicit statement declaring employment at will as company policy; this statement usually safeguards the employer's position. A well-written disclaimer, which I will provide later in Chapter 13, can prevent an employee handbook from creating an implicit contract.

constructive discharge A type of wrongful discharge exemplified when an employer intentionally or unintentionally creates or allows conditions to exist that lead an employee to believe he or she has only two options: (1) to accept a personally adverse situation or (2) to resign.

waiver A signed document in which a terminated employee agrees not to sue the organization in return for a sum of money not required by law or contract, for example, a month's extra severance pay, an immediate severance payment, and an official statement or reason for firing the employee.

> Under the Older Workers Benefit Protection Act of 1990, in a buyout or mass layoff, older employees have up to forty-five days to consider the waiver and seven days afterward to reconsider a decision to sign. Executives responsible for producing personnel policies should be familiar with this legislation, which makes it illegal to deny older workers benefits at least equal to those for younger employees. Unless carefully crafted, the wording of a waiver could be self-invalidating, as recently demonstrated by a case in which the U.S. Supreme Court ruled that the employer failed to follow the rules set down by the Age Discrimination in Employment Act (ADEA).[12] The rules stipulate the following:

> › The waiver must be part of your agreement with the employee.
> › It must be written in simple English.
> › It must refer specifically to the employee's rights in ADEA that are being waived.
> › The waiver must be limited to claims or rights that arose before the employee signed the release.
> › To make the release a binding contract, it must be in exchange for something of value (for example, cash or benefits) that is more than what is offered without the signed waiver.

> The waiver agreement must also advise the employee in writing to talk with an attorney before signing the waiver.
> The employee must be allowed a seven-day period in which to revoke the agreement after he or she has signed it.
> If the release is related to an early retirement incentive plan (ERIP) offered to a specific group or worker category, the law requires you to disclose in writing, in plain English, the class, unit, or group of individuals affected by the ERIP, and the eligibility, time limits, job titles, and ages of affected individuals.
> Each employee affected by an ERIP must have at least forty-five days to mull over his or her decision; if not related to an ERIP, each employee is entitled to twenty-one days.

Waivers won't prevent lawsuits. In fact, in the spring of 1997, the EEOC stated that an employee's promises not to file a discrimination lawsuit are null and void as far as the commission is concerned. "Agreements extracting such promises from employees may also amount to separate and discrete violations of the antiretaliation provisions of the civil rights statutes." A waiver may prevent an individual from suing, this EEOC notice says, but it doesn't prevent the commission from enforcing the ADEA or any other law that prohibits employment discrimination,* and the Sixth Circuit Court agreed.[17] No, waivers won't prevent lawsuits, but if they are entered into voluntarily and with full knowledge of the facts, terms, and conditions, you have a better chance of prevailing than you would without them.

arbitration A neutral forum for handling complaints that can often prevent large damage awards associated with jury trials. Courts have ruled that in exchange for a signed waiver of the right to sue, the company *must* provide mandatory arbitration of disputes, and the company *must* explain the rules and provide employees with a copy of any agreement they sign.[12] Before implementing arbitration agreements, it's advisable to train managers in preventive measures.

Be aware, however, that by signing an agreement to submit their cases to arbitration, employees do not *automatically* forgo

*EEOC Notice No. 915.002 (April 10, 1997).

their right to sue under ADEA or Title VII of the Civil Rights Act.[13] In addition, courts have contradicted each other regarding whether mandated arbitration—for example, in the securities industry—is unfair as a result of a bias in favor the employers.[14] The Supreme Court didn't clarify matters for arbitration in all union environments, insofar as it decided a case sent to it from the Fourth Circuit Court of Appeals on narrow, local grounds; however, the unanimous Court agreed with earlier decisions that employees who pursue a discrimination claim through arbitration under a collective bargaining agreement may still take their claim to court.[15] In a nonunion setting, however, the Supreme Court refused to hear a case from the Ninth Circuit Court, allowing the lower court's ruling to stand that the Civil Rights Act of 1991 prohibits employers from requiring employees to submit their claims to compulsory arbitration as a *condition of employment*; the law intends its arbitration clause to give employees only the option of choosing an alternative venue for complaints. Employers cannot require them to do so.[16]

But, oh what a weirdly winding web the judicial system weaves. On March 21, 2001, the Supreme Court justices changed their minds. In a case sent to the Court by the Ninth Circuit, and in spite of attorneys general from twenty-two states asking the Court not to rule in favor of the employer, by a vote of 5–4, they sent the case back to the Ninth Circuit saying that a company can require applicants to sign an arbitration agreement. They based their decision on the grounds of their interpretation of the Federal Arbitration Act of 1925, the clause that makes contractual agreements that call for arbitration of disputes. The attorneys general, however, believe that this ruling will limit the states' ability to enact laws in relation to forcing workers to sign agreements as a condition of employment.[18]

Case closed? No. In its second look at the claims and counterclaims, the Ninth Circuit, on February 4, 2002, ruled that the employer's arbitration agreement was unenforceable. Parts of the agreement were too one-sided to be enforceable under applicable California law. In particular, the court found the agreement onerous when it requires employees to arbitrate their claims against the company but that the company not arbitrate its claims against the employees.[19] Before adopting an arbitration agreement as a condition of employment, talk it over with your attorney. No telling what the laws of your state may require.

separation agreement A document that identifies the employee's last day of employment and includes provisions for:

> Unused vacation pay
> Bonuses
> Commissions and other compensation due
> Savings or profit-sharing entitlement
> Insurance coverage conversion plans and procedures
> A plan for repaying outstanding advances
> Tax consequences of the severance settlement
> Reemployment rights

Severance policies covered by ERISA may be better left unpublished, although they are embodied in what is called a summary plan description (SPD) and distributed to all employees. The plan should cover the benefits formula(s), methods of payment, eligibility, severance triggers, a description of waivers, and settlement rights.*

service letter A letter required by at least six states (maybe more by the time you read this) describing an ex-employee's work history and, in some cases (for example, Minnesota and Missouri), a reason for dismissal. Check to see whether your state requires a service letter. A possible trap: A written statement of termination for cause can be used in a self-defamation lawsuit. Make sure the letter states only the facts and states them in a manner that cannot be construed as a deliberate or malicious attempt to prevent the ex-employee from future employment.

letter of understanding A letter written by a former employee identifying his or her understanding of why he or she was fired and requesting that you sign the letter or correct the reason stated in the letter. You are not under a legal obligation to sign or respond to this document. The same possible self-defamation trap exists here that exists in a service letter.

*See also Robert J. Nobile, "The Law of Severance Pay," *Personnel*, 67:11 (November 1990), p. 15; August Bequal, *Every Manager's Guide to Firing* (Homewood, Ill: Business One Irwin, 1991).

Our review of essentials of wrongful discharge should help you grasp many of the things you can and cannot do with respect to disciplining and firing employees. It should also help you to examine your own organization's stance vis-à-vis employment-at-will issues and help you understand how employment at will is being attacked.

Cases

1. 779 F.2d 101, 121, L.R.R.M. (BNA) 2169 (2d Cir. 1985).
2. 456 Pa. 171, 319 A.2d 174 (1974).
3. 408 Mich. 579, 292 N.W.2d 880 (1980).
4. 495 F. Supp. 344, 117 L.R.R.M. (BNA) 2702 (Mich. 1980).
5. 373 Mass. 96, 364 N.E.2d 1251, 115 L.R.R.M. (BNA) 4658 (1977).
6. 181 Cal. App. 3d 813, 226 Cal. Rptr. 570 (Cal. Ct. App. 4th Dist. 1986).
7. 226 Mont. 69, 733 P.2d 1292 (1987).
8. 666 P.2d 1000, 115 L.R.R.M. (BNA) 4254 (1983).
9. See also 393 Mass. 231, 471 N.E.2d 47, 118 L.R.R.M. (BNA) 2406 (Mass. Sup. Ct. 1984).
10. 63 Or. App. 1423, 664, P.2d 1119, 118 L.R.R.M. (BNA) 3019 (Or. App. 1983).
11. No. 92–7506 (2d Cir.).
12. No. 88–1591 (4th Cir. 1990); 114 L. Ed. 2d 26, 111 S. Ct. 1647 (1991); No. 98–1246 (1st Cir., Dec. 22, 1998).
13. 500 U.S. S. Ct 20 (1991); Nos. 97–7801, 97–7839, 1998 (2d Cir. July 9, 1998); No. 97–15698 (9th Cir. May 8, 1998).
14. No. 97–15698 (9th Cir. May 8, 1998); see also, "Mandatory Arbitration Upheld for Securities Worker's Claim," *New York Law Journal*, citing a case in a federal district court; "Arbitration Decision to Reinstate Driver Who Failed Drug Test Violated Public Policy," *Transportation Update News Letter* (Fall, 1997), citing a case in the First Circuit Court of Appeals.
15. No. 97–889 (4th Cir. 1998); U.S. S. Ct., November 16, 1998; 415 U.S. 36 (1974); 55 U.S. 20 (1991).
16. No. 97–15698 (9th Cir. 1998).
17. No. 97–1698, 6th Cir. (April 23, 1999).
18. U.S. S. Ct., No. 99–1379 (March 21, 2001).
19. 9th Cir., No. 98–15992 (February 4, 2002).

13

Safe Discipline and Firing Practices

Economic and political winds create new or different judicial tides that ebb and flow over time and with the economy and state of the nation. During periods of high unemployment, for example, people are reluctant to quit in a fit of pique and go to court. Likewise, newly elected judges or new federal court appointments take the tides on still another turn; what direction they will take is often anyone's guess. All I can say is that eddies in these legal tides have weakened the foundations of the employment-at-will doctrine.

Until recently, the creed of employment at will seemed impregnable, a ready-made defense against employee retaliation for unfair or outrageous treatment. But the growth in human rights, especially since the turn of the twentieth century, has generated a new legal climate in the United States that produced not only the civil rights laws of 1964 but also frequent judicial reviews of the at-will defense, especially where legal rights are involved. Inspired by the human rights movement, employees now look to their own interests under the common laws of contract.

Workers defend themselves in court against breach of contract or wrongful discharge more frequently than before, and the courts have sided with employees in almost any kind of personnel decision a manager might possibly make. No longer merely bitter and resentful, resigned to their fate when they feel improperly treated in compensation or promotion or when fired, employees don't just get angry, they get even.

The days when employers could treat employees however they wished have become a relic of history. Pressures created by the labor movement have stayed the employer's free hand. Managers today must pause before punishing or discharging an employee, whether or not they believe they have just cause. Both common law and statute law, including the various EEO laws I have already discussed, have balanced the employer-employee relationship; *how* one goes about disciplining or discharging an employee, the subjects of this chapter, can become a court matter.

Does your organization reserve the right to fire someone with or without cause, with or without notice? Has it published an employee handbook that spells out terms or conditions of employment that could lead to lawsuits? Has it trained you and other managers how to administer its policies and how to avoid making loose promises or implied threats? You should be prepared to deal with the changes time has wrought.

What You Cannot Do

Managers' hands have been stayed in two broad areas: discipline and policy administration.

Discriminatory Discipline

You cannot administer disciplinary policies and procedures that could in themselves have "a meaningful adverse effect on an employee's working conditions."[1-5] Reprimands, especially if filed in a personnel jacket, may affect an employee's future promotion opportunities and have a permanent impact on his or her ongoing work life. This in turn could affect the employee's daily life and psychological well-being. When a disciplinary action affects a person's terms or conditions of employment, it could have a discriminatory effect if the person's status places him or her in a protected group.

Let's take wage garnishment, which minority employees (given their social conditions) experience more frequently than do others, as an example. A policy that would discipline an employee for numerous garnishments could have a disparate impact on minorities, and that policy, even if it results in just a reprimand, may constitute an unlawful employment practice because of the disparate impact. Personnel policies and decisions should have a clearly defined business basis and should not have an adverse impact on people whose social status makes them especially vulnerable.

Provisions of the Employee Handbook

You cannot ignore the provisions of an employee handbook *if* the employee can show that:

> ' The employee handbook has become a part of an employment contract.
> ' The job security provisions in an employee handbook are enforceable.
> ' A summary dismissal is a breach of an employment contract.[6]

Personnel handbook provisions can form a *unilateral contract* and therefore become enforceable as an employment contract if they are distributed to the general population of employees, or if they are used for any purpose other than as a guide for supervisors, or if they are not delimited by a disclaimer that can prevent a printed policy manual from suggesting promises you do not intend to keep. Policy statements should then be used only as a general guide for *managing supervisory behavior.*

You cannot promise job security. Phrases such as *career situation* or *job security* might not form the basis of a contract, but specific job security provisions in an employee handbook, disseminated to all employees, can be so construed. Those provisions could then override a terminable-at-will construction of an employment contract. Check your manual to see if a job security provision could affect your ability to fire someone, and if so, call the situation to your personnel officer's attention.

Replacing or amending the old manual presents you with another situation. A second employee handbook or an amendment does not necessarily usurp the earlier one. In a 1987 case, a federal court ruled that a company's at-will revisions of its original employee manual did not *automatically* supersede the termination-for-cause contractual relationship embodied in the handbook's earlier version.[7]

For the court to accept the revisions, you must show that an employee contesting an at-will discharge had accepted the new handbook as his or her amended contract. If, at the time you issue the second handbook, you require employees to sign an acknowledgment that they have read it, that they understand the terms that affect the conditions of employment, and that they are willing to work according to those terms, you are on safer ground.

If your employee handbook promises that certain procedures will be followed before an employee is discharged, then your disciplinary policy contains sufficiently *definite language* to form an offer of a *unilateral contract.* Under those circumstances, according to some courts, a summary dismissal can constitute a breach of contract. Check out the key words in one specific policy statement that lost in court:[6] "If an employee has violated a company policy, the following procedure *will apply* [italics added]."

That this policy with those words was distributed to all employees nailed down the contract. In this case, the court held that the employer's argument that employees are at-will was without merit because the termination procedures were contractually binding.

Read your policy manual carefully. Ask your personnel officer to check the state's legal precedents in cases such as these. A goodly number of states agree with these decisions.[8-16] How you administer policies is as important as the policies themselves. If you have a personnel policy that creates enforceable contract rights, it is essential to follow it to the letter; failure to do so can be seen by the courts as a breach of contract.[17]

Let's say that your organization's employee handbook prescribes a five-step progressive disciplinary procedure. The first two steps call for counseling, the third for a written reprimand, the fourth for a three-day suspension, and the fifth for discharge if another incident occurs. The handbook also includes statements that promise fair and objective consideration for employees with job-related problems, and that you, the employer, will adhere to a policy of progressive discipline tempered by the seriousness of the offense. Let's also say that your organization has published these statements but has not trained your managers in the proper application of the rules or monitored your *management performance.*

All those policy statements could form the basis of a contract that supersedes employment at will, or so the Wyoming Supreme Court concluded. If, under the circumstances I outlined, you follow all the steps but discharge the employee even though he or she did not commit another offense warranting discipline, which violates the rule of the fifth step ("if another incident occurs"), you probably will be sued and lose.

Substantial compliance with the discipline procedure is an insufficient defense. In the court's opinion, *strict* compliance can be the only standard by which the procedures can be judged. You cannot follow most, but not all, of the steps. You must follow *all* of them. The failure to do so is a breach of contract for which the wrongfully discharged employee could possibly receive damages.

The little things are important as well, especially if an employment contract has been reduced to writing. The following language can cause you much trouble if you fail to adhere to it closely:

> Unless you, or the company, give written notice of termination, this agreement will be automatically extended on December 31 of each year.

If the contract calls for *written* notice, the courts have said that oral notice is not sufficient.[18] If you have any doubts as to how your personnel policies commit you and the other managers, ask your personnel officer to get a professional opinion from an attorney who specializes in employee relations in your state (opinions will differ from state to state). You might also ask that the attorney conduct a seminar for you and your fellow managers. In the meantime, there are things you can do personally to improve your safety.

What You Can Do

That the courts have come to recognize employee contract rights as well as civil rights is not an occasion for managerial hand-wringing. The courts also recognize employer rights as long as policy books are properly written and policies properly administered. In what follows, I try to show you some ways in which you can protect yourself with well-written disclaimers and policy statements that have withstood many court challenges.[20–43]

Protecting Your Right to Fire

If your organization has published an employee handbook, check to see if it contains language that specifically reserves to you your right to employ at will or to modify the organization's employment rules. If the handbook says there is no employment contract, then you cannot breach any contract.[43]

Even though courts in different states, at different times, disagree with the Pennsylvania Supreme Court, that court's basic outline of what constitutes the at-will doctrine provides a clear statement of what to consider when looking at your own organization's published rules under which employees can be discharged:

1. If the employer publishes a handbook, the at-will policy is preserved if the book includes specific language that assumes the employer's unilateral right to modify its policies. That reservation of rights precludes the possibility of creating a just-cause contract.
2. The at-will policy is further protected if the employer states that published reasons for discharge are merely illustrations, not exclusive causes. That claim then gives the employer the right to decide on a case-by-case basis what constitutes just cause or to ignore just cause altogether.
3. If, when they receive the handbook, employees are required to sign an acknowledgment that they received it, they give up their right to being discharged for only just cause.

Publishing Disclaimers

Well-written disclaimers and policy statements offer some protection against lawsuits. Check out your organization's job application or handbook to make sure the disclaimers do the following:

> Uphold the idea of employment at will
> Explain that employment is for no specific duration
> Explain that either party can end the relationship at any time, with or without cause, with or without notice
> Explain that no one but the highest management authority in

the group can alter the terms described in the organization's documents

Check any written policy manuals that have been distributed to any of the nonmanagement employees for language that does the following:

› Clearly spells out the limitations on employment
› Explains to both managers and employees that the personnel policies in the manual act as guidelines for conduct, not as a contract

Finally, make sure that if your organization has published disclaimers and policies, the employees have also acknowledged by their signatures that they have read and understood them. If your managers rewrite anything that could materially change the conditions or terms of employment, ask that they have the employees sign a written acknowledgment of having read and understood the revisions as well, and ascertain that they are willing to work under the new terms and conditions.

The recommended disclaimer and acknowledgment shown in Figures 13-1 and 13-2 have been modeled after several that have

Figure 13-1. Recommended disclaimer for employee handbook.

About This Handbook

This handbook spells out the goals, standards, values, attitudes, beliefs, and benefits that [company name] believes are important and that management encourages. The standards of conduct govern all employees, including management personnel, and are intended to help us all get along in a friendly and productive atmosphere. [Company name]'s policies are also designed to promote your personal productivity and career advancement.

At the same time, this handbook serves only as a general guide to what we can reasonably expect from each other in the conduct of our business. Therefore, neither this handbook nor any of its provisions constitute an employment agreement or contract of any kind or a guarantee to continued employment. Because circumstances and situations change, we will have to change or amend these guidelines from time to time. We will notify you in writing when we do.

Figure 13-2. Recommended acknowledgment by employee.

Acknowledgment

I have read the *Employment Handbook* and understand and agree that it is only a general guide that does not constitute an employment contract or guarantee of continued employment. I also understand and agree that my employment is for no definite period; that my employment and compensation can be terminated with or without cause, with or without notice, at any time, at the option of either [*company name*] or myself; that no representative of the organization other than [*name of person heading organization*] has any authority to enter into any agreement for employment for any specified period of time or make any agreement contrary to the foregoing.

passed court tests, and should, in most cases, hold up if ever challenged. Even if you use them verbatim, have a labor attorney check the statement for consistency with what has been upheld in your state. Local precedent is the only valid test, although favorable precedents are not guarantees that you will win in court.

Effectively Written Policies and Procedures

If your organization has or develops a personnel manual, your personnel officer should distribute it to each manager in your organization and ask for a signed acknowledgment that the manager has received and read it. A seminar on how to read, interpret, and use the manual would be a good idea.

The manual should identify a set of guidelines with regard to goals and objectives (policies) and procedures or rules. It should explain the values the organization holds and what work-related values and conduct it expects of employees. It also should detail for managers what they are supposed to do in the event an employee does not follow the rules. If your organization does not distribute such a manual, you should discuss the matter with your personnel officer; there may be a good reason for not doing so. Then, again, there may not be.

The sample antiharassment policy statement that appears in Chapter 9 on sex discrimination (Figure 9–1) illustrates what a well-written and complete policy and procedures statement should look like. If your organization publishes policies and procedures, you can use the guidance that follows to measure just how well written and complete they are (or aren't).

At the same time, each new employee should receive a copy of an employee handbook that distills information from the personnel manual. This abridged version of the personnel manual should consist primarily of policy statements (the goals and objectives) hedged in disclaimers, some procedures, and the organization's values, expectations, and basic rules of conduct.

Policy Statements

A policy by itself is a guideline for thinking or for making decisions, not necessarily a guide to specific actions, and it should not make any promise that can be construed as establishing a contractual obligation. Check your organization's policy statements to see if they meet the criteria described next.

A complete policy should follow a format that includes separate sections for each part of the policy:

Policy:	The policy statement itself
Procedures:	Steps used to apply or implement the policy
Management Responsibilities:	What managers are expected to do, methods for monitoring or controlling how the policy statement is implemented
Consequences:	Statements concerning what will happen in the event the policy is not enforced, as well as statements concerning consequences if policies are not followed; positive statements related to the value of following the policy would be helpful (for example, "To ensure the cooperation of all employees, this policy . . .")
References:	Quotes or summaries of specific legal documents if legislation or common law is involved

A policy should be:

› *Broad,* in the manner of a goal statement, and leave room for discretion and interpretation, making application flexible but under the direction of the policy. It could start with "It is [*organization's name*] intent to . . ."

> *Comprehensive,* covering every aspect of the relevant personnel activities. Words such as "all cases of this kind," "in no circumstance can anyone authorize a contract other than . . ." should be prominent.

> *Livable,* fitting the realities of both the organization and the world around it. For example, a policy statement can begin with "Given the ratio of minority employees to majority employees in [*organization's name*] . . ."

> *Inviolate,* allowing no exceptions unless the policy itself fails to apply in special circumstances. In some cases, the policy might read, "This policy does not apply to employees on an unpaid leave of absence."

> *Authoritative* (though not authoritarian), identifying responsibilities, accountabilities, and both positive and negative consequences of decisions made within the context of the policy. For example: If you are a first-line supervisor, you will be held responsible for the daily attendance of the employees reporting directly to you. Failure to take timely corrective action for unexcused absences could result in disciplinary action for you as well as for the employee. If you report 100 percent attendance for the quarter, you will receive one day's time off in the quarter immediately following the quarter in which the 100 percent attendance occurred.

> *Applicable,* used frequently by managers to ensure that their decisions are fair, consistent, and in line with executive management's thinking and wishes. A policy might deny a supervisor the right to offer full-time permanent employment to an applicant without the agreement of human resources: "To prevent the appearance of contractually obligating the organization to any one applicant, you must discuss all decisions to hire with the vice president of human resources, and an agreement to extend an offer to that person must be reached."

Even if the policy statements are broad and comprehensive, they could still fail to communicate their intent to everyone because either they do not say what they mean or they are expressed poorly.

Figure 13-3 lists the right way and the wrong way to write policy statements. In which column would you say your organization's policy statements fall?

Procedures

A procedure is a sequence of steps to be performed and, in this context, usually describes how to implement a policy. Policies usually evolve slowly, but procedures are subject to frequent, sometimes sweeping, changes or amendments. Whereas a policy statement is a broad statement of intent (a goal), procedures are specific and action-oriented. They explain how a rule of conduct (which is a requirement for action or inaction) is enforced and how managers are supposed to use their authority or exercise their control. For example, a procedure related to hiring policies might say, "If an applicant does not fill out all relevant blanks in the application for employment (for example, a gap appears between employments), you should ask the person what happened during those years between employments."

Figure 13-3. Rights and wrongs of policy statements.

Right Way	*Wrong Way*
Short sentences that use an economy of language	Technical jargon or other language that might not be readily understood by everyone
A friendly, responsive tone	Legalistic language, even when talking about the law
Personal pronouns (for example, *you*) rather than impersonal words (for example, *managers*) to allow readers to see how the policy applies to them	A choppy or abrupt style
Clear, ordinary language that says what the organization really means	Ambiguity or fuzziness that allow managers to make inappropriate or improper decisions by implication
Action-oriented language expressed by active verbs	Overuse of lists or outlines

Miscellaneous Items

Other materials can be added to a personnel manual to help managers understand what they cannot or can do. For example, the manual should include a section in the back that contains summaries of relevant pieces of legislation or common law concepts (such as those in this book). That and other devices can help an organization protect itself, its managers, and its line employees from wrongful discharge suits.

Conclusion

Employees have found their voice through the courts and other government agencies, a voice long reserved for employers. On the bright side, the new balance struck by the courts between employee and employer rights, if maintained, will help you develop effective management standards and practices that will benefit all concerned. You and your organization can help yourselves if you follow these suggestions.

Use and follow progressive disciplinary procedures whenever possible. When you do have to fire someone, make sure you have backup documentation that you have shared with higher management before making your final decision. In short, do not get caught "building a file," which can lead to an assessment of damages.

Check your policy manual to see if it lists clearly stated offenses for which immediate discharge is possible. Make sure the list is accompanied by a disclaimer saying that the list only illustrates the types of offenses that could result in immediate discharge; that it is not exclusive of other possibilities. The list coupled with a well-written disclaimer makes employment at will an organizational policy; discharge for cause is not necessary and is not restricted to rules of conduct spelled out in a policy manual.

Decide whether you have been given appropriate guidelines about what to say to other people once you have discharged an employee. If you fire someone for cause—for example, theft, destruction of property—you need merely mention the incident in brief, neutral, matter-of-fact terms to those employees who have a need to know, such as immediate coworkers. Firing someone for poor performance can be acknowledged merely by saying that the organization and the employee agreed to disagree and separate. Both ways of explaining things should help you avoid charges of defamation.

But written policies are not enough. Your organization should train you and your co-managers in how to enforce company codes of conduct and how to follow the guidelines for avoiding litigation when hiring, appraising, promoting, or firing employees. If the organization does not offer the training, ask for it.

You can discipline or fire an employee. No one says you cannot. But, if you do, you have to ensure that in the process you have not breached a contract, explicit or implicit, or violated public policy (which I will discuss in Chapter 14), and that the action is not illegal under other laws.

At issue is the balance between employer and employee rights, rights governed by laws of contract as well as civil rights laws. As employer, you have the right to dismiss any employee you want, for whatever reason you want, and with whatever notice you want to give as long as you do not have a definite employment contract limiting your actions.

On the other hand, where no definite employment contract exists, you should be prepared to defend yourself against any charges an employee you dismiss brings against you or your organization. Although no law requires your organization to publish specific personnel policies, they are still good protections against lawsuits. However, they can also be the source of lawsuits, if those policies, as you have read, produce disparate treatment or adverse impact— or, more likely, if they are not carefully implemented.

CASEBOOK

Although I could produce many volumes with breach-of-contract cases, I will include only a few illustrative samples through which you can test your own awareness and against which you can test your organization's disciplining and firing policies.

How Can You Preserve Your Right to Fire?

When Barbara Price ran her "for sale" advertisement in the newspaper published by her employer's competitor, she had no idea she would lose her job over it. In court, she claimed that the language of the employee handbook created a contract that limited employee discharge to "just cause,"—that is, actions that violate very specific rules or expectations: "The following actions violate the standards of conduct of the *Tribune and therefore represent cause for disciplinary action.*" The handbook then listed eleven separate actions common to most handbooks: dishonesty, possession of intoxicants or illegal substances, unexcused absences, and so on.

The publication's attorney argued that the employer had the right to terminate anyone at any time, with or without cause, or to determine what other than the eleven items listed could be called just cause. To bolster the employer's case, the defendant read into the record two other excerpts from the handbook:

> [The eleven separate actions] enumerat[ed] here [are] by way of illustration and shall not be deemed to exclude any other just causes.
>
> It must be remembered that as circumstances change, rules often must change. Therefore, the *Tribune* may from time to time amend some rules to meet changing needs.

Does your organization list reasons for discharge? How does the employee manual protect your freedom to discharge someone?

At-Will Supported

The Pennsylvania courts provide the basic outline of what constitutes the at-will doctrine. The Pennsylvania Superior Court decided for the defendant, refusing to undermine the at-will employment doctrine prevalent in that state. According to the court, without a clear statement of the *employer's* intent to agree to any other arrangement, at-will must prevail.

In this case, because the handbook's language specifically reserved the right to modify the employment *rules* (not at-will employment), the employer's right to discharge at will held.[43] Discharging the employee was not in breach of contract because *no such contract existed,* either implicitly or explicitly. In addition, because the employee signed an acknowledgment, the employer had protected itself completely. On the other hand, in different states, decisions go against the traditional doctrine of termination at-will when, without *written agreements* to say differently, an employee manual gives rise to *implied* contract rights. If the company fails to follow its own rules, it thereby violates the contract established in its own manual.[44]

To sum up, the substance of the employment-at-will doctrine consists of the employers' right to hire and fire people for and at their own convenience. In the absence of a written agreement, an employer may hire someone for an unspecified period of time and fire him or her with or without reason (cause), with or without notice. But, don't forget, the employee has the equal right of quitting at any time, with or without cause, with or without notice.

Changing Terms in Midstream

Felix and Gene had worked for Defense First Corporation for thirty and twenty-eight years respectively. Over the years, the two hourly employees had received copies and updates of the company's employee handbook, most recently in 1989. Each version of the handbook stated that layoffs in each division would be made in reverse order of seniority, which appeared to Felix and Gene to give assurances of their job security.

The 1989 version of the handbook also included a clause that reserved to the employer "the right to amend, modify or cancel this handbook, as well as any or all of the various policies, rules, procedures and programs outlined in it." The clause also promised to inform any affected employees of "any amendment or modification."

In 1993, the company notified all hourly employees that layoff guidelines wouldn't be based on seniority, but rather on each employee's "abilities and documentation of performance." Felix and Gene were laid off less than two weeks later.

The federal court hearing the case alleging a breach of the implied-in-fact contract that guided the layoff procedures of the pre-1989 handbooks granted a summary judgment to Defense First Corporation, citing the company's 1989 handbook authorizing its right to amend its procedures.

What do you think the Ninth Circuit Court had to say about this situation?

Unilateral Contract Action a No-No

If you said the Ninth Circuit said there was no federal action here—
get thee to the state court—you'd be right. If you said the state court
agreed that the Defense Corporation's claim was correct, you'd be
wrong.

In the actual case on which this story is based,[19] the court ruled
that an implied-in-fact contract can be found "when a reasonable
person could conclude that both parties intended that the employer's (or the employee's) right to terminate the employment relationship at-will had been limited." Given that implied-in-fact contract,
neither party may alter the contract without the consent of the
other. Just issuing a new handbook doesn't constitute legally adequate notice or explanation of the way the new book affects employees' rights; likewise, just showing up for work the day after the
handbook is published isn't proof of consent. Employers "cannot be
free to only selectively abide by" its communications and handbooks.

In short, bilateral agreements can't be altered unilaterally.

Can Your Disciplinary Procedures Form a Contract?

Peter Strauss had worked as a loan officer for State Bank for a year
and a half when a routine audit uncovered a number of technical
exceptions in its loan portfolio. Without a hearing, he was fired.

In turn, he took the bank to court, claiming that it breached his
employment contract by dismissing him without cause and in violation of the bank's prescribed disciplinary procedures. To bolster his
case, he cited three provisions of the employee handbook that the
bank had adopted and distributed to the employees while Strauss
was employed but that it did not follow when it discharged him:
performance review, job security, and a four-stage disciplinary action
procedure. The first provision said:

> All employees want to know "where they stand." Our
> performance evaluation program is designed to help you
> to determine where you are, where you are going, and how
> to get there. Factual and objective appraisals of you and

your work performance should serve as aids to your future advancement.

The second citation, "job security," extolled the stability of employment in the banking industry.

> Employment in the banking industry is very stable. It does not fluctuate up and down sharply in good times and bad. . . . We have no seasonal layoffs and we never hire a lot of people when business is booming only to release them when things are not as active.
>
> The job security offered by [*State*] Bank is one reason why so many of our employees have five or more years of service. In return for this, management expects job security from you, that is, the security that you will perform the duties of your position with diligence, cooperation, dependability, and a sense of responsibility.

The third provision described a four-stage "disciplinary policy."

> In the interest of fairness to all employees, the company establishes reasonable standards of conduct for all employees to follow. . . . [They] are not intended to place unreasonable restrictions on you but are considered necessary for us to conduct our business in an orderly and efficient manner. If an employee has violated a company policy, the following procedure will apply:
>
> 1. An oral reprimand by the immediate supervisor for the first offense, with a written notice sent to the executive vice president
> 2. A written reprimand for the second offense
> 3. A written reprimand and a meeting with the executive vice president and possible suspension from work without pay for five days
> 4. Discharge from employment for an employee whose conduct does not improve as a result of the previous action taken

State Bank's attorney argued that all three provisions were irrelevant inasmuch as Strauss was employed at will.

A jury awarded Strauss $27,675 in damages for being termi-
nated in breach of contract and without good cause. The bank took
its case to the state supreme court.

What has your organization published with respect to performance appraisal, job security, and disciplinary procedures? If it lost a
case before a jury, how could your state supreme court possibly rule?

Got 'Em, Follow 'Em

The Minnesota Supreme Court ruled in favor of the plaintiff on all
three counts and provided me with the answers to the three broad
questions I discussed in the text: (1) Can an employee handbook
become a part of an employment contract? (2) Can job security provisions in an employee handbook be enforced? (3) Can a summary
dismissal, as in this case, breach an employment contract? The court
answered yes to all three.[16]

First, personnel handbook provisions can form a *unilateral contract* and may therefore become enforceable as an employment contract if they are distributed to the general population of employees,
or if they are used for any purpose other than as a guide for supervisors, or if they are not delimited in some manner (for example, with
a disclaimer).

Second, phrases such as *career situation* and *job security* might not
form the basis of a contract, but job security provisions in an employee handbook, disseminated to all the employees, can be so construed. The job security provisions in the employment contract
would then override a terminable-at-will construction of the contract.

Third, a disciplinary policy is binding when it contains sufficiently *definite language* to form an offer of a *unilateral contract* promising that certain procedures will be followed before an employee is
discharged. The phrase "if an employee has violated a company policy, the following procedure will apply" is definite language in this
case.

Cases

1. 707 F.2d 1274, 32 F.E.P. Cases (BNA) 142 (11th Cir. 1983).
2. 99 Lab. Cas. (CCH) 10,639 (N.W. Ohio 1983).

3. 99 Lab. Cas. (CCH) 10,640 (D. Mass. 1983).
4. 122 L.R.R.M. 2344 (E.D. Miss. 1986).
5. Reported in *Resource,* The Journal of the American Society for Personnel Administration, 8:1 (January 1989).
6. (Minn. Sup. Ct. April 29, 1983).
7. 753 F. Supp. 871 (E.D. Va. 1987).

Examples of Employee Manuals as the Basis of
Enforceable Contracts
8. No. 84–2554 (1st Dist. Ill. September 15, 1985).
9. 708 P.2d 110 (Ariz. Ct. App. 1985); see also 141 Ariz. 544, 688 P.2d 170 (1984).
10. No. 49592–1 (Wash. Sup. Ct. July 5, 1984).
11. 215 Neb. 677, 340 N.W.2d 388 (Neb. 1983).
12. 672 P.2d 629 (Nev. 1983).
13. No. 84-CA-1508-MR (Ky. Ct. App. April 12, 1985).
14. 486 A.2d 798 (Md. Ct. App. 1985).
15. No. WD 36426 (Mo. Ct. App. April 9, 1985).
16. No. A-98–82 (May 9, 1985).
17. 704 P.2d 702 (Wyo. 1985).
18. 609 F. Supp. 627 (N.D. Ill. 1985).
19. *Demasse v. ITT Corp.,* No. CV-97–0177-CQ (Arizona, May 1999); see also, "Handbook Created Contract Employer Can't Unilaterally Alter," *HR News,* (July 1999), p. 8; and "Handbook Headache," *Personnel Legal Alert,* Alexander Hamilton Institute, Inc. (May 2, 1999).

Cases Upholding a Disclaimer or Other Employee
Manual Procedures
20. 100 Lab. Cas. 10,793 (Ala. Sup. Ct. 1983).
21. 474 So. 2d 1069 (Ala. 1985).
22. 495 So. 2d 1381 (Ala. 1986).
23. 199 Cal. Rptr. 613 (Cal. App. 2d Dist. 1984).
24. 113 Idaho 581, 746 P.2d 1040 (Idaho App. 1987).
25. 2 I.E.R. Cases 1568 (Ill. App. Ct. 1987).
26. No. 87–1622 (Ill. App. Ct. June 24, 1988).
27. 738 S.W.2d 824 (Ky. Ct. App. 1987).
28. No. 84–824 (La. Ct. App. Dec. 12, 1985).
29. 495 F. Supp. 344 (E.D. Mich. 1980).
30. C.A. No. 81–73233 (E.D. Mich. October 18, 1982).
31. N.W.2d 529 (Mich. App. 1984).
32. No. 71,773 (Mich. Ct. App. Nov. 4, 1985).
33. No. 76,014 (Mich. Ct. App. 1985).
34. 122 L.R.R.M. 2153 (6th Cir. 1986).
35. 417 N.W.2d 496 (Mich. Ct. App. 1987).
36. 413 N.W.2d 146 (Minn. App. 1987).
37. 2 I.E.R. Cases 1799 (Mo. 1988).
38. 220 N.J. Super. Ct. 135, 531 A.2d 757 (N.J. Super. Ct. 1987).
39. 356 S.E.2d 357, 2 I.E.R. Cases 269 (1987).
40. No. 49,770 (Ohio Ct. App. December 5, 1985).

41. 1 I.E.R. 476 (Pa. 1986).
42. 715 S.W.2d 60 (Tex. Ct. App. 1986).
43. 116 L.R.R.M. (BNA) 3092 (Wis. Ct. App. 1984).
44. 354 Pa. Super. 199, 511 A.2d 830, 1 I.E.R. 476 (Pa. 1986); see also No. 97–1726,
    8th Cir. (1999).

14

Public Policy

In Chapter 13, I made a reference to *public policy* without defining or explaining the concept. The reason should now be obvious: Any discussion of firing someone in violation of public policy requires its own chapter.

Giving employees time off for voting or for serving on a jury is the best-known public policy issue, but it represents only the surface of a constantly expanding body of issues. The concept covers every aspect of a citizen's social and political rights and obligations; firing someone in violation of public policy, if the charge is substantiated, is always an exception to termination at will.

It pays, therefore, to define this key term before grappling with the questions regarding what you cannot and can do that the concept raises. You need to see if your organization's policies and practices could, in some way, jeopardize you or the organization itself.

public policy Laws and resolutions of the state, common law, the state's constitution, judicial decisions, and public morals form public policy and create rights and obligations. Society believes it cannot function effectively without essential social standards, such as honesty in business dealings. To satisfy this social demand, the courts have established the concept of public policy. The matter of violations of public policy ranges far and wide because most states, including those that accept employment-at-will as their theory of management—for example, Pennsylvania and Illinois—have specific laws protecting a person's rights and always *except* actual violations of public policy.

What You Cannot Do

Particular violations of public policy deserve special consideration. Managers commit the following sins too frequently:

› *The obvious.* You cannot refuse to give someone time off for voting if the polls are not open during the person's nonworking hours. You cannot refuse to give a person time off to answer the call for jury duty. You cannot fire someone for meeting his or her civic obligations. Employers abridge or interfere with voting rights, jury duty, courtroom testimony, and so on at their own risk, and very few employers today abridge these rights; but, from our definition it is clear that matters of public policy do not stop here. Most cases where someone feels abused for exercising rights preserved or mandated by law relate to more subtle issues: the right to answer a subpoena, the right to file a workers' comp claim, the right to refuse to violate a standard of conduct, and so forth.

› *Fire someone for refusing to violate public morals.* You cannot fire someone who refused to do anything he or she believes is contrary to *public* morals (as distinguished from *personal* morals, which by themselves do not define or form a source of public policy). Values created by social and legal processes determine public morals and can be used to call you to court if you discharge someone who feels wrongfully discharged in violation of public policy.[1]

› *Fire someone for refusing to violate a law.* You cannot ask someone to violate or conspire to violate a local, state, or federal statute and fire him or her for refusing to do so. It does not matter if the law was actually violated or if the employee can prove conclusively that a law was broken. The employee does not even have to take the complaint to the authorities, which action is also protected under law. The employee need only show in court that he or she was fired for discussing with management his or her reasonable belief that certain actions are illegal. The firing itself is an instance of wrongful discharge in violation of public policy.[2]

› *Fire someone for refusing to commit perjury.* You cannot ask someone to lie in court or in a sworn document, or to lie in the normal course of doing business, and fire him or her for refusing to do so.[3] This rule also covers instances in which a statement could possibly be false.[4] A person has a social obligation to refrain from making statements the truth of which is unclear or questionable,[5] and firing him or her for not making them would be retaliatory.

› *Fire probationary employees if they are fulfilling a legal obligation.* Let's say you have an employee, a woman employee, you have placed on probation for excessive absences and tardiness. You have given her written warning that she will be fired if she misses work during the probationary period. Let's also suppose she receives a subpoena to make a deposition in a lawsuit in which she is the defendant. Feeling caught between the proverbial rock and hard place, she answers the subpoena. Can you fire her for being absent during her probationary period?

No, say the courts. You cannot. An employer must give a person time off to make deposition or answer a subpoena regardless of the circumstances.[6] It makes no difference if the request to attend a deposition hearing is oral, delivered by counsel, or under subpoena. The employee's attendance record notwithstanding, the *threat* of the loss of a job because he or she fulfills her legal obligation interferes with the judicial process and injures the public.

  › *Prevent an employee from exercising legal rights.* Asking an employee to sign a waiver of rights, for example, to sign away his or her right to file a workers' compensation claim, could be seen as an attempt to deny that employee his or her legal rights. Firing the person after he or she signs the waiver can be seen as an exception to termination at will in violation of public policy.[7]

Managers should be on guard anytime an employee is entitled to exercise legally protected rights. If a waiver of rights is used, especially if the person cannot read English, advising the employee of the agreement's contents and having him or her acknowledge the explanation could help protect the release's proper wording. Even so, it might not stand up in court. The wisest course of action in a situation such as this is for you or your organization to adhere to the spirit and letter of the law.

This is particularly important in the case of workers' compensation because the purpose of such statutes is to provide medical cost protection in the event an employee is injured during the conduct of the employer's business. To infringe on the remedial spirit of the law not only jeopardizes your employees, it also injures your ability to hire and retain employees.

  › *Violate an employee's First Amendment rights.* You cannot fire someone for whistle-blowing—that is, complaining to authorities about illegal, immoral, or dangerous-to-the-public business practices.[8] Connecticut, for example, has two laws that apply.

The first, the Free Speech Act, enjoins employers from retaliating against someone exercising his or her First Amendment rights:

> [Any] employer . . . who subjects any employee to discipline or discharge on account of the [employee's exercising his or her] rights guaranteed in the first amendment of the United States Constitution or section 3, 4, or 14 of article [1] of the [state's] constitution, provided [that] activity does not substantially or materially interfere with the employee's bona fide job performance or the working relationship between the employee and the employer, shall be liable to [the] employee for damages caused by [the] discipline or discharge.

The second law, the Connecticut Whistleblowing Statute, extends the first law to cover whistle-blowing:

> No employer shall discharge, discipline, or otherwise penalize any employee because the employee . . . reports . . . a violation or suspected violation of any state or federal law or regulation or any municipal ordinance or regulation to a public body, or because an employee is requested by a public body to participate in an investigation, hearing, or inquiry held by that public body, or a court action.

The Connecticut District Court gave teeth to these statutes when, in an important case in 1986, it ruled that rather than conflict with each other, one law complements the other.[8] This way, a court could award the plaintiff two different sets of remedies. Under the Whistleblowing Statute, relief is limited to reinstatement, back pay, and benefits. The Free Speech Act entitles the aggrieved to collect damages, including punitive damages. Interfering with an employee's guaranteed rights anywhere, not just in Connecticut, could get expensive. Today, with the chicanery found in corporate America—for example, "cooking the books" or suppressing or destroying damaging information—whistle-blowing has become a moral imperative to protect the public good and individuals' lives and welfare.

You cannot require someone to lobby on your organization's behalf, and fire him or her for refusing. Because public policy compels employers to recognize society's interest in an employee's freedom of political expression, such action could be seen as interfering with an employee's freedom from discharge because of his or her political beliefs. A person can be a loyal employee even if he or she does not hold the same political opinions as his or her employer does.

In a landmark case,[9] the Third Circuit Court in Pennsylvania weighed an employee's right to political freedom against the employer's right to effectively conduct business by asking these four questions:

1. Did the employee's behavior prevent the employer from fulfilling its responsibilities?
2. Did the employee's behavior prevent him from carrying out his responsibilities?
3. Did the employee's behavior interfere with necessary, close working relationships?
4. Did the employee's behavior occur at a time, in a manner, and in a place to interfere with the employer's business operations?

If the court had answered any one of those questions in the affirmative, the employee would have lost his case. Because none of them were applicable to his behavior, he won. Before you let anyone go in a situation such as this, make sure you base your decision on rational rather than emotional grounds.

Even if you don't fire or otherwise discipline a whistle-blower, you and your organization could be sued under the False Claim Act by your employees-as-taxpayers if your company has allegedly defrauded the government—even if the government has not brought suit. In some cases, the employees may ask for damages for the "stress, anxiety, and mental anguish" they experienced from their fear of being fired or otherwise disciplined.[14] Damages could run into the millions; therefore, don't take any of this lightly.

› *Deny someone due process.* You can fire someone you merely suspect of wrongdoing, but you should not deny him or her due process when you do it. You should give him or her the opportunity to show that he or she did not commit the wrongful act.

Appearances can sometimes deceive. It is dangerous to assume that you are in the right when you think someone did harm or injury to your organization. While in many courts around the country employers have won the right to discharge employees suspected of wrongdoing, even though the case against the employee was not proved, in many other courts the failure to extend *due process privileges* to the accused has cost employers the right to terminate for cause.

What You Can Do

When it comes to public policy, your best bet is to understand your limits under local, state, and federal laws. What you cannot do translates into what you can do to manage safely within the constraints of public policy.

At the same time, you can protect yourself if you think an employee's actions or failure to act interferes with your business operations. The decision to which I referred earlier (by the Third Circuit Court in Pennsylvania) highlights several important tests of self-defense.[9]

Before even thinking of taking action against someone who has engaged in some arguably protected activity, especially a political activity, consider whether or not *you* have the *protections* you need. Consider the following elements:

› The nature and motive(s) of the employee's conduct
› The sorts of interests both you and the employee are trying to advance
› Your countervailing interests against those of the employee
› How near or close the employee's conduct is to the time and act of interference you allege
› What in the nature of the particular relationship between you and the employee might lead you to expect the employee to comply with your organization's agendas?
› Society's interest in protecting freedom of belief and action against any contract interests that may exist between you and the employee

Your defense would have to show that the employee intentionally and maliciously acted in a manner to harm your ability to conduct business: that your business interests have greater social and economic value than the employee's personal interests do, that the employee acted adversely on or about the time of the harm, that the employment contract created an expectation of loyalty (including political loyalty), and that society's interests are better met by the organization's agenda than by the employee's. That defense is as tough to create as the sentence describing it is long.

To practice safe management with regard to dealing with whistle-blowers, I offer you the following words of advice from New York attorneys John P. Furfaro and Gregg A. Gilman:*

> Encourage employees to report any wrongdoing by creating a reporting system that, if necessary, bypasses their immediate supervisor (who may be the culprit).
> Write clearly stated policies, distribute them to all employees, and enforce them.
> Respect confidentiality and reassure employees that they will not be disciplined for reporting suspected wrongdoing.
> Conduct prompt and thorough investigations into all complaints.
> Take corrective action when necessary.
> Obey the three rules of safe management I've stressed before: document, document, document—especially in cases involving disciplining or firing of employees who have made whistle-blower claims.

Again, it is in your own interest to pay attention to what the law protects before firing someone for anything other than poor performance or gross misconduct.

Conclusion

The recognition of contract rights comes at the same time that employees have learned that they cannot be denied the right to vote, serve on a jury, apply for workers' compensation or unemployment

*See "The New Whistleblower Risks," an interview with John P. Furfaro and Gregg A. Gilma, attorneys with the firm Skadden, Arps, Slate, Meagher & Flom, in *Boardroom Reports* (August 15, 1991), p. 2.

insurance, or attend to other legal matters. They also know they have the right to protest or refuse if they have been asked to violate a law or a standard of social conduct. All such strictures violate the rights granted by the dictates of public policy. But what constitutes public policy?

No matter how morally outraged an employee may be by what the employer requires or does, undesirable personal morals *alone* cannot define or become the source of *public* policy. Rather, public policy is based on common law, the state and federal constitutions, state and federal statutes, judicial decisions, and public morals. Only by looking at values created by those processes can public policy be determined.

Inasmuch as public policy issues vary from state to state and jurisdiction to jurisdiction, no blanket prescriptions can be written for keeping your decisions out of court. There are no guarantees.

Rather, in matters where running up against public policy is possible, give yourself a chance to reflect on your decision before acting on it; perhaps call an attorney before doing something about a decision that seems jeopardized by the judicial tide of the time or place.

—— CASEBOOK ——

Most personnel officers can talk knowledgeably about public policy, but few managers can. Their ignorance of the law often puts them at risk and jeopardizes their organizations; and that is why you should read each case carefully and grapple with the question that begins each one.

Compare your decisions with those of the courts in the following cases. Could you or your organization be jeopardized in some way similar to the one described in the cases? How can you use the court's ruling in a given case to help you or your organization protect or defend yourselves?

Can You Fire Someone for Refusing to Go Along with a Prank?

A camping trip in the Arizona desert with your supervisor and coworkers should be a lot of fun. At least that is what paramedic coordinator Ellen Braun thought until the party began. To her embarrassment, everyone was expected to defecate and urinate in public. She was also expected to take part in a skit, a parody of the song "Moon River," that would end with all the performers pulling down their pants and mooning the audience, exposing their bare backsides to the spectators. Braun would not go along with any of that.

Before the camping trip, so the plaintiff claimed, she had received consistently favorable performance appraisals. Afterward, her supervisor regularly criticized her performance and attitude. The relationship between the paramedic coordinator and the supervisor deteriorated, culminating in Braun's discharge.

The aggrieved claimed retaliatory discharge. The hospital countered with charges of a lack of cooperation and poor performance.

Assuming that such a skit is acceptable, how would you react if an employee refused to go along with it? With whom do you think the court sided?

No Laughing Matter

This case seems trivial and extreme, but because it carried all the way to the Arizona Supreme Court it helps clarify the meaning of the public policy exception to termination at will that I described in the beginning of this chapter. Its importance, therefore, cannot be emphasized enough.

The court ruled that the employee should not have been fired; the supervisor's actions *were* punitive and retaliatory. Firing someone who refuses to engage in a prank he or she thinks is contrary to *public morals,* as well as contrary to his or her own morals, may violate public policy and form the predicate for a wrongful discharge lawsuit.[1]

While individual cases or violations of public policy may differ, the general rules for application created by the Arizona Supreme Court seem essentially the same for all courts in all states. The court agreed that in one sense the incident was trivial (people at play), but in a larger sense, it was quite serious. As Braun claimed, the act of mooning itself could be considered a violation of the criminal code: Exposing one's anus or genitals is contrary to public standards of morality. Firing the plaintiff for refusing to moon the audience there-fore violates public policy.

So people at play turned into a major court case. One person's fun can turn out to be another's discomfort and the source of every-one's great misery. Managers have to take care that pranks do not get out of hand, and if they do, take care of how people who do not want to join in on the so-called fun are handled.

That does not mean that every disagreement leads to a violation of public policy. Another case underscores the importance of *public* perceptions of right and wrong.

In this instance, the court found that an employee, fired for complaining about his employer's mismanagement, had the right to disagree with management's decisions, but management also had the equal right to fire him. Even if the employee was right to be offended by poor management, the court said, the employer violated no matter of public policy; the conflict was over *personal values,* not over public morals, conscience, or policies.[10]

Can You Fire Someone for Refusing to Violate a Law?

"The plan may not be legal," Eric Freedman complained to his CEO. "The methods are definitely not generally accepted accounting pro-cedures, and they may violate federal securities law."

The company's stony-faced president mulled over the problem before answering his chief financial officer. "Just restate some ac-counts. Discount the purchase of production equipment as income and restate the African safari accounts to bring things back into line."

"I'm sorry, Gene. That won't work. It overstates income and inflates asset valuation, which, in my opinion, violates federal law."

"We need team players here, Eric. You should know that."

Freedman steadfastly refused to accept the accounting proce-dures the company finally used. In response to his complaints to management, he was fired.

In court, when Freedman sued Worldwide Publishing for wrong-ful discharge in violation of public policy, the company's attorney argued that *state* law does not mandate a set of accounting proce-dures; therefore, public policy is not at issue here. In addition, no one ever proved that the company's procedures violated any laws. In accordance with the company's termination-at-will policies, they fired Freedman for not complying with the company's wishes.

What do you think? Do you think the company has a case? Do you think your organization would fire a senior vice president for complaining internally about accounting procedures?

No Gaps in GAAP

Your company might not have fired Freedman, but the one for whom the plaintiff worked did, and the Illinois Court of Appeals, Fifth District, took it to task.[2] Basing its judgment partially on an earlier Illinois decision,[11] the court ruled that not just state statutes apply to the principle of public policy. Federal laws duly enacted in Congress, national in scope, mandate public policy in all the states.

Federal law mandates the use of GAAP (generally accepted accounting principles). Therefore, asking the finance officer to accept deviations from GAAP amounted to asking him *to conspire to violate a federal law as well as accepted social standards.* Firing him for protesting unaccepted standards violated public policy with regard to reporting practices: full disclosure, truthfulness, and accuracy in the financial reports made to governments. In making this decision, the Illinois court applied federal law to issues of public policy in the states.

This decision is one of several that demonstrate that taking refuge behind the doctrine of employment at will does not always work. Both the violation of public policy and the promise not to discharge an employee without cause constitute exceptions to the doctrine.

The moral of this story might be: If you are going to violate the law yourself, do not try to drag anyone along with you or fire him or her for not cooperating. You will be hit twice, once for breaking the law in the first place and second for firing someone for not helping you do it.

How about your organization? What safeguards prevent a manager from ever asking someone to commit a possible felony?

Can You Fire Someone for Refusing to Possibly Defame Someone Else?

Frank Sullivan was fired. When he applied for unemployment insurance, Ed Polanski, a supervisor, refused to sign upper management's statement describing the reasons for dismissal. Polanski claimed that the report, falsely accusing Sullivan of poor work habits and immoral behavior, was untrue. Without Polanski's signature, management could not file its counterclaim; they fired the supervisor as well.

But Polanski went to court, arguing that his discharge was retaliatory and was the same as cases in which an employee is fired for refusing to commit perjury or for refusing to alter Office of Safety and Health Administration (OSHA) or Environmental Protection Agency (EPA) reports. His attorney also argued that accepted standards of social conduct and public policy require honesty in business relationships and that the employer fired the supervisor for his honesty.

The company defended itself by claiming that the truth or falsity of the statement was a factual question that management resolved internally. It was Polanski's opinion against theirs. They had good cause to fire him: insubordination.

How would your organization handle this type of situation? Who do you think won after a long, difficult fight?

Honesty Is the Best Policy

Here's the question: Is refusing to make a *possibly* false statement protected by public policy?

A jury said it was and awarded the plaintiff damages. But the appeals court reversed, ruling that even though public policy favors honesty in business, refusing to sign the report on the basis of one's personal opinion of what constitutes honesty or dishonesty is not protected. The report's honesty is a factual matter that was settled. An exception would undermine the doctrine of termination at will.

Furthermore, the opinion said, this case does not resemble wrongful discharge claims in which someone is to asked to commit perjury. *Statutes* protect such instances, but no statute protects honesty per se. Damages need not be paid.[4]

Not so, answered the Oregon Supreme Court in a decision one year later. Pay the plaintiff damages. Oregon *case law* protects him from being discharged because he refused to sign a report that is *arguably defamatory*. Given the nature of the allegations against his colleague's work habits and moral conduct, the plaintiff had a social obligation not to defame him. Public policy *is* violated by discharging someone on that ground.[5]

The debate between the courts in this case shows how significant the issue is and how dependent upon definitions court rulings can be. The Oregon Supreme Court's decision further extends the meaning of public policy by calling upon social obligations instead of laws against perjury. The decision seems to say, "Honesty in business is merely good business, for both employers and society. Why compound dishonesty in doing business with wrongfully discharging someone for refusing to be dishonest?"

Does a Signed Waiver of Workers' Comp Rights Protect You if You Fire the Person?

Jack Berkowitz, an Eastern European immigrant, hurt himself on the job badly enough to require hospitalization and time off. Not even the doctors were sure he would be able to return to the job he had. After his employer, Handicraft Industries, had him sign a severance agreement in which he waived all his rights, including the right to file a workers' comp claim, he was fired.

A year later Berkowitz filed the workers' comp claim. When the company fought back, he went to court stating that his firing was retaliatory in violation of public policy, designed to prevent him from filing his claim.

In response, the company signed severance waiver and asked for a summary dismissal of the case.

Berkowitz's attorney responded that since the immigrant could not read or write English, some manager or another was obligated to read and explain the document to him, which no one had done.

What do you think? Should this case go to trial? Would your organization do something to prevent an employee from filing a bona fide workers' comp claim? Under what conditions?

Make It Clear

A waiver of rights, such as the one contained in the severance agreement, may not head off a retaliatory discharge lawsuit—especially if the employee does not understand the terms of the agreement.

The Illinois Appellate Court in this 1985 case said, "Go to trial." The allegations were sufficient to create factual questions about the employer's intent. The court pointed out that the employee need not show that he, in fact, had filed a claim. He need merely show that he was fired to *prevent* him from exercising his legally guaranteed rights. If the employee did not understand he was signing a waiver that jeopardized his rights, and the employer knew the man could not read or write English, the waiver could appear to have been an intentional ploy to have the man relinquish his right.[7]

When it comes to an employee's legal rights, beware any attempt to interfere. If you are not sure of where you stand, check it out with an attorney. The time and expense of safe management shrink in the face of a possible lawsuit.

Can You Fire Someone for Refusing to Reimburse Your Organization for a Work-Related Loss?

When an allegedly stolen payroll check showed up in the Community Credit Union's statements, it bore an apparently forged endorsement. Diana Bonds, a teller, cashed the check, and for that, without having an opportunity to explain how she came to do it, she was told to reimburse the credit union for the loss. When she refused to do so, management discharged her.

Her attorney complained in court that the discharge violated Section 103.455 of the Wisconsin statutes, which prescribes procedures for imposing the burden of paying for a work-related loss on an employee accused of causing the loss. Under this law, the accused must be given the opportunity to show that the loss was not his or her fault. Community Credit Union failed to follow those statutorily prescribed procedures, the suit alleged.

The employer retorted that the cashing of a fraudulently endorsed payroll check falls outside the purview of the law cited. The possible felony justifies immediate dismissal.

What do you think? Was immediate dismissal justified? Is that how your organization would handle this sort of situation?

Due Process

The Wisconsin Supreme Court did not think that immediate dismissal was justified. It agreed that the statute did not expressly prohibit firing someone in this sort of situation, but that was beside the point. Rather, firing the employee contravened the public policy embodied in the legislation.

According to the court, the law's main purpose is to avoid coercing an employee to carry the full burden of a work-related loss without due process, which includes the opportunity to show that he or she did not cause the loss through either carelessness, negligence, or willful misconduct.[12]

What Can You Do if Someone Tells the Painful Truth?

Kristine Shultz responded to a subpoena in a coworker's insurance claim against Health Care Associates, their employer, and told the truth. Her testimony helped the coworker to win the case.

Her employer, seeing her testimony as an act of disloyalty, went as far as to say, "Maybe you should seek other employment because you testified against us." That's what Schultz alleged in court after quitting.

To her attorney's charge that his client was forced out, the employer answered that Schultz quit voluntarily.

How would you react to Kristine's testimony? Would you have fired her? Whose side do you think the court took?

To Tell the Truth

You can find yourself in the same deep trouble that the employer brought on itself if you fire someone in violation of some aspect of public policy. The court ruled that the employer forced the plaintiff to quit by telling her to find employment elsewhere because she fulfilled her obligation to testify honestly when subpoenaed to do so. Continued employment there would only have led to intolerable conditions for her. For the court, this was a case of both *constructive discharge* and a violation of *public policy*.[13]

Cases

1. No. 17646-PR (Ariz. Sup. Ct. 1985) (en banc); see also 125224-93 (N.Y. S. Ct. 1994) under appeal at this time.
2. 101 Ill. Dec. 251, 498 N.E.2d 575 (Ill. App. Ct. 5th Dist. 1986); see also 940 F.2d 184 (7th Cir. 1992).
3. 328 S.E.2d 818 (N.C. Ct. App. 1985).
4. 670 P.2d (Or. Ct. App. 1983).
5. 681 P.2d 114 (Or. Sup. Ct. 1984).
6. 2 I.E.R. Cases 589 (Mo. Ct. App. 1987).
7. 478 N.E.2d 1039 (Ill. App. Ct. 1985).
8. 105 Lab. Cas. 55.608 (D. Conn. 1986).
9. No. 83-5101 (3d Cir. October 26, 1983).
10. 489 A.2d 828 (Pa. Super. Ct. 1985).
11. 108 Ill. 2d 502, 92 Ill. Dec. 561, 485 N.E.2d 372 (1985), *cert. denied,* 106 S. Ct. 1641 (1986).
12. 104 Lab. Cas. 55,555 (Wis. 1986).
13. 620 F. Supp. 1268, 120 L.R.R.M. (BNA) 3233 (D. Kan. 1985).
14. 929 F.2d 1416 (9th Cir.); see also no. 25480-4-1 (Wash. 1990), (9th Cir. 1993), litigated.

15

Managing a
Reduction in Force

In August 2003, while I was writing these revisions, the official unemployment rate had seen a blip or two on the upswing, yet thousands of workers were still receiving pink slips. As in most recoveries from a recession, recovery in the workforce lags behind all other figures. Nevertheless, we cannot take constant layoffs lightly, and managers have obligations to ensure that workers are not rudely harmed by their decisions.

What with mergers, downsizing, and buy outs, the risks involved in laying off members of protected groups have increased. For example, large defense and aerospace companies have been sued for age discrimination; although most have settled out of court, the costs of defending themselves against the suits have taken a toll. Many companies face racial discrimination suits, class-action suits taken by specific classes of employees, and individual and class-action suits of gender discrimination.

What You Can Do

There are ways, however, to protect yourself and your company from such attacks, while treating laid-off employees fairly. Follow the nine court-recognized steps I describe in detail in Chapter 16, which are briefly listed here:

1. You have an appropriate business plan with business-driven goals for laying off employees.
2. You know your workforce well enough to recommend who

to dismiss without its having an adverse impact on any protected group(s) or violating a contractual commitment or an
employee benefit plan.
3. You have objective methods for selecting employees.
4. You're in a position to document the business purpose of subjective decisions and have well-defined, written performance
criteria to offset subjectivity.
5. You are able to identify and document:
   › Marginally performing employees
   › Superfluous employees identified by a work or process rede-
     sign program
   › Employees with the least amount of knowledge or skills
     related to newly created work
6. You can apply the criteria of a fair and evenhanded seniority
system.
7. You have records that document the grounds for your decisions.
8. Your company has a plan that helps to protect members of
protected groups during an RIF or other cost-cutting actions.
9. You and your company can communicate effectively with all
people affected by your actions.

But what about plant closings? Those nine steps don't always
apply. That's where the Worker Adjustment and Retraining Notification (WARN) Act comes into play.

Since February 1989, hourly and salaried workers, their families
and communities have been protected by the WARN Act from sudden closings or layoffs from private companies or public and quasi-
public entities with 100 employees or more (not including recent
hires and part-timers). The act requires companies to give employees
or their unions sixty days' notice before the closing of a plant or a
division of the company or the company itself.

› Notice is triggered if an employment site will be shut down,
which will result in an employment loss—that is, a termination
other than for cause, voluntary departure, or retirement, or a
layoff exceeding six months, or a reduction in hours of more
than 50 percent in each month of any six-month period—for
fifty or more employees during any thirty-day period.

> Notice is triggered if there is to be a mass layoff that does not result from a site closing but that caused an employment loss during any thirty-day period for 500 or more employees, or for 50–499 employees if those employees constitute 33 percent or more of the active workforce.
> Notice is triggered if, during a ninety-day period, two or more groups of workers affected reach the threshold number of either a plant closing or mass layoff, unless the employer can show that the employment losses during that period are the result of separate and distinct actions and causes.
> In the event of the sale of a business, the seller must provide notice of any covered site closing or mass layoff that occurs up to and including the date and time of the sale; the buyer is responsible after that date and time.
> Notice is not required for the closing of a temporary facility or at the conclusion of a project or specific undertaking as long as the employees knew at the start that their employment was limited to the duration of the site or project; however, an employer cannot claim that an ongoing project is "temporary" in order to sidestep this Act.
> Notice is not required for strikers or workers of a collective bargaining unit involved in negotiations leading to a lockout that closes a plant or to a mass layoff; other employees affected are entitled to notice.
> Notification is required to reach affected employees at least sixty days before a closing or mass layoff.
> If terminations occur on more than one day, notices are due to the affected employees or their representatives, the state dislocated worker unit, and local government at least sixty days before *each* separation.
> Exceptions to the sixty-day notice are if a faltering company seeking new capital or business would be adversely affected by notice, unforeseeable circumstances, and natural disaster.

Whereas the WARN Act requires certain employers to give employees or their union sixty days' written notice of a plant closing or mass layoff, it doesn't provide for a statute of limitations period. This has led courts to divided opinions as to whether to apply state law statutes of limitations for similar laws or apply the six-month statute of limitations period found in the National Labor Relations Act.

In 1995, the Supreme Court decided that state statutes have provided a limitations period for federal cases when federal legislation doesn't, except when the state limitations period would interfere or frustrate national policy. Therefore, the Supreme Court justices said that the failure of Congress to provide a limitations period in WARN justified the presumption that courts are to borrow a limitations period from the most closely analogous state statute.

I advise you and your company that by relaxing the deadlines in lawsuits brought under WARN and favoring employees the court's message is to comply strictly with WARN. Why make yourselves vulnerable in some faraway state where the statute of limitations may be as long as six years?[1]

Effects of the WARN Act

The WARN Act is enforced by United States district courts. An employer found in violation of the Act can be penalized for up to $500 a day for each day of the violation. While the DOL (Employment and Training Administration, 202-219-557) can answer general questions about these regulations, it cannot provide specific advice or guidance with regard to any individual case.[2]

Waivers

Since even sound business reasons and releasing only the worst employees still won't protect you from a lawsuit under some circumstances, it's in your best interest to have employees sign an attorney-reviewed waiver of all claims in return for a severance package they wouldn't otherwise have a right to receive.

When offering a severance package to workers in the protected age category in exchange for a release, check to see whether that release meets the criteria of the Older Workers Benefit Protection Act (OWBPA), which require the following:

> › The waiver must be part of your agreement with the employee.

› It must be written in simple English.
› It must refer specifically to the employee's rights under the Age Discrimination in Employment Act (ADEA) that are being waived.
› The waiver must be limited to claims or rights that arose before the employee signed the release.
› To make the release a binding contract, it must be in exchange for something of value—for example, cash or benefits—that is more than what is offered without the signed waiver.
› The waiver agreement must advise the employee in writing to talk with an attorney before signing the waiver.
› The employee must be allowed a seven-day period in which to revoke the agreement after he or she has signed it.
› If the release is related to an early retirement incentive plan (an ERIP) offered to a specific group or worker category, you are required by law to disclose in writing, in plain English, the class, unit, or group of individuals affected by the ERIP, eligibility, time limits, job titles, and ages of affected individuals.
› Each employee affected by an ERIP must have at least forty-five days to mull over his or her decision; if not related to an ERIP, each employee is entitled to twenty-one days.[3]

Realistic Effects of Waivers

These agreements won't prevent lawsuits, but if they are entered into voluntarily and with full knowledge of the facts, terms, and conditions, you have a better chance of prevailing than you would without them. However, if you ask an employee to waive his or her right to sue the company for discrimination or any other negative reason, make sure that you have all your bases covered. If dismissed employees can show disparate impact or other hostile reasons for being fired, you will most likely lose. If they can show a history of abuse in the workplace, you will most likely lose. Managers must manage safely to protect their decisions to fire people.

In fact, in the spring of 1997, the Equal Employment Opportunity Commission (EEOC) stated that an employee's promises not to file a discrimination lawsuit is null and void as far as the commission is concerned. "Agreements extracting such promises from employees may also amount to separate and discrete violations of the anti-retaliation provisions of the civil rights statutes." A waiver may prevent an individual from suing, this EEOC notice says, but it doesn't prevent the commission from enforcing the ADEA or any other law that prohibits employment discrimination.

Conclusion

Nothing prevents a company from closing or moving offshore. That happens regularly these days. Whereas previously the closings affected blue-collar workers almost exclusively, white-collar workers are beginning to feel the pain, too. Call your credit card company for information, and it isn't unlikely that you'll talk to someone in India. It happened to me just two weeks ago. Call tech support for your software, and you may speak to someone in Taiwan. That also happened to me not too long ago.

These realities are the price we pay for expanding into a global economy, where we'll find people just as bright and as capable as Americans but who will work for a small fraction of the pay we demand for ourselves in our high-tech, high-priced consumer society. The WARN Act and the OWBPA are only two ways, two inadequate ways, of protecting workers in the United States from total devastation as they watch their jobs fly overseas. More must be done to ensure that jobs are created that will allow our workers to live in the style to which they have been too accustomed.

Cases

1. U.S. Supreme Court, 515/29, May 30, 1995.
2. See "The Worker Adjustment and Retraining Notification Act: A Guide to Advance Notice of Closings and Layoffs," U.S. Department of Labor, Employment and Training Administration Fact Sheet, www.doleta.gov/programs/factsht/warn.htm.
3. EEOC Notice No. 915.002 (April 10, 1997).

16

Safe Management of Older Employees

Americans used to look up to and, in some cases, revere the elderly. Ironically, today, when longevity has become more the rule than the exception, young people often think of the older generation as economic obstacles. As one writer aptly states, "America is no place to age gracefully."* Resentment then expresses itself in forms of prejudice usually associated with racism: discrimination in hiring, promotion, and firing. Although less litigious than other protected groups, older employees are harassed, belittled, and mistreated in the workplace rather than sought out for their experience, skills, and wisdom. "Move over, old person. Make way for younger blood."[1] In spite of all that, a reason for the decrease in age discrimination cases may be due to a 1993 Supreme Court decision that makes age discrimination more difficult to prove rather than from a decrease in harassment or disparate impact of layoffs on people over age 40.

According to the opinion written by Justice Sandra Day O'Connor for the unanimous Court, since the Age Discrimination in Employment Act (ADEA) affords an employer a " 'bona fide occupational qualification' defense . . . [i]n a disparate treatment case, liability depends on whether the protected trait—under the ADEA, age—actually motivated the employer's decision. When that decision is wholly motivated by factors other than age, the problem that prompted the ADEA's passage—inaccurate and stigmatizing stereotypes about older workers' productivity and competence—disappears. Thus, it would be incorrect to say that a decision based on years of service—which is analytically distinct from age—is nec-

*Nina Munk, "Finished at Forty," *Fortune* (February 1, 1999), p. 20.

essarily age-based."[2] On the other hand, the Court did *not* say that *any* decision that has a disparate impact on older employees is justified.

The Court's silent disapproval of just any old lawsuit found a soft voice in 2002 when it dismissed with a one-sentence decision that it acted "improvidently" when it accepted the case heard in and denied by the Eleventh Circuit Court of Appeals.[44] The lower court had ruled that older workers couldn't sue under ADEA unless on the grounds of "disparate impact" and the plaintiffs could prove intent. But, wait.

Didn't that same court rule in 2000 that employees suing over age bias under ADEA didn't have to prove intent?[45] In that case, Justice O'Connor wrote that the lower court had wrongly relied on "the premise that a plaintiff must always introduce additional, independent evidence of discrimination." That this supervisor was over 40, that he had shown that another supervisor said that he was "too damn old to do the job" was sufficient to establish a prima facie case of age discrimination.

In spite of all the confusion, since the last edition of this book, age bias complaints have risen again, by 40 percent since 1999, according to the *AARP Bulletin,* citing federal government figures. The article identifies David Grinberg, a spokesperson for the EEOC, as saying that "the increase . . . is linked to a confluence of factors including more older people staying on the job longer and the economic downturn that has led to worker layoffs, [and] 'blatant discrimination based on age.'"* These factors lead the EEOC to file more and more claims on behalf of older employees, many of which are settled out of court.

So, it seems, we still need special interest laws (such as the ADEA) to protect our aging but still productive workers. That is also why you need to consider how to prevent *ageism* when you make personnel decisions, especially when laying off employees during a

---

*"Age Bias Complaints Up 40 Percent Since '99," *AARP Bulletin* (February 2003), p. 2. See also, "Tales of Woe from Older Workers," *St. Louis Post-Dispatch* (February 11, 2001), p. E6; "2000 Census Reflects the Graying of America," *op. cit.,* (May 15, 2001), pp. A1 and A7; "High Noon for Older Writers," *AARP Bulletin* (June 2001), pp. 32 and 17; Trish Nicholson, "50-Plus Workers Hit by Cutbacks," *The Nation* (AARP, October 2001), pp. 1, 22; "Justice for Some," AARP, *The Magazine* (May and June, 2003), p. 22.

reorganization or downsizing effort. First, let's see what the law says it protects before I look at what you cannot and can do.

What the Law Says

I can sum up the statute as it pertains to this chapter by saying that since the law intends to promote the employment of older persons, to prohibit age discrimination in employment, and to help employers and workers find ways of meeting problems arising from the impact of age on employment, it protects all persons age 40 years or older. As do other EEO laws, this one requires you to make employment opportunities available to its protected group, and it prevents you from otherwise discriminating against any person over 40 with respect to compensation, terms, conditions, or privileges of employment merely because of age. The terms "otherwise discriminate" means that you cannot use age as a basic consideration for discharging someone or forcing someone to retire.

If you do fire, lay off, or otherwise discriminate against employees age 40 or over, tuck this fact into the back of your mind: They have the incentive to fight back. ADEA provides it by awarding significant damages if the aggrieved can prove age discrimination: *double* the amount of pay *and benefits* an employee *would have* earned between the time he or she was turned out and the time the court decides in his or her favor. Some juries have levied damages of more than a million dollars on defendants.* ADEA also permits jury trials, and juries tend to allow the older person's age to work to his or her advantage. The very reason you might let him or her go becomes the motive for ruling against you.

What You Cannot Do

You cannot fire or lay off older employees as freely as you might wish. The law makes that abundantly clear. And ways around it can

---

*Cited in "Age Case Costs Employer Over a Million Dollars," *Missouri Employment Law Letter,* edited by Vance C. Miller and Robert A. Kaiser, (November, 1988) pp. 1–2, no case number cited; see also "Poor Performance or Age Discrimination?" *The EEO Review: The HR Professional's Guide to Managing Lawfully in the Workplace,* (New York: Panel Publishers) pp. 1–2, citing S.D. Ia. 1996.

be easily blocked, mainly because length of service, higher salaries, and age usually go hand in hand. If high salaries, seniority, or tenure enter into your employment decisions—for example, demotions or layoffs—you run the risk of discriminating against employees on the basis of age; any additional reasons you invoke can be judged to be pretextual—for example "overqualified,"[41]—especially if the employees involved have had long records of unimpeachable service.[3, 4]

As in other forms of discrimination, beware retaliatory motives. Harassment, building a case against an employee, or otherwise making his or her working conditions intolerable after he or she threatens to or has brought action against you for age discrimination can provide your employee with a so-called smoking gun.[5] What you say or do to an older employee can, and probably will, be used against you in a court of law or before the EEOC.[6]

The EEOC often considers seemingly innocuous statements as evidence of age harassment, such as "more accident prone than younger employees," "unable to learn new tasks because he or she is too old," "less efficient than younger employees." Making older employees the butt of jokes or barbs because of their age, poor health, or other medical problems, while younger employees' illnesses are overlooked, are more shots from the gun. Other forms of evidence include:

› Identifying performance problems only after an employee reaches a certain age (for example, age 65)
› Suggesting that an employee sign up for Social Security or take early retirement
› Expressing concerns about the cost of health benefits of older employees
› Taking action against older employees with supposedly poor performance records (for example, demoting or discharging them), but not taking similar action against younger employees with as bad or worse records
› Basing personnel decisions on so-called employee potential— that is, that the older employees do not have the career or income-generating possibilities that younger employees do
› Placing unreasonable standards on older employees that make it difficult or impossible to meet the demands placed on them[7-11]

Safe management demands that managers handle work-related matters or act on the basis of legitimate business interests in a timely and reasonable manner. Arbitrarily replacing a member of a protected group, in this case an older employee, by a member of a non-protected group, a younger employee, can open up an organization to a lawsuit. (*Arbitrary replacement* means the lack of a sound business reason for taking the action.) Offhand remarks about older employees and "new blood" policies can be used as evidence of discrimination. The facts underlying an action determine the value of that action.[12]

The courts want facts and documentation. For example, ADEA provides employers with an exemption for bona fide employee benefit plans in which the employer is not required to provide identical benefits to all employees regardless of age. The law requires only that the employer *spend* equally on all employees, but the exemption is limited to achieving *equivalency* in the cost of providing benefits to younger and older workers alike. To take advantage of the exemption, an employer must demonstrate that the nature and extent of the cost savings realized by specific reductions in its benefit plan merely *balanced costs*.[13]

The ability to balance the needs of the organization against the needs of its employees provides one mark of effective management. Particularly, the way in which management handles layoffs, an ever-present fact of contemporary economic life, to prevent an adverse impact on a protected group (especially on people over age 40) separates effective managers from those who are likely to wind up in court.

Demoting Older Employees to Save Money

You cannot reduce your costs at the expense of older employees' salaries. Older employees usually enjoy the seniority and higher compensation scales that tempt managers to manipulate those earnings in order to cut corners. However, do not count on the demoted employees or the courts agreeing with you.[14, 15]

Using a Reorganization as an Excuse

You cannot vindicate laying off older employees on the basis of a need to reorganize, as long as they are the only target of the reorganization. In addition, if your organization must downsize or shift people around, take care that neither you nor your fellow managers shoot yourselves in the foot by discussing the "reorg" in discriminatory terms—for example, "can't adapt to change" or "need a few good, young people."[16]

What You Can Do

Once more it seems that your hands are tied. But that is not true. You can demote or fire employees if they merit it, regardless of their age, but you must guarantee that your actions are bona fide and legitimate by keeping records of poor performance, written warnings, and so forth.[17]

Implementing Reductions in Force

You can downsize if financial difficulties require it. However, be sure that the decision makers have as much distance as possible and are insulated from the people about whom they are making the layoff decisions. Lower-level managers can recommend people to lay off, but they must base their recommendations on business-related factors only.[18, 19]

Making Legitimate Business Decisions

Follow these six commonsense rules to guide what you can do when managing older employees, especially if you have to make tough demotion or firing decisions:

1. *When managing anyone, keep detailed records of all disciplinary actions.* In the event that an older employee feels mistreated because of age, your documentation of a history of performance problems is your best defense.[20] The practice of building a file is clearly a case of too little too late.[21]

And keep your records until the statute of limitations runs out (or longer): two to three years from a firm date of termination. Failure to identify a firm date or to maintain production or other records could work against you and your organization.[22, 23]

2. *Offer older workers the same counseling or training opportunities you offer younger employees.* You can certainly teach older people new tricks. Most of them have the education, training, or experience necessary for transferring old skills to new jobs, and they should be allowed the opportunity to try. Especially if you are faced with a reduction in force (RIF) or job discontinuance, consider other alternatives for your employees with the greatest amount of seniority before letting them go. A layoff based on seniority is not solid grounds if the older employees are capable of performing other jobs or learning how to do them.[24]

At the same time, you are not *obligated* to retrain or relocate an employee whose job is eliminated by a RIF if to do so would create an unacceptable burden for you, the employer. If retraining or relocation would cost more than your organization can reasonably afford or if no other positions exist, so that such a position would have to be created, you can justify your decision. As long as *age itself* is *not* a criterion, the issue becomes a matter of "legitimate business reason."[25–27, 42]

3. *Prevent harassment on the basis of age.* If you are in a policy-making position and your organization does not have an antiharassment policy, create one. Use the guidelines in Chapters 2 and 9. And train your managers to prevent harassment on the basis of age, just as you would train them to prevent harassment on the basis of sex, race, disability, or veteran's status. Calling people "old and overpaid" is not only unfair and cruel, it can also be used as evidence against you of having a hostile work environment, especially if an older employee quits and sues for constructive discharge or if you fire him or her for some other reason. Your comments *condition* the discharge; employees not involved in the situation may be allowed to testify against you.[28]

4. *Help protect older employees during an RIF or other cost-cutting actions.* Even if you do not make the layoff decisions, give careful consideration to whom you recommend for demoting or cutting and how you execute the decisions. Listing employees' ages and years of service could be used as direct evidence of age discrimination.[29] However, under the Older Workers Benefit Protection Act (OWBPA), your company *must* give all mass layoff victims a list of all potentially affected employees, even those not laid off. Using a proportion-

ate classification system in which you lay off and also retain a proportionate representation of women, minorities, and employees over age 40 could be seen as a pretextual scheme rather than an affirmative action plan.[30] Such a plan could also pose a problem in states, such as New York, that prohibit discrimination against young workers.

At the minimum, use the following checklist to determine whether a planned RIF will pass muster:*

☐ When faced with laying off employees (a reduction in force, or RIF), the layoff should meet business-driven goals and fit an appropriate business plan. Once management identifies and documents the business purposes for the RIF, consider possible alternatives to laying off people, such as a hiring freeze, reduced hours, reassignment, natural attrition, and voluntary retirement or exit packages.

☐ If the layoff is necessary, know your workforce before recommending whom to dismiss. Concentrating the layoff on a specific protected group—for example, older employees or African-American employees—can be construed as evidence of discrimination. Knowing your people is the only way to determine if the RIF will have an adverse impact on any protected group(s) or violate a contractual commitment or employee benefits plans that could constrain what you do.

☐ Where possible, use objective methods of selecting employees to dismiss, such as employees made superfluous by a process redesign program and not to be replaced by other employees.

☐ If you use any subjective criteria, be sure to document their business purpose, such as relative performance, and ensure that well-defined, written performance criteria offset the degree of subjectivity that performance appraisals or ranking systems tend to have. The Fourth Circuit Court of Appeals, in 1991, provided these guidelines: Deciding to lay off someone based on a company-wide performance rating system, which has been in place for many years and which has not

*Adapted from Donald H. Weiss, *Fair, Square, and Legal: A Manager's Guide to Safe Hiring, Managing, and Firing Practices,* Second Edition (New York: American Management Association, 2004) p. 155.

been shown to be discriminatory, and choosing to lay off all those who were among the lowest rated, must count as "an articulation of a legitimate nondiscriminatory reason."[45]

☐ Consider the following as relatively objective criteria that will meet the court's guidelines:
  › Marginally performing employees
  › Superfluous employees identified by a work or process redesign program
  › Employees with the least amount of knowledge or skills related to newly created work

☐ Apply the criteria of a seniority system where appropriate. However, because women and minorities have sometimes been the last hired and first fired, they may see decisions based on seniority as discriminatory. Therefore, it's wise when looking at employees with the least amount of time in service or seniority also to take into account simultaneously a lack of or only marginal skills.

☐ Have records that document your grounds for your decisions, and avoid declarations such as "We need new blood around here," or "We have to downsize regardless of how it affects [members of some protected group]." Anything that smells of using business decisions as an excuse to discriminate against a protected group will be seen by the courts as a smoking gun.

☐ Help to protect members of protected groups during a RIF or other cost-cutting actions to the extent possible. Historically, older employees, members of minority groups, and women have been first fired during a RIF. However, it can be hard to balance "the need to promote diversity" when trying to decide whom to fire or to lay off. Until now, courts have accepted protecting minorities and women where it can be shown that company decisions have historically had a disparate impact on them—that is, affected them to a greater extent than nonminorities. If they can support a "but for" argument—that but for the color of their skins, their gender, or their age they wouldn't have suffered the impact of the decisions—they will probably win. Your documentation must show that you have done all things possible to ensure that your firing decisions don't have a disparate impact on protected groups.

☐ As in the case of dismissing an employee for cause, when introducing cost-cutting measures, when reengineering, reorganizing, or downsizing, you and your company must communicate clearly but cautiously with all people affected by those actions. Follow the same guidelines described in Chapter 11 when informing people of the layoff and that they are to be let go.

Because a variety of other supportable methods for making layoff decisions exist, you should also check with your attorney.

Offering early retirement, based on an existing pension plan, to people who want to take advantage of it is acceptable as long as the following are true:

› No other avenues for cost saving are available.
› Employees are not pressured or coerced into accepting it or being fired.
› Employees are given sufficient time to study and accept or reject the offer.
› Employees are given sufficient and proper counseling as to the terms of the offer.
› Exceptions are based on bona fide business reasons, for example, essential employees or employees covered by a collective bargaining agreement that you cannot unilaterally alter.
› Criteria for eligibility are clearly spelled out and do not discriminate against the older retirees in favor of the younger ones.[31–34]

I cannot overemphasize the need for rational, legitimate business reasons for taking cost-cutting actions that adversely affect older employees. Time and again the courts have ruled that if an employer eliminates an employee's job for legitimate business reasons, it is not obligated to create or locate another job for the employee. ADEA does not demand that heavy obligation, even if the organization has an informal policy that offers that assistance.[35] Should the appearance of discrimination lead you into court, the documentation of nondiscriminatory reasons can lead you safely out of court as well.[38]

5. *Ask employees taking early retirement to sign a release in which they acknowledge having read and understood the terms of the agreement, having received sufficient time and counseling for making a reasoned decision, and having voluntarily accepted or rejected the offer of early retirement.*[38] A release is *useful* in the event you are challenged in court, but it is not a surefire defense. Your release should clarify all the terms of the plan, explain realistically the consequences of signing the release, leave open the opportunity to negotiate the terms and conditions of the plan, and make it clear that coercion was not used (that acceptance was voluntary). Compare the two *actual* release statements shown in Figures 16-1 and 16-2 and decide which one survived the court challenge.

Legal language or not, Release 1 cannot bind the terms of the retirement package the company offered its employees. Vague and ambiguous, the document falls far short of binding language. Release 2 holds its own not because it is more complicated but rather because it is more thorough.

The first paragraph in Release 2 dates the document, clarifies its purpose, and signals that its signing is voluntary: "The Employer and Employee mutually desire to enter into this Agreement whereby the Employee voluntarily elects . . ." It indicates that a bona fide and established pension plan exists: "early retirement under the Employer's retirement plan." This paragraph also refers to a valuable consideration, an essential ingredient for binding any contract, when it says "in consideration of an additional sum of money, specified in paragraph 2, below."

The release specifies an effective date from which tolling begins (two to three years). It also names the plan to which the first para-

Figure 16.1 Release statement 1.

In consideration of the foregoing, you, [*employee name*], hereby release [*company name*] and all of its subsidiaries, divisions, and related corporations from any and all actions, causes of action, claims, and demands, whatsoever, which you, your heirs, executors, or administrators ever had, now have, or may have against such entities by reason of any matter, course, or thing whatsoever.[37]

Figure 16-2. Release statement 2.

Special Early Retirement Incentive Program Agreement

This Agreement is entered into this _____ day of _____,
20_____ between [*company name*] ("the Employer") and [*employee name*]
("the Employee"). The Employer and the Employee mutually desire to enter
into this Agreement whereby the Employee voluntarily elects early retirement
under the Employer's retirement plan in consideration of an additional sum
of money, specified in paragraph 2, below.

1. The Employee's retirement will become effective on _____,
    20___. The Employee will thereafter receive his or her monthly retire-
    ment allowance as provided in the Pension Program for Nonunion
    Employees.
2. In addition to the monthly retirement allowance described in para-
    graph 1, above, the Employee will receive $_____ in one lump-
    sum payment.
3. The Employee has been advised to consult an attorney and has been
    given [*depending upon the circumstances, from twenty-one to forty-
    five*] days to make a decision.
4. The Employee has been advised that he or she has seven days after
    signing this agreement to revoke his or her decision.
5. The Employee and the Employer agree that any disputes with regard
    to compensation or benefits or other issues pertaining to this agree-
    ment must be taken before a mutually acceptable arbitrator.
6. The Employee and the Employer acknowledge that this agreement
    does not cover any issue arising after the effective date of this agree-
    ment.
7. The Employee releases and discharges [*company name*], its officers,
    agents, and successors, from any and all claims arising under Title VII
    of the Civil Rights Act of 1964, as amended, 42 U.S.C. 2000 *et seq.*,
    The Age Discrimination in Employment Act, 29 U.S.C. §621 *et seq.*
    [*and any relevant state law*].
8. The Employee has read this Agreement, understands its terms and the
    release in it, and voluntarily accepts its provisions.[35]

---

graph refers, Pension Program for Nonunion Employees, and binds the retirement allowance to the terms of the program. It specifies the consideration given in return for signing the release before asking the signer to release and discharge the company, *et al.*, from any and all claims arising under the laws pertinent to such causes: Title VII of the Civil Rights Act of 1964 and the Age Discrimination in Employment Act. The last paragraph then affirms that the "Employee has read this Agreement, understands its terms and the release in it, . . ." and it reaffirms that the employee "voluntarily accepts its provisions." Before the passage of the Older Workers Benefits Protection Act (OWBPA), that waiver was sufficient without paragraphs 3 through 6; now those paragraphs are essential. (See Chapter 15 for additional details concerning safe and fair waivers.)

Measure any similar document your organization has used or is considering using against the standards set by our models. If it lacks any of the terms we identified, it too will fail in court. Should an employee threaten to sue no matter what efforts were made to help or protect him or her, an early settlement out of court may be a more humane as well as less expensive tactic. Do not forget that the employee, not you, has the incentive to fight. However, if you (or your organization) believe that you are in the right, take whatever action you deem appropriate. Do not forget our constant warning: Before doing anything, consult an attorney.

Why consult an attorney? The EEOC doesn't believe in just agreeing to arbitration or signing a waiver. The commission has brought a lawsuit against Allstate Insurance "accusing it of forcing thousands of agents to give up their right to sue . . . for age discrimination or other issues."

6. *Communicate clearly but cautiously with all your organization's constituencies.* Everyone with a need to know, that is, everyone who will be affected by cost cutting, reorganization, or downsizing (officers, board members, employees), should know what is happening. Communications should include the organization's economic condition and the steps being taken to improve it or to do away with the organization or some part thereof. However, be careful that when you produce communiqués, you do not trigger another smoking gun by using discriminatory language or by penetrating the insulation that protects the top management decision makers (which I will talk about in the Casebook).

Conclusion

It is not only in society's best interest to hire, train, and promote all possible workers regardless of sex, race, national origin, creed, or *age,* it is also in your best interest as a manager.

Isaac Newton, when writing about his discovery of the universal laws of gravity, refused to take credit for his own genius. Instead, he gave credit to those geniuses who came before him. "I stood," he said, "on the shoulders of giants." Your older employees, because of their years of training and experience, are the giants on whose shoulders you stand.

CASEBOOK

Employees are getting older. That is not just a mindless truism about the average age of employees. It is, rather, a warning.

Before the end of the first decade of the twenty-first century, all the baby boomers will have crossed age 60, most of them will be into their retirement years, and most of them will be "plateaued"—that is, will have reached the highest level in the organization they can. At the same time, they will be healthy, energetic, and productive. You may be one of them. How will your managers and your organization treat you?

Study these cases and see how prepared your organization is for safely managing a graying workforce. Consider the issues that surface from the point of view of what you yourself are doing and what will happen in the future with respect to how older employees are treated.

Can You Save Money by Demoting Employees?

Milt Jonah lost his supervisory position and was demoted to lead worker just after his fifty-third birthday. He was still smarting from the news when he found out he was being replaced by someone forty years old. "They demoted me just to save money," he told the court. "They're going to close the plant in a few years, and they'd have to pay me more separation pay than they will my younger replacement. Our seniority plan requires it. To prove it, I found out that when they made the decision to demote me, they called in a benefits expert who reviewed who would get what when the closing came."

The company responded that money saving was an issue, but still, because Jonah was the least experienced supervisor in the group and had poor performance evaluations, they had a reasonable and legitimate business reason for demoting him.

If faced with a closing, how would your organization go about reducing costs? What are some of the issues it would consider?

Pretext

If the plaintiff had received such poor reviews in the past, why did the organization wait until now to do something about it? That was the question asked by the courts. The evidence linked the demotion to save money to age discrimination, because the saving of money purportedly stemmed directly from the supervisor's greater seniority.[14]

An employee is not required to take a demotion to satisfy a company's cost-saving plan. If an employee quits under those circumstances, he or she could also charge constructive discharge, that is, making or allowing the employee's work conditions to become so intolerable that he or she has no choice but to quit.[15]

Yet your hands are not entirely tied if you can demonstrate that the demoted or fired employee merited that treatment, for example, through poor productivity records, written warnings, and so forth.[17] Also, if an employee's salary is higher than those of peers in other companies in your industry, the court may allow you to cut costs by bringing that salary down so that it is in line with the market—as long as each individual case is considered on its merits and is not facially biased.[43] Just ensure that any personnel decision you make, especially if you plan to demote an older employee, can be backed by valid business reasons.

Does Your Need to Reorganize Vindicate You?

In 1971, a major consumer goods company found its 50 percent decline in sales sufficient reason to cut costs by making a substantial structural reorganization and firing a large number of executive employees within a relatively short time span: more than one hundred employees between 1971 and 1973. It just so happened that most of the laid-off employees were older than age 40.

The company argued that nondiscriminatory business reasons justified its actions: Key accounts had not been called upon, some managers had not worked with their salespeople for several years, no new methods had been adopted for ten years or more, and the managers did not even know their business had been falling off. Age had nothing to do with the decisions.

What criteria would your organization use for identifying people for discharge?

Loose Lips and Pink Slips

Without a doubt, the company had pressing needs for a drastic reorganization and had indeed considered factors other than age in making its firing decisions. However, age was one determining factor in choosing which particular employees to discharge. How did the court come to this conclusion *ten years later?*

Company pay recommendations and discharge reports made too many offhand comments and age-related statements. Some had less-than-obvious relationships to age, but implied them nevertheless: "unable to conform to the new [company] philosophy," "inability to adapt to change . . . [or] to the new configuration." Others made blatant references to age: "really good young man," "outstanding young buyer." If you couple those statements with the fact that a vast majority of sales reps hired during the reorganization were in their twenties while the majority discharged were older people, you do not need the wisdom of a judge to draw the conclusion that the company intended to discriminate on the basis of age.[16]

"A pattern of discrimination" coupled with several smoking guns brought a defense industry giant to an out-of-court settlement in March 1993. A white paper by a key executive called for continually attracting and retaining young people in order to remain competitive, and a house organ article stated that in spite of thousands of layoffs, "We are still hiring people, mostly out of college." Of those thousands laid off, a disproportionate number of them were age 55 or older, the EEOC charged in its lawsuit. How much did these acts of discrimination cost? In cash and enhanced benefits to roughly 950 former workers in the St. Louis area, the cost was $20.1 million. The company also had to rehire ex-workers, at comparable pay levels, for at least four years.* Now, add in attorney and other costs.

Yes, this case was settled in 1992, but don't think a whole lot has changed since then. For example, courts have levied more than $1 million in damages in other, very similar cases to the one here.† On the other hand, according to one court, if a reduction in workforce meets the standard of business necessity, nothing in ADEA prohibits employers from using subjective criteria in deciding whom to let go, as long as smoking guns are absent.[36]

If you are in charge and your motives are pure, under some circumstances someone else's loose lips could sink your ship.

Who Should Make the Decisions?

When ten older employees of Sangrita, Inc., found themselves suddenly on the streets and replaced by younger employees, they wasted no time in taking their former employer to court. Because they had all received performance ratings of satisfactory or better throughout their tenure with Sangrita, the only reason they could find for their dismissal was age.

No, the company retorted. It was just a matter of money. The reduction in force was necessitated by financial difficulty. Upper management, where the final cutback decisions were made, had never made discriminatory remarks, even though the supervisors, who had submitted the names, had.

The plaintiffs alleged that the people who headed up the division in which the plaintiffs worked—the plant's general manager, Steve Rowan, and his direct report, Dan Horton (the director of the data system division)—influenced the company to terminate older employees by repeatedly making age-related references, such as "older

---

*Christopher Carey, "Laid-Off Defense Workers on the Attack," *St. Louis Post-Dispatch* (July 5, 1993), pp. 10B–11B.
†See earlier note: "Age Case Costs Employer over a Million Dollars," *Missouri Employment Law Letter*, (November, 1998).

employees," "older farts," and "old bastards." At one meeting, Rowan commented on his surprise that so many of the "old guard" and "old faces" were still around and that he would "like to see new blood or new ideas." At yet another meeting, Rowan allegedly told an employee, "Bob, you've been with the company a long time. You're too old to go any further. It's my policy that I'm going to make room for younger men."

The employees used that evidence to argue that, in spite of the fact that neither Rowan nor Horton was directly involved in the decisions concerning whom to lay off, the name-calling and other remarks created a bias against older employees.

How do you feel about older employees? If you think you would like to replace them, could your feelings be held against you and your organization's decision makers? If you are the decision maker, could your direct reports get you in trouble with your older employees?

Insulating the Decision Maker

Best leave layoff decisions to people far removed from the employees directly affected. That is how Sangrita, Inc., defeated the claims against it.

According to the courts in the case, the comments made by Rowan and Horton could not be considered direct or substantial evidence, not even circumstantial evidence, of discrimination on the basis of age. Their positions of authority notwithstanding, they did not have the complete authority to lay off employees in the reduction in force without approval from top management. The list they submitted was sent to the headquarters office, in a different location, and reviewed by upper management, which then made the final decisions. The court could find no connection between the biased remarks and the layoff decisions.[18, 19]

In its opinion, the court emphasized that to show age discrimination, a plaintiff must draw a connection between what was said and an adverse action taken against him or her. To make that showing, the age-related comments or statements have to come from someone *directly responsible for the dismissal decision.* That another person in the chain of command makes biased remarks or statements is not sufficient evidence to conclude that the decision was the result of that person's bias.

In this case, the decision makers were insulated from the charge of age bias. But do not think that you can always hide behind that kind of insulation.

In the previous case, it seemed that distance made the managers safe, but that defense may not always work.

Can Your Decisions Hide Behind Other Managers' Biases?

When Max Bowman, age 61, was laid off from the television station where he worked, he charged management with age discrimination, even though he could not attribute age-biased remarks to anyone making the decisions. Instead, he could claim only that one of his own managers, the one who signed his pink slip, had made the biased statements.

The trial court dismissed the case, emphasizing that it does not matter who implements the firing decision; what is important is who makes the decision. In this case, even though higher management consulted with the biased manager, the higher-level managers made the final decision on strictly business-related grounds.

Bowman appealed to the Seventh Circuit Court, where he showed that younger employees were transferred to other positions while he was let go even though he volunteered to work in another capacity. In response to his request for a transfer, his exit interviewer told him that the news bureau had grown too complex for him to handle another job and that a hiring freeze precluded using him in some other capacity. Younger employees were more favorably treated than he was; therefore, age was a determining factor in the decision that affected him adversely.

The company disagreed. The station's ratings were third among the major network stations in the community. Each department was reviewed (1) to improve the ratings and (2) to eliminate overstaffing. Fifteen vacant positions were eliminated, and a few months later the entire news bureau was closed, leaving Bowman without a job. The discharge decision, the company concluded, arose from its efforts to achieve a leaner, more efficient company.

Why would you or your organization lay off any specific employee? Have you considered the implications of such reasons?

The Value of Silence

That the television station's upper management did not make biased remarks made no difference. The Seventh Circuit Court ruled that the triable issues concerned whether the plaintiff's age was a factor in the decision to lay off that specific employee rather than consider him for other available positions for which he was qualified.[39]

The station may have had economic reasons for its decision, but at the time management discharged the plaintiff, two vacancies for which he was qualified existed in the newsroom. They were later filled by younger people. In addition, management's hiring freeze was subject to considerable discretion rather than absolute. Although more than fifteen jobs were eliminated after they became vacant, fifteen people between the ages of 34 and 44 were hired within a year to fill yet other vacancies. The court agreed with Bowman: The television station's cost-cutting actions were selective and had more of an adverse impact on him than on younger employees.

Consider two points: The TV station had legitimate business reasons for a cutback, yet the court ruled against it. Why? Because management could not answer the question "Why wasn't the older employee retained in an alternative position, as were some of the younger employees?" The managers should have considered other available positions into which they could have transferred the protected employee.

Especially if you allow younger (nonprotected) employees to transfer or offer them the opportunity to transfer to or assume another available position, you must consider the older (protected) employee as well. *Offering* the older employee the opportunity, even if it happens to be lower-paying (in some cases), will prevent the assumption that he or she does not want to accept it. In this case, it was age protection, but the same applies to issues such as race, sex, disability, or military status.

If the employee turns down the offer, then you should document the fact that you offered a choice but the employee rejected it.

If you do not do this, the employee can come back and claim that he or she would have taken the alternative if it had been offered.

The second point underscores the issue raised at the start of this discussion: What you say can strip away the decision maker's insulation. Regardless of who makes discriminatory remarks or comments and who makes the layoff decision, if the remarks or comments *follow* the discharge decision, it can be presumed that whoever makes the remarks or comments *has been authorized* to make them. This court decision means that if your CEO makes the discharge decision and you execute it, if you make a discriminatory remark such as "You probably could not learn the new technology" during the exit interview, your CEO could be held liable for age discrimination. This is only one chip in the insulation; others are likely to follow.

Insulation works two ways: Federal laws also insulate most older employees, and most states have statutes as well. The Vermont Supreme Court, before the state had a law prohibiting discrimination on the basis of age, invoked public policy in a wrongful discharge suit when an efficiency consultant recommended that a company change its "retirement-home image" by hiring "young gogetters." On the basis of that advice, the company fired several older employees and defended itself on the grounds that the state lacked a legal barrier to the decision.

The Vermont Supreme Court answered that the absence of statutes against discrimination does not imply the license to discriminate. Instead, there exists a clear and compelling public policy against age discrimination. An employee can sue for wrongful discharge in violation of public policy.[40] This decision therefore suggests that antidiscrimination statutes codify and acknowledge what is best for society.

Cases

1. 772 F.2d 799, 39 F.E.P. Cases (BNA) 14 (11th Cir. 1985).
2. 507 U.S. S. Ct. 604 (April 20, 1993).
3. 702 F.2d 686, 31 F.E.P. Cases (BNA) 376 (8th Cir. 1983).
4. 46 F.E.P. Cases (BNA) 519 (S.D.N.Y. 1987).
5. 822 F.2d 1249, 44 F.E.P. Cases (BNA) 268 (2d Cir. 1987).
6. 710 F.2d 76, 33 F.E.P. Cases (BNA) 977 (2d Cir. 1983).
7. 643 F. Supp. 779, 42 F.E.P. Cases (BNA) 1144 (E.D. Pa. 1986).

8. 821 F.2d 489 (8th Cir. June 17, 1987).
9. 803 F.2d 202, 42 F.E.P. Cases 185 (5th Cir. 1986).
10. 822 F.2d 52 (3d Cir. June 19, 1987).
11. 785 F.2d 458, 41 F.E.P. Cases (BNA) 714 (7th Cir. 1986).
12. 785 F.2d 584, 40 F.E.P. Cases (BNA) 508 (7th Cir. 1986).
13. 842 F.2d 1480, 46 F.E.P. Cases (BNA) 857 (3d Cir. 1988).
14. 772 F.2d 374 (8th Cir. 1983).
15. 781 F.2d 173, 39 F.E.P. Cases (BNA) 1201 (10th Cir. 1986).
16. 690 F.2d 1072 (E.D.N.C. 1982).
17. 688 F.2d 547, 29 F.E.P. Cases (BNA) 1491 (7th Cir. 1982).
18. 744 F.2d 1464, 41 F.E.P. Cases 562 (M.D. Fla. 1986).
19. See also 750 F.2d 1405, 36 F.E.P. Cases 913 (7th Cir. 1984).
20. 609 F. Supp. 1003, 38 F.E.P. Cases (BNA) 79 (N.D. Ill. 1985).
21. 768 F.2d 402, 247, 38 F.E.P. Cases (BNA) 773 (D.C. Cir. 1985).
22. 603 F. Supp. 1035, 37 F.E.P. Cases (BNA) 193 (D. Conn. 1985).
23. 833 F.2d 1406, 45 F.E.P. Cases 608 (10th Cir. 1987).
24. 832 F.2d 258 (E.D. Pa) 45 F.E.P. Cases (BNA) 212 (3d Cir. 1987), *cert. denied,* 109 S. Ct. 782 (1989).
25. 40 F.E.P. Cases (BNA) 1227 (W.D. Ky. 1986).
26. 643 F.2d 914, 25 F.E.P. Cases (BNA) 355 (2d Cir. 1981).
27. 673 F.2d 34, 29 F.E.P. Cases (BNA) 937 (2d Cir. 1982).
28. No. 953243 (6th Cir. September 24, 1996; 84 F.3d 1074 (8th Cir. 1996). See also, 708 F.2d 233, 31 F.E.P. Cases (BNA) 1532 (6th Cir. 1983).
29. 679 F. Supp. 751, 46 F.E.P. Cases (BNA) 1050 (N.D. Ill. 1988).
30. 424 Mich. 675 (1986).
31. No. 82–1697 (6th Cir. May 16, 1984).
32. No. 82-C-7277 (N.D. Ill. January 7, 1987).
33. 843 F.2d 190, 46 F.E.P. Cases (BNA) 1086 (5th Cir. 1988).
34. 782 F.2d 1421, 40 F.E.P. Cases (BNA) 201 (7th Cir. 1986).
35. C.A. No. 82-C-1576 (June 14, 1984).
36. 82 F. 3d 980 (10th Cir. May 1, 1996).
37. 714 F.2d 556, 32 F.E.P. Cases (BNA) 1451 (5th Cir. 1983).
38. 633 F. Supp. 13, 46 F.E.P. Cases (BNA) 174 (E.D. Tex. 1988).
39. No. 87–2065 (7th Cir. May 9, 1988).
40. 1 I.E.R. Cases 800 (Vt. 1986).
41. 2d Cir. No. 90–7318 1990.
42. Nos. 91–1591 and 91–1614 (1st Cir. 1993).
43. 936 F.2d. 112 (2d Cir. 1991).
44. U.S. Supreme Court No. 01–584.
45. 933 E2d 231,234 (4th Cir. 1991).

Appendix

What Civil Rights and Other Personal Protection Laws Say

Despite legislation and despite a regular procession of cases before the U.S. Supreme Court, equal opportunity battles continue into this twenty-first century, and probably will continue well into the next hundred years.

Numerous magazine and newspaper reports on the economy can be cited to demonstrate how close to accurate my predictions in the third edition were. The rate of new job creation and the growth of the workforce has been in negative numbers between 2000 and 2003, 90 percent of the new jobs created are in service sectors, and the gender distribution of the workforce has evolved to roughly 50 percent women. Inasmuch as the majority of new entrants into the labor pool since the year 2000 has been women and minority workers, employers should be offering equal opportunities by default, but as the recent cases in this book has shown, generally speaking they don't. With attention to cultural and social diversity and to a wide variety of needs and sensitivities fast becoming a management necessity, hiring women, minorities, disabled people, and older people will be the easy part; managing them will be the hard part.*

I will not add to the many thousands of pages already written about the laws governing equal opportunity. Instead, I will summarize the most important of them to provide a context to which you can relate the cases and the answers I cite about separate management issues: hiring, management practices, discharging, and so on.

Generally, each summary is divided into six parts:

1. Purpose
2. Whom/What the Act Protects
3. What Managers Cannot Do

*For more information, see the Web site of the Department of Labor at www.dol .gov.

4. What Managers Can Do
5. Penalties for Intentional Violation
6. Enforcement

These summaries supply only a thumbnail sketch of what has been ruled impermissible and what has been ruled acceptable, at least up to this point in time (mid-2003). If you have any doubt about any specific situation, a call to your organization's personnel department or attorney is in order.

If a complaint is lodged against you personally, you would be well advised to say nothing to your employees; discuss the matter only with your personnel officer and your attorney.

Title VII, Civil Rights Act of 1964
(as amended)

Purpose

To protect constitutional rights, to extend the Commission on Civil Rights, to establish a Commission on Equal Employment Opportunity (EEOC), and for other purposes

Whom/What the Act Protects

Protected groups covers:

1. People of race or color other than white (now defined by the Supreme Court in terms of the Civil Rights Act of 1866: all ethnic minorities)
2. People of any bona fide religious persuasion
3. Members of either sex
4. People whose national origin is other than the United States

What Managers Cannot Do

1. Fail or refuse to hire any person or otherwise discriminate against any person with respect to compensation, terms, conditions, or privileges of employment because he or she is a member of a protected group
2. Discharge any person because he or she is a member of a protected group
3. Limit, segregate, or classify employees or applicants for employment in any way that would deprive or tend to deprive a person of employment opportunities or have an adverse effect on the person's status as an employee
4. Fail to provide training to a person because he or she is a member of a protected group

5. Retaliate against any employees or applicants for employment because they made a charge, testified, assisted, or participated in any manner in an action protected by this law
6. Print or publish (or have someone else print or publish) any notice or advertisement relating to employment that may adversely affect members of a protected group
7. Fail to post and keep posted in an obvious place a notice concerning the contents of this law

What Managers Can Do

1. Hire or employ people on the basis of a bona fide occupational qualification (BFOQ), that is, a qualification demanded by the conditions of the position—for example, an unusual or special skill, or being male in order to play a male role
2. Apply different standards of compensation or different terms, conditions, or privileges of employment as part of a legally acceptable seniority or merit system, or a system that pays for piecework or on commission or in different locations, as long as the distinctions are not the result of deliberate discrimination
3. Set up different compensation packages if the differences are authorized by the provisions of Section 6(d) of the Fair Labor Standards Act of 1938, as amended, if they are based on factors other than sex—for example, seniority or merit system or piecework or quality bonuses.
4. Hire without regard to quotas or preferential treatment
5. Fire or otherwise discipline someone for good cause

Penalties for Intentional Violation

1. A court order stopping the company from conducting unlawful employment practices and ordering affirmative action, which may include but not be limited to reinstating or hiring employees with or without back pay, or any other fair relief the court rules is appropriate
2. Court action to force an organization to comply (if necessary)
3. Reasonable attorney fees and other costs

Enforcement

1. Equal Employment Opportunity Commission (EEOC)
2. Attorney General of the United States (AG)

A person may file charges within 180 days after the alleged unlawful practice took place, and notice of the charge will be served within ten days afterward. If the person filing the claim has filed charges with a state or local agency, then he or she has 300 days in which to file, or may file within thirty days after the state or local agency finishes its action, whichever is earlier.

If, within thirty days, the EEOC is not able to arrange an agreement it finds acceptable, it may bring civil action through the AG. Employee/applicant may file suit within ninety days after the right to sue notice has been issued.

[*Note:* The terms and conditions of the Civil Rights Act of 1964 have been extended to cover harassment in the workplace on the basis of race, color, religion, sex, and national origin. Not only may the individual defendant be held liable, but the organization can be held liable also if it has not taken reasonable steps to prevent harassment. The organization is particularly liable if it can be shown that organization policies or indifferences have created a "hostile environment."]

Executive Order No. 11,246
Covering Government Contractors
and Subcontractors
(as amended by Executive Orders
11,375 and 12,086)

Purpose

To extend the equal opportunity provisions of Title VII of the Civil Rights Act of 1964 by specifically prohibiting job discrimination based on race, color, religion, sex, national origin, handicap, or veteran's status by:

1. Contractors and subcontractors operating under federal service, supply, and construction contracts
2. Contractors and subcontractors who perform under federally aided construction contracts and who have contracts in excess of $10,000 with the federal government
3. Nonconstruction contractors and subcontractors with fifty or more employees who have prime contracts or subcontracts with the federal government in excess of $50,000; such employers must develop and maintain written affirmative action programs

Whom/What the E.O. Protects

Protected groups covers:

1. People of race or color other than white (now defined by the U.S. Supreme Court in terms of the Civil Rights Act of 1866: all ethnic minorities)

2. People of any bona fide religious persuasion
3. Members of either sex
4. People whose national origin is other than the United States
5. Handicapped persons as defined by the Rehabilitation Act
6. Veterans as defined by the Veterans Readjustment Act

What Managers Cannot Do

1. Fail or refuse to hire any person or to otherwise discriminate against any person with respect to compensation, terms, conditions, or privileges of employment because he or she is a member of a protected group
2. Discharge any person because he or she is a member of a protected group
3. Limit, segregate, or classify employees or applicants for employment in any way that would either deprive or tend to deprive a person of employment opportunities or have an adverse effect on the person's status as an employee
4. Fail to provide training to a person because he or she is a member of a protected group
5. Retaliate against any employees or applicants for employment because they made a charge, testified, assisted, or participated in any manner in an action protected by this law
6. Print or publish (or have someone else print or publish) any notice or advertisement relating to employment that may adversely affect members of a protected group
7. Fail to post and keep posted in an obvious place a notice concerning the contents of this law or to notify any labor union or representative of employees with which it has a collective bargaining agreement or other contract or agreement of its commitment under E.O. 11,246
8. Fail to include the following information in a written bid:
   a. Whether the organization has an affirmative action program and supporting documentation on file, unless exempted by E.O. 11,246 or by an administrative exemption
   b. Whether it has participated in any previous government contract or subcontract subject to E.O. 11,246 and its equal opportunity clause
   c. Whether it has filed all reports due under the applicable filing requirements
9. Fail to require prospective prime contractors and subcontractors to submit a written certification that the contractor does not and will not maintain segregated facilities
10. Fail to complete accurate annual reports of compliance
11. Deny the administering agency and the secretary of labor access to its books, records, and accounts to investigate or determine compliance

What Managers Can Do

1. Apply for an exemption if the exemption is in the national interest—for example, security clearance requirements
2. Hire or employ people on the basis of a bona fide occupational qualification (BFOQ)
3. Apply different standards of compensation, or different terms, conditions, or privileges of employment, as part of a legally acceptable seniority or merit system or a system that pays for piecework or on commission or in different locations as long as the distinctions are not the result of deliberate discrimination
4. Hire without regard to quotas or preferential treatment
5. Fire or otherwise discipline someone for good cause

Penalties for Violations

1. Sanctions imposed by the Office of Federal Contract Compliance Programs (OFCCP), which could include loss of any part or the whole of a federal contract, debarment from further contracts, publication of violators' names, recommendations to the Justice Department for action under E.O. 11,246 and to the Equal Employment Opportunity Commission or the Justice Department for action under the Civil Rights Act of 1964, Title VII
2. Criminal action for furnishing false information in connection with the procurement of a federal contract
3. Injunctions stopping the company from conducting unlawful employment practices and ordering affirmative action, which may include but not be limited to reinstating or hiring employees with or without back pay or any other fair relief the court rules is appropriate
4. Court action to force an organization to comply (if necessary)
5. Reasonable attorney fees and other costs

Enforcement

1. OFCCP, Department of Labor
2. Attorney General of the United States (AG)
3. Federal district court

A person may file charges within 180 days after the alleged unlawful practice took place, unless the time limitation is extended by the OFCCP upon a showing of good cause and notice of the charge will be served within ten days.

Sex Discrimination Guidelines Under E.O. 11,246
(41 C.F.R., Pt. 60–20)

Purpose

To interpret legislation banning preference, limitation, or discrimination based on sex

Whom the Guidelines Protect

Anyone, regardless of gender, unless gender is a bona fide occupational qualification (BFOQ)

What Managers Cannot Do

1. Specify sex in recruiting, job posting, or advertising to hire, unless sex is a BFOQ
2. Distinguish in any manner on the basis of sex in personnel policies
3. In any way prohibit, limit, or discriminate on the basis of sex when filling available positions, unless sex is a BFOQ
4. Make distinctions based on sex in employment opportunities, wages, hours, or other conditions of employment
5. Favor married over unmarried people, people with no children over people with young children, or people of one sex over people of another sex
6. Use limitations of physical facilities to accommodate people of both sexes as a reason for discrimination
7. Rely on state labor laws that protect women in order to deny them employment for which they are qualified
8. Penalize women because of their need for time away from work for childbearing
9. Use mandatory or optional retirement age to discriminate on the basis of sex
10. Use seniority lines or lists based solely on sex

What Managers Can Do

1. Distinguish on the basis of sex, where sex is a BFOQ
2. Assign jobs on the basis of differences in capabilities

Civil Rights Act of 1991

Purpose

To amend the Civil Rights Act of 1964 to strengthen and improve federal civil rights laws and for other purposes

Specifically, the law:

1. Provides remedies for intentional discrimination and unlawful harassment
2. Codifies the concepts of "business necessity" and "job related" as criteria for hiring and management decisions
3. Provides statutory authority and guidelines for bringing disparate impact suits to court under Title VII of the Civil Rights Act of 1964
4. Expands the scope of various civil rights statutes in order to provide adequate protection to victims of discrimination

Whom the Act Protects

The groups protected under the Civil Rights Act of 1964 are covered by this act as well. The Act does not protect individuals who are currently and knowingly using or possessing a controlled substance, unless rules discriminating against drug users are used with the intent to discriminate because of race, color, religion, sex, or national origin. The Act exempts employers or agencies operating in foreign countries if compliance would violate the law there. And the Act is not retroactive to cover actions prior to enactment. (See also two U.S. Supreme Court decisions, April 26, 1994.)

What Managers Cannot Do

1. Conduct business practices that have a disparate impact on protected groups. Disparate impact exists if:
   a. The complaining party (the EEOC, the attorney general, or an individual) *demonstrates* (meets the burdens of production and persuasion)
   b. That an employer (or employment agency, labor organization, joint labor-management committee, or federal entity)
   c. Uses a particular employment practice to deny members of a protected group the benefits of employment
   d. *And* the employer fails to demonstrate that the challenged practice is job-related for the position in question and is consistent with business necessity
   e. Or has refused to adopt an alternative employment practice that would meet job-related and business necessity criteria and would not have a disparate impact on protected groups.
2. Use "business necessity" as a defense against a claim of intentional discrimination.
3. Adjust the scores of, use different cutoff scores for, or otherwise alter the results of employment-related tests on the basis of race, color, religion, sex, or national origin; that is, "race norming" is illegal.

4. Use factors other than race, color, religion, sex, or national origin for establishing an employment practice when it can be demonstrated that discrimination against a protected group was the motivating factor.
5. Encourage or be a party to challenges against employment practices that execute and are within the scope of a litigated or consent judgment or order that resolves a claim of employment discrimination under the Constitution or federal civil rights laws.
6. Adopt a seniority system that intentionally discriminates against a protected group.
7. Create artificial barriers (for example, "the glass ceiling") that prevent women and minorities from advancing into management and decision-making positions.

What Managers Can Do

1. If challenged, demonstrate that a specific employment practice does not cause a disparate impact; in this case, they do not have to demonstrate that the practice is required by business necessity.
2. Demonstrate that compliance with the law in a specific case—for example, hiring a person with a disability—would cause an undue hardship on the business.
3. Demonstrate that compliance with the law when operating in a foreign country would violate the law of that country.
4. Create an environment conducive to diversity in the workplace.

Enforcement

Enforcement resides in the EEOC and the Justice Department; however, the act created a new study commission—the Glass Ceiling Commission—to study and promote programs for eliminating artificial barriers and creating opportunities for women and minorities in management and other decision-making positions.

Penalties

1. In the case of unlawful, intentional discrimination with malice or reckless indifference to the law (which unifies claims under the Civil Rights Act of 1964, the Americans with Disabilities Act of 1990, and the Rehabilitation Act of 1973), compensatory damages, punitive damages, and legal expenses (including attorney fees and expert testimony costs).
2. Grounds for compensatory damages may include future pecuniary losses, emotional pain, suffering, inconvenience, mental anguish, loss of enjoyment of life, and other nonpecuniary losses.

Exemptions from Penalties

1. These penalties do not apply to an employment practice that is unlawful because of its disparate impact, to which the penalties under the Civil Rights Act of 1964 apply.
2. Damages might not be awarded in a suit brought under the Americans with Disabilities Act of 1990 or regulations implementing Section 501 of the Rehabilitation Act of 1973, if the employer can demonstrate a good faith effort at reasonable accommodation.
3. Punitive damages cannot be awarded in claims against a government, a government agency, or a political subdivision.

Limitations on Awards for Compensatory Damages

1. Employers of between 14 and 100 employees in each of twenty or more calendar weeks in the current or preceding calendar year: $50,000.
2. Employers of between 101 and 200 employees in each of twenty or more calendar weeks in the current or preceding calendar year: $100,000.
3. Employers of between 201 and 500 employees in each of twenty or more calendar weeks in the current or preceding calendar year: $200,000.
4. Employers of more than five hundred employees in each of twenty or more calendar weeks in the current or preceding calendar year: $300,000.
5. Jury trials may be requested by any party when compensatory or punitive damages are at issue. The court shall not inform the jury of the limitations set by law.

Age Discrimination in Employment Act of 1967
(as amended)

Purpose

To promote employment of older persons, to prohibit age discrimination in employment, and to help employers and workers find ways of meeting problems arising from the impact of age on employment

Whom the Act Protects

All persons age 40 or older

What Managers Cannot Do

1. Fail or refuse to hire any person or otherwise discriminate against any person with respect to compensation, terms, conditions, or privileges of employment because of age

2. Discharge or require retirement of any person because of age
3. Limit, segregate, or classify employees or applicants for employment in a way that would deprive or tend to deprive a person of employment opportunities or have an adverse effect on the person's employee status on the basis of age
4. Reduce anyone's wages in order to comply with this Act
5. Retaliate against any employees or applicants for employment because they made a charge, testified, assisted, or participated in any manner in an action under this title
6. Print or publish (or have someone else print or publish) any notice or advertisement relating to employment that indicates a preference, limitation, specification, or discrimination based on age
7. Deny an employee or a spouse over age 65 the same health care coverage offered to employees and their spouses under age 65
8. Fail to post and keep posted in an obvious place a notice concerning the contents of this law

What Managers Can Do

1. Discriminate where age is a BFOQ.
2. Observe the terms of a bona fide seniority system or any bona fide employee benefit plan as long as the plan is not a subterfuge; this exception does not excuse the organization's failure to hire someone in this protected group or requiring his or her involuntary retirement because of age.
3. Fire or otherwise discipline someone for good cause.

Penalties for Intentional Violation

1. A court order stopping the organization from conducting unlawful employment practices; ordering affirmative action, which may include but not be limited to reinstating or hiring employees with or without back pay; or providing any other fair relief the court rules is appropriate
2. Court action to force an organization to comply (if necessary)
3. Liquidated damages as well as the penalties in item number 1
4. Reasonable attorney fees and other costs

Penalties for Unintentional Violation

1. Appropriate legal and fair relief, including judgments compelling employment, reinstatement or promotion, or unpaid wages

Enforcement

1. Equal Employment Opportunity Commission (EEOC)
2. Attorney General of the United States (AG)

A person may file charges of unintentional discrimination within two years after the alleged unlawful practice took place, and within three years for intentional violations. Notice of the charge will be served afterward within ten days, unless the person filing the claim has filed charges with a state or local agency; then, the person has 300 days in which to file, or else must file within thirty days after the state or local agency finishes its action, whichever is earlier.

If the EEOC is not able to arrange an agreement it finds acceptable within thirty days, it may bring civil action on behalf of the individual through the AG.

[*Note:* The terms and conditions of the ADEA have been extended to cover harassment in the workplace on the basis of age. Not only may the individual defendant be held liable, but the organization can be held liable also if it has not taken reasonable steps to prevent harassment. The organization is particularly liable if it can be shown that its policies or indifference has created a "hostile environment."]

Rehabilitation Act of 1973

Purpose

To protect the constitutional rights and employment opportunities of disabled people applying to or working for a federal agency, or a business or an institution under contract or receiving federal funds

Whom/What the Act Protects

Any person who:

1. Has a physical or mental disability or impairment that constitutes or results in a major handicap to employment; *and*
2. That largely limits one or more of the person's major life activities;
3. Can reasonably be expected to benefit from vocational rehabilitation services;
4. Has a record of an impairment; or
5. Is regarded as having an impairment.

This definition is used to cover many different conditions, such as obesity, drug abuse, alcoholism, and facial skin problems common among black men that prevent them from shaving.

What Managers Cannot Do

1. Fail or refuse to hire any person or to otherwise discriminate against any person with respect to compensation, terms, conditions, or privileges of employment because he or she is disabled

2. Discharge any person because he or she is disabled
3. Limit, segregate, or classify employees or applicants for employment in any way that would deprive or tend to deprive them of employment opportunities or have an adverse effect on their status as an employee
4. Fail to provide training to a person because he or she is disabled
5. Retaliate against any employees or applicants for employment because they made a charge, testified, assisted, or participated in any manner protected by this law
6. Print or publish (or have someone else print or publish) any notice or advertisement relating to employment that may adversely affect people who are disabled
7. Fail to post and keep posted in an obvious place a notice concerning the contents of this law

What Managers Can Do

1. Deny employment where the disability or impairment would interfere with the person's ability to perform the duties of the job
2. Deny employment to any person whose alcohol or other drug abuse would prevent him or her from performing the duties of the job in question or would be a direct threat to property or to the safety of other people
3. Hire without regard to quotas or preferential treatment
4. Fire or otherwise discipline someone for good cause

Penalties for Intentional Violation

1. A court order stopping the organization from conducting unlawful employment practices; ordering affirmative action, which may include but not be limited to reinstating or hiring employees with or without back pay; or any other fair relief the court rules is appropriate. However, the court takes into account the reasonable costs of any necessary workplace changes to accommodate disabled people and the availability of options for accommodation or other relief in order to achieve a fair and proper solution.
2. Court action to force an organization to comply (if necessary).
3. Reasonable attorney fees and other costs.
4. The burden of proof is on the employer.

Enforcement

1. Equal Employment Opportunity Commission (EEOC)
2. Attorney General of the United States (AG)

A person may file charges within 180 days after the alleged unlawful practice took place, and notice of the charge will be served within ten days, unless the person filing the claim has filed charges with a state or local agency; then the person has 300 days in which to file, or else must file within thirty days after the state or local agency finishes its action, whichever is earlier.

If the EEOC is not able to arrange an agreement it finds acceptable within thirty days, it may bring civil action through the AG.

[*Note*: The terms and conditions of the Rehabilitation Act have been extended to cover harassment in the workplace on the basis of disability and to include failure to provide reasonable accommodation. In a case of harassment, the individual defendant can be held liable, but the organization can be held liable also if it has not taken reasonable steps to prevent harassment. The organization is particularly liable if it can be shown that organization policies or indifference has created a "hostile environment."]

[*Note*: The Americans with Disabilities Act extends coverage to the private as well as to the public sector and affects all but the smallest of employers (fourteen or fewer employees) and an estimated 43 million people. More precisely worded and more comprehensive than the Rehabilitation Act, it also requires service companies—for example, restaurants—to improve their accommodations for disabled people.]

Americans with Disabilities Act of 1990

Purpose

To provide a clear and comprehensive plan for eliminating discrimination against individuals with disabilities and to provide clear, strong, consistent, and enforceable standards addressing discrimination against individuals with disabilities, including the power to enforce the Fourteenth Amendment and to regulate commerce with regard to discrimination faced daily by people with disabilities

Whom/What the Act Covers

1. Individuals with a disability, defined as any person who has a physical or mental impairment that substantially limits one or more major life activities, has a record of such impairment, or is perceived as having such an impairment.
2. "Qualified individual with a disability" refers to any person with a disability as defined above who, with or without reasonable accommodation, can perform the essential functions of the job that he or she holds

or wants. Not qualified is any individual who poses a direct threat to the health or safety of other people in the workplace or among the employer's other constituencies (for example, customers), where "direct threat" means a significant risk that cannot be eliminated by a reasonable accommodation.

3. Also covered are rehabilitated drug users who are not currently using drugs, or who are participating in a supervised rehab program and are no longer using drugs, and people who are erroneously regarded as using drugs.

4. The act specifically excludes any employee or applicant who currently, knowingly uses a controlled substance, if the employer acts on the basis of such use. It also excludes homosexuals, bisexuals, transvestites, and persons whose sexual behaviors do not stem from physical impairments. It likewise excludes persons who experience compulsive gambling, kleptomania, or pyromania; and people who experience psychoactive substance use disorders resulting from current use of illegal drugs. Since 1992, employers of fewer than fifteen employees for each working day in twenty or more calendar weeks in the current or preceding calendar year have been exempted, along with the U.S. government, corporations wholly owned by the U.S. government, Indian tribes, and bona fide private membership clubs (other than labor organizations) exempt from federal taxation.

What Managers Cannot Do

1. Limit, segregate, or classify a job applicant or employee in a way that adversely affects that person's opportunities or status solely on the basis of the person's disability.

2. Participate in a contractual or other arrangement or relationship that subjects a qualified applicant or employee to prohibited discrimination. This includes contracts or other arrangements with employment agencies, labor unions, providers of fringe benefits, and training or apprenticeship programs.

3. Use standards, criteria, or methods of administration that discriminate on the basis of a disability or that perpetuate discriminatory practices against persons under common administrative control.

4. Exclude or otherwise deny equal employment or benefits to a qualified person solely because of the disability of a person with whom the qualified individual has a relationship or association, as in the case of a disabled spouse.

5. Fail to make "reasonable accommodation" for known physical or mental limitations of a qualified applicant or employee, or deny job opportunities to a qualified applicant or employee based on the need to make reasonable accommodation, unless the employer can demonstrate that

the accommodation would impose an "undue hardship" on the operation or management of the organization. "Reasonable accommodation" includes making existing facilities readily accessible to and usable by individuals with disabilities; job restructuring; part-time or modified work schedules; reassignment to a vacant position; acquisition or modification of equipment or devices to meet the needs of the person with the disability; appropriate adjustment or modification of examinations, training materials, or policies; and similar accommodations. The definition also includes the provision of "auxiliary aids and services," such as qualified readers or interpreters, and other methods of making materials and communications (for example, taped texts) available to the aurally or visually impaired. The law makes tax credits and other financial considerations available to employers for making accommodations that are unusually expensive.

6. Use qualification standards, employment tests, or other selection criteria that adversely affect or screen out individuals with disabilities or a class of individuals with disabilities unless the standards, tests, or other criteria are shown to be job-related for the position in question and are consistent with business necessity. This prohibits the employer from considering possibilities with regard to future positions in the organization during the screening process.

7. Fail to select and administer employment tests whose results accurately reflect the skills, aptitudes, or other factors they are supposed to measure for people with disabilities that impair sensory, manual, or speaking skills, except where those are the skills to be measured.

8. Require medical examinations or ask job applicants whether they have a disability. Combine information from postjob offer or postemployment examinations with other personnel information, except to inform first aid and safety personnel, supervisors, and managers with regard to work restrictions or accommodations for the employee.

What Managers Can Do

1. Use their own judgment, subject to conditions created by a collective bargaining agreement, as to which functions of a job are essential to that job and write an appropriate, functional job description before advertising or interviewing applicants for that position.

2. Adopt procedures and policies, including drug tests, to ensure that former drug users are no longer engaged in the use of controlled substances.

3. Adopt policies that require an individual not pose a direct threat to the health or safety of other individuals in the workplace or to other constituencies of the employer (for example, customers).

4. Deny employment opportunities to applicants or employees if making

accommodation creates undue hardship, defined as an action requiring significant difficulty or cost. Conditions stipulated by a collective bargaining agreement—for example, shift work assignments—may be taken into consideration.

5. Ask applicants about their ability to perform job-related functions and conduct voluntary medical examinations as part of an employee health program.

6. Require medical examinations after making an offer but prior to the applicant's first day of work and condition the offer on the result of the examinations (but only if all entering employees must undergo such examinations and if they are job-related and consistent with business necessity).

7. Use qualification standards, tests, or other selection criteria—including the requirement that an individual not pose a direct threat to the health and safety of others—as a defense as long as they are job-related and consistent with business necessity, and no reasonable accommodation is possible.

8. Use religious qualifications and preferences if the organization is a religious corporation, association, educational institution, or society.

9. Deny employment opportunities in food-handling positions when an individual has a disease listed on the Department of Health and Human Services' list of infectious and communicable diseases that may be transmitted through food handling.

10. Establish policies and practices that prohibit the use of alcohol or controlled substances at the workplace by all employees, require that employees not be under the influence of alcohol or illegal drugs at the workplace, and require that all employees conform to the Drug-Free Workplace Act of 1988.

11. Hold users of controlled substances or alcohol to the same qualification standards for employment or job performance and behavior as other employees, even if unsatisfactory performance or unacceptable behavior is related to the drug or alcohol use.

12. Post notices accessible to job applicants, employees, and members describing the applicable provisions of the Act, in the manner prescribed by the Civil Rights Act of 1964.

Enforcement

Equal Employment Opportunity Commission, as set forth in the 1964 Civil Rights Act, the attorney general, or any person who believes that he or she has experienced discrimination on the basis of a disability

Penalties

ADA incorporates by reference the remedies and procedures of the Civil Rights Act of 1964 (see Appendix, Title VII, Civil Rights Act of 1964, as amended)

and the injunctive relief and pay remedies of the Civil Rights Act of 1991 (see Appendix, Civil Rights Act of 1991).

Family and Medical Leave Act of 1993

Purpose

To establish minimum standards for employment—namely, to:

> Balance workplace demands with the needs of families
> Promote the stability and security of families
> Promote the national interest in preserving family integrity

The Act is to Accomplish Those Goals By:

> Entitling employees to take reasonable unpaid leave of up to twelve weeks in a twelve-month period for medical reasons, for the birth or adoption or care of a son or daughter, and for the care of a son or daughter, spouse, or parent who has a serious health condition
> Accommodating the legitimate interests of employers
> Minimizing the potential for employment discrimination on the basis of sex by ensuring generally a gender-neutral basis for making leave time available for eligible medical reasons (including maternity-related disability) and for compelling family reasons
> Promoting the goal of equal employment opportunity for women and men, pursuant to the Equal Protection Clause

Whom the Act Protects

Employees of employers where fifty or more workers commute within seventy-five miles of the work site, who have been working for that employer for at least twelve (not necessarily consecutive) months before the leave request, and who have worked at least 1,250 hours during that twelve-month period.

What Managers Cannot Do

Managers cannot "interfere with, restrain, or deny the exercise or the attempt to exercise, any right" under the Act. Specifically, employers cannot:

1. Deny eligible employees a total of twelve workweeks of leave during any twelve-month period when leave is taken for one or more of the following reasons:
   a. The birth of a son or daughter and to care for the child.

    b. The placement of a son or daughter for adoption or foster care.

    c. To care for the employee's spouse, son, daughter, or parent, if the family member has a serious physical or mental health condition, even if another family member is available to give needed care.

    d. The employee is unable to perform the functions of the position because of his or her own serious health condition.

2. Deny unmarried domestic partners working for the same employer their own twelve weeks' leave time as long as the time is requested for the care of their child or parent (but not for the care of a child or parent of the unmarried partner)

3. Deny intermittent or reduced schedule leave in cases involving a serious health condition of the employee or a family member, when such leave is medically necessary

4. Modify an exempt employee's status under the Fair Labor Standards Act or deny such an employee intermittent leave or a reduced leave schedule or dock such an employee's pay

5. Deny eligible employees returning from family and medical leave the position they held when they went on leave, or an equivalent position with equivalent pay, benefits (including benefits accrued while on leave), and other terms and conditions of employment

6. Deny, reduce, or modify "group health plan" coverage or any other benefits to which an eligible employee would have been entitled had he or she been working continuously during the period of leave

7. Fail to contribute to a multiemployer health plan (one to which more than one employer is required to contribute and that is maintained through one or more collective bargaining agreements) during the leave period, unless the plan expressly provides for alternative methods of coverage for the period of the leave

8. Deny employees of public and private elementary and secondary schools the same rights, remedies, and procedures as other eligible employees, except as specified by the Act (Paragraphs 132–135)

9. Deny federal government civil service employees equal rights under the Act, except as specified by various provisions of the Act

10. Interfere with an employee's right to:

    a. Complain to anyone (for example, management, unions, other employees, or newspapers) about allegedly unlawful practices

    b. Participate in a group that opposes discrimination

    c. Refuse an order that the worker believes is unlawful under the Act

    d. Oppose unlawful acts by persons other than the employer (for example, former employers, unions, and coworkers)

11. Discharge or discriminate against someone for:

    a. Filing charges or instituting or causing to be instituted any proceeding under the Act

b. Giving or deciding to give any information in connection with an inquiry or proceeding relating to any right under the Act

c. Testifying or agreeing to testify in any inquiry or proceeding relating to any right under the Act

What Managers Can Do

1. Take all reasonable steps to avoid the risk of discriminatory treatment with regard to meeting the family and medical needs of their employees.
2. Limit the right of employees to take leave for the birth of or placement of a son or daughter to twelve months after the birth of or placement with the employees.
3. Limit total leave time of both spouses in any twelve-month period to twelve weeks if both work for the same employer and if their leave is taken for the birth or adoption of a son or daughter or for the care of a sick parent.
4. Deny leave to employees for the care of an unmarried domestic partner.
5. Deny employees an intermittent or reduced schedule leave for the birth or placement of a son or daughter, except by a formal agreement between the employer and the specific employee.
6. Require employees seeking leave (continuous, intermittent, or reduced schedule) for planned medical treatment to provide thirty days' notice (or as much notice as is practical) and medical certification outlining the dates on which treatment is expected and the duration of the treatment.
7. Require employees seeking leave (continuous, intermittent, or reduced schedule) for planned medical treatment to make a reasonable effort, with the health care provider's approval, to schedule medical treatment in a manner that will not unduly disrupt the employer's operations.
8. Require, if the employer has a reasonable doubt as to the validity of an eligible employee's certification, a second opinion from a health care provider designated or approved by the employer, provided that:
   a. The employer pays for the second opinion.
   b. The health care provider is not employed on a regular basis by the employer.
   c. In the event of a conflict of opinion, the employer pays for a third opinion approved jointly by the employer and employee; this third opinion would be final and binding.
9. Require employees seeking leave time for a foreseeable event (for example, the birth or placement of a son or daughter) to give thirty days'

notice, or as much notice as is practical (for example, in the event of a premature birth or availability of a child).

10. Require anyone who has requested foreseeable intermittent or reduced schedule leave for planned medical treatment to transfer temporarily to an available alternative position if:
    a. The employee is qualified for the alternative position.
    b. The position has equivalent pay and benefits.
    c. The alternative position better accommodates recurring periods of leave than the employee's regular position.

11. Offer exempt employees substitute arrangements for any part of the twelve weeks of leave granted under the Act, depending on the reason for the leave, for example, accrued paid vacation, personal, family, or medical or sick leave.

12. Require an employee on leave to report periodically on his or her status and intent to return to work.

13. Require each training employee to provide certification from the health care provider that he or she is able to resume work.

14. Deny to restored employees accrued seniority or employment benefits or any other right, benefit, or position of employment to which the employees would have been entitled had he or she not taken the leave (although eligible employees, as defined in the Act, retain all accrued benefits while on leave).

15. Deny eligible employees among the highest paid 10 percent of employees within seventy-five miles of work site restoration to their prior or equivalent position if:
    a. Denial is necessary to prevent substantial and grievous economic injury to the employer's operations.
    b. The employees have been notified that the employer intends to deny restoration, as soon as the employer determines that such injury to the operations would occur.
    c. In the case of an employee already on leave, he or she elects not to return to work after being notified of the employer's decision.

16. Deny health care benefits if the employer does not already offer them; however, they must be provided for employees on leave if they are made available while those employees are on leave.

17. Recover the premium paid for maintaining employees' health plan coverage during any period of unpaid leave if:
    a. Employees fail to return from leave after their entitlement has expired.
    b. Employees fail to return to work for a reason other than (1) the continuation, recurrence, or onset of a serious health condition that would entitle the employee to leave, or (2) other circumstances beyond the employee's control.

18. Require employees to support their claim to inability to return to work, from a health care provider, because of the continuation, recurrence, or onset of a serious health condition that would entitle the employee to leave, or other circumstances beyond the employee's control.

Enforcement

Secretary of Labor, Wage and Hour Division of the Department of Labor. This Act does not modify or affect any federal or state law prohibiting discrimination on the basis of race, religion, color, national origin, sex, age, or disability; it does not preempt state and local laws providing greater leave rights now in effect or passed in the future. It does not affect collective bargaining agreements or employment benefit programs or plans providing greater family or medical leave rights. On the other hand, collective bargaining agreements or employers' plans cannot pre-empt the provisions of this Act.

Penalties from Civil Action by Employees: Willful Violations

An employee's right to civil action is terminated when the secretary of labor files an action seeking monetary relief on that employee's behalf, unless the secretary dismisses his of her action without prejudice.

Damages:	An amount equal to the wages, salary, employment benefits, or other compensation denied or lost to the employee because of the violation. In the absence of losses of compensation, the employer is liable for an amount equal to the actual monetary losses sustained by the employee as a direct result of the violation, for example, the cost of providing care, up to an amount equal to twelve weeks of the employee's wages or salary.
Interest:	To be added to the amount of damages, calculated at the prevailing rate.
Liquidated damages:	An additional final settlement of damages, equal to the sum of the damages awarded and interest on those amounts, that can be awarded unless the employer proves to the satisfaction of the court that its conduct or omission, in violation of the Act, was done in good faith and that the employer had reasonable grounds for believing that it was not in violation of the Act.
Equitable relief:	Other awards to the employee—for example, employment, reinstatement, promotion, etc.

| *Fees and costs:* | Reasonable attorney fees (mandatory and unconditional), reasonable expert witness fees, and other costs of the action. |

Penalties from Civil Action by Secretary of Labor

Recoverable damages are identical to those available in employee suits. The secretary must bring action no later than two years after the date of the last event constituting the alleged violation, or within three years of the last event if the violation is willful. The courts may, at the request of the secretary of labor, restrain by injunction any employer from interference violations.

Vietnam Era Veterans Readjustment Assistance Act of 1974 Title IV: Veterans, Wives, and Widow Employment Assistance and Preference and Veterans' Reemployment Rights

Purpose

To protect the constitutional rights and employment opportunities of veterans, especially of veterans of the Vietnam era

Whom the Act Protects

1. Any veteran of the Vietnam era, which means anyone who served in the armed forces for 180 days or more between 1964 and 1991
2. Any member of the Active Reserves or National Guard
3. Any person discharged or released from active duty because of a service-connected disability or who is entitled to compensation under the laws administered by the Veterans Administration

What Managers Cannot Do

1. Deny reemployment to a veteran who is still qualified to perform the duties of his or her position, as long as he or she applied for reemployment within ninety days after release from military service and has satisfactorily completed that military service
2. Deny a veteran his or her benefits, seniority, status, or pay
3. Deny a disabled veteran reemployment in another position for which he or she is qualified if that person is no longer able to perform the duties of his or her previous position, or deny the person his or her benefits, seniority, status, or pay, or any similar condition of employment
4. Deny military leave time to any person called to active duty by the

armed forces, the Ready Reserve, the National Guard, or the Public Health Service

5. Deny military leave time to any person fulfilling his or her obligation to the Reserve or National Guard or other component of the armed forces, or who is called upon to take additional training

6. Deny a member of the Reserve or National Guard or other component of the armed forces seniority, status, or pay as a result of his or her obligations

7. Deny benefits to any person serving in any component of the military or armed forces except in regard to military leave pay if the person and the employer agree to a partial payment plan

Penalties for Intentional Violation

1. Court order requiring compliance
2. Compensation for loss of wages or benefits
3. Reasonable attorney fees and other costs
4. The burden of proof is on the employer

Enforcement

The Office of Veterans' Reemployment Rights in the Department of Labor

[*Note:* The terms and conditions of the Vietnam Era Veterans' Readjustment Act have been extended to cover harassment in the workplace on the basis of military status and to include failure to provide reasonable accommodation. In a case of harassment, the individual defendant can be held liable, but the organization can be held liable also if it has not taken reasonable steps to prevent harassment. The organization is particularly liable if it can be shown that organization policies or indifference has created a "hostile environment."]

Uniformed Services Employment and Reemployment Rights Act (USERRA)

Purposes

1. To encourage noncareer service in the uniformed services by eliminating or minimizing the disadvantages to civilian careers and employment that can result from such service

2. To minimize the disruption to the lives of persons performing service in the uniformed services as well as to their employers, their fellow employees, and their communities, by providing for the prompt reemployment of such persons upon their completion of such service

3. To prohibit discrimination against persons because of their service in the uniformed services
4. To ensure that members of the uniformed services are reinstated with the seniority, status, and rate of pay they would have obtained had they remained continuously employed by their civilian employer
5. To protect individuals from discrimination in hiring, promotion, and retention on the basis of present and future membership in the armed services

Whom/What USERRA Protects

1. Any qualified person employed by an employer, which includes any person who is a citizen, national or permanent resident alien of the United States employed in a workplace in a foreign country by an employer that is an entity incorporated or otherwise organized in the United States or that is controlled by an entity organized in the United States regardless of whether or not that uniformed service is voluntary or involuntary.
2. A person who is a member of, applies to be a member of, performs, has performed, applies to perform, or has an obligation to perform service in a uniformed service. An employee no longer needs to request permission to be absent for military leave but instead provides notification of pending military service.
3. Any person whose absence from a position of employment is necessitated by reason of service in the uniformed services shall be entitled to the reemployment rights and benefits and other employment benefits if:
   a. The person (or an appropriate officer of the uniformed service in which such service is performed) has given advance written or verbal notice of such service to such person's employer; no notice is required if giving such notice is precluded by military necessity or, under all of the relevant circumstances, giving such notice is otherwise impossible or unreasonable.
   b. The cumulative length of the absence and of all previous absences from a position of employment with that employer by reason of service in the uniformed services does not exceed five years.
   c. The law shall apply to someone who is absent from a position of employment if his or her cumulative period of service in the uniformed services:
      (1) Is required, beyond five years, to complete an initial period of obligated service
      (2) If the person was unable to obtain orders releasing him or her from a period of service in the uniformed services before the expiration of such five-year period through no fault of his or her own

(3) Is ordered to or retained on active duty (other than for training) under any provision of law because of a war or national emergency declared by the president of the United States or Congress, as determined by the secretary concerned

(4) Ordered to active duty (other than for training) in support, as determined by the secretary concerned, of an operational mission for which personnel have been ordered to active duty

(5) Ordered to active duty in support, as determined by the secretary concerned, of a critical mission or requirement of the uniformed services

(6) Called into federal service as a member of the National Guard

(7) Is required as a member of a reserve component if called upon to perform funeral honors duty

What Managers Cannot Do

1. Deny initial employment, reemployment, retention in employment, promotion, or any benefit of employment on the basis of that membership, application for membership, performance of service, application for service, or obligation.

2. Deny a person reemployment if he or she provides appropriate documentation or if the person cannot provide that because it does not exist or is not readily available at the time of the employer's request; if, after reemployment, documentation comes available that establishes that the person does not meet one or more of the requirements, the employer may terminate his or her employment.

3. An employer shall not discharge a person covered by this law from such employment, except for cause:
   a. Within one year after the date of such reemployment, if the person's period of service before the reemployment was more than 180 days
   b. Within 180 days after the date of such reemployment, if the person's period of service before the reemployment was more than thirty days but less than 181 days

4. An employer may not require any person covered by this law to use vacation, annual, or similar leave during such period of service. Any person whose employment is interrupted by a period of service in the uniformed services shall be permitted, if requested, to use during his or her period of service any vacation, annual, or similar leave with pay accrued by the person before the commencement of his or her service.

5. An employer cannot count military service as time away from the employer for retirement purposes.

6. An employer may not retaliate against or take any adverse employment action against anyone because he or she has:

a. Taken an action to enforce a protection afforded any person under this law.
b. Testified or otherwise made a statement in or in connection with any proceeding under the law.
c. Assisted or otherwise participated in an investigation under this law.
d. Exercised a right provided for in this law. This prohibition applies regardless of whether that person has performed service in the uniformed services.

What Managers Can Do

1. Deny the benefits of this law if:
   a. The person's separation is with a dishonorable or bad conduct discharge.
   b. The person's separation is under other than honorable conditions.
2. An employer is not required to reemploy a person under this chapter if:
   a. The employer's circumstances have changed in any way that makes reemployment impossible or unreasonable.
   b. Reemployment would impose an undue hardship on the employer.
   c. The employment from which the person leaves to serve in the uniformed services is for a brief, nonrecurrent period and there is no reasonable expectation that such employment will continue indefinitely or for a significant period.
   d. If the person who completes a period of service in the uniformed services fails to notify the employer of his or her intent to return to a position of employment not later than the beginning of the first full regularly scheduled work period on the first full calendar day following the completion of the period of service and the expiration of eight hours after a period allowing for the safe transportation of the person from the place of that service to the person's residence; or as soon as possible after the expiration of the eight-hour period referred to in clause unless reporting within that period is impossible or unreasonable through no fault of his or her own.
   e. If the person is hospitalized for, or convalescing from, an illness or injury incurred in, or aggravated during, the performance of service in the uniformed service until the person recovers from that illness or injury.
3. An employer may deny retention, preference, or displacement rights if any other person has a superior claim.
4. An employer can deny a person's claim if he or she proves that the person knowingly provided clear written notice of intent not to return to a position of employment after service in the uniformed service and was aware of the specific rights and benefits to be lost under the law.
5. An employer can deny any benefits to which the person would not

otherwise be entitled if the person had remained continuously employed.

Enforcement

Enforcement is carried out by the Department of Labor, the Veteran's Employment and Training Service (VETS), and the Attorney General of the United States (AG).

National Labor Relations Act, 1935
(as amended)

Purpose

To lessen the causes of labor disputes that interfere with interstate or foreign commerce, to create a National Labor Relations Board (NLRB), and for other purposes

Whom/What the Act Protects

The rights of employees to organize themselves; to form, join, or assist labor organizations; to bargain collectively through their own representatives. It also allows all workers, nonunion as well as union, to engage in other concerted activities for the purpose of collective bargaining or other mutual aid or protection. It prevents nonunion employees from being forced or coerced into joining a labor organization or engaging in collective bargaining except where membership in a labor organization is a condition of employment and is created by contract.

What Managers Cannot Do ("Unfair Labor Practices by Employers")

1. Interfere with, restrain, or coerce employees exercising their rights.
2. Dominate or interfere with the formation or administration of a labor organization or contribute financial or other aid to it; however, managers are required to allow employees to meet with them during working hours without a loss of time or pay to discuss issues of collective interest.
3. Discriminate in hiring or tenure on the basis of union or nonunion membership; managers cannot use the terms or conditions of employment to encourage or discourage membership in a labor organization, except where an agreement exists that requires membership.
4. Fire or otherwise discriminate against an employee for filing charges or giving testimony under this Act.

5. Refuse to bargain collectively with the employees' representative (however, see item 2 under "What Managers Can Do").
6. Enter with employees into any contract, express or implied, that would cause the employer to stop or refrain from handling, using, selling, transporting, or otherwise dealing in any of the products of any other employer or person (Hot Cargo Clause).

What Managers Can Do

1. Freely express viewpoints, arguments, or opinions in writing, print, graphics, or visuals about unions or collective bargaining as long as they do not threaten reprisal or force for forming or joining a collective bargaining unit and do not promise benefits for not forming or joining one
2. Under Section 9a of the Act, hear employee grievances and adjust them without union representation, as long as the adjustment is consistent with the terms of a contract or agreement in effect and as long as the bargaining representative has been given an opportunity to be present
3. Reject proposals or requests for concessions
4. Appeal any ruling of the NLRB in any appropriate circuit court of appeals of the United States

Penalties

1. Injunction or restraining order stopping an alleged unfair labor practice while in arbitration or adjudication
2. A fine of not more than $5,000 or imprisonment for not more than one year or both for interfering with the activities of the NLRB or any of its members, agents, or representatives
3. Specific remedies on a case-by-case basis ruled on by the NLRB and/or the courts

Enforcement

The National Labor Relations Board

Fair Labor Standards Act, 1938
(Wage-Hour Act, as amended)

Purpose

To establish fair labor standards in employment in and affecting interstate commerce, and for other purposes

Whom the Act Protects

All workers, including children and women

What Managers Cannot Do

1. Employ children under age 16 ("oppressive labor") and certain categories of children ages 16 to 18
2. Pay wages under the minimum hourly rate (currently $5.25 per hour)
3. Use sex as a basis for discriminating in wages, although where wages are based on a factor other than sex, such as a seniority system, members of one gender group may be adversely affected
4. Lower the wage rate of any employee to comply with this Act
5. Employ nonexempt workers for more than forty hours a week unless they are paid at least time and a half their "regular rate of pay" for the overtime
6. Discharge or otherwise discriminate against any employee for filing, instituting, or causing to be instituted a complaint relating to this Act or for testifying or being about to testify in an action protected by this Act
7. Discharge or otherwise discriminate against any employee for taking part in a collective action with respect to wages or other working conditions

Exclusions from "Regular Rate of Pay"

1. Gifts, special bonuses, rewards for service
2. Payments made for occasional periods in which no work is performed, travel expenses, or other reimbursable expenses
3. Recognition for service awards
4. Contributions irrevocably made to a trustee or third party in a retirement, pension, or insurance plan
5. Extra compensation paid on a premium rate for:
   a. Overtime after a regular eight-hour day
   b. Overtime on a nonworkday
   c. Work outside normal hours as agreed upon through collective bargaining
6. Compensation through a guaranteed wage plan based on a bona fide individual contract or collective bargaining agreement

Exempt Employees

1. Executives, managers, and first-line supervisors
2. Employees whose jobs require making decisions—using personal judg-

ment, creativity, or innovativeness—but who are not classified as managers

3. Teachers and educational administrators
4. Salespeople and other people working on commission or for tips for service
5. Employees of service organizations in which more than 50 percent of the organization's gross income derives from *intra*state as opposed to *inter*state commerce

Criminal Penalties

For willful violation, up to $10,000 or imprisonment for up to six months or both

Civil Penalties

1. Unpaid minimum wages or unpaid overtime or both, and an equal amount of liquidated damages
2. Fair relief, including employment, reinstatement, promotion, payment of lost wages, liquidated damages, and reasonable attorney and court fees
3. A court order stopping an unfair labor standards practice (injunctive relief)

Enforcement

The Wage and Hour Division of the Department of Labor

Labor Management Relations Act, 1947
(Taft-Hartley Act)

Purpose

To amend the National Labor Relations Act, providing additional support for mediation in labor disputes that affect interstate commerce; to equalize legal responsibilities of labor organizations and employers; to give the president of the United States emergency powers; and for other purposes

What the Act Protects

The nation's general welfare

What It Forbids

1. Unwarranted or sudden lockouts
2. Paying, loaning, or delivering money or other assets by an employer to

a union, union official, union welfare fund, or employee involved in a labor dispute
3. Employers and unions making contributions to political candidates

Mediation Process

1. The Federal Mediation Service was created to try to avoid industrial controversy by offering services either on its own initiative or by request from one or more of the parties involved in the dispute.
2. If the service's director cannot produce an agreement through conciliation within a reasonable time, he or she will try to get the parties to find other means of settling the dispute without resorting to a strike, a lockout, or other coercion (for example, submitting the employer's last offer to a secret ballot of the employees).
3. Failure to agree is not a violation of any duty or obligation imposed by this Act.

Duties of Employers and Employees

1. Make every reasonable effort to agree on rates of pay, hours, and working conditions, including notice of changes.
2. Arrange promptly to hold a conference to settle any differences between them.
3. If a conference is not successful, participate fully in meetings called by the service.

National Emergencies and Presidential Powers

1. The Federal Mediation Service will advise the president of the United States of a serious threat to the general welfare of the nation.
2. The president is empowered to direct the attorney general to petition any appropriate district court to stop a threatened strike or lockout or to end one or the other in progress.
3. If a federal court agrees that a strike or a lockout will adversely affect an entire industry or substantial part of it or would threaten the national health, safety, or security, it can stop the strike or lockout or take other appropriate measures.

Penalties (Other Than Injunctions Described Above)

1. Fine of $5,000 for an organization making illegal contributions to political candidates
2. Fine of up to $1,000 or one year in prison or both for officers of any organizations making illegal contributions

Enforcement

1. The attorney general acting on orders from the president
2. Federal district courts

Labor-Management Reporting and Disclosure Act, 1959 (Labor Reform Act)

Purpose

To prevent labor organizations, employers, or their officers and representatives, including labor relations consultants, from distorting and defeating the policies of the Labor Management Relations Act, 1947, as amended (LMRA)

Whom the Act Protects

Nonsupervisory union and nonunion employees

What Managers Cannot Do

Interfere with employees' right to work, organize, choose representatives, bargain collectively, and engage in concerted action for their mutual aid or protection

What Managers Must Do

Under this Act, employers must file a number of reports with the secretary of labor, including the following reports relevant to our subject matter:

1. Reports of any payments, loans, promises, or other agreements to any labor organization, or to an officer, agent, shop steward, or other representative of a union. The report must list pertinent details concerning the transaction.
2. Reports of any person who attempts to persuade employees in favor of or against unionism.
3. Reports of any agreements with a third party who supplies information about a labor dispute involving the employer, unless that information is used solely for administrative, arbitral, or judicial proceedings; also exempted from reporting is anyone who is not a direct or indirect party to the agreement. Regular officers, supervisors, or employees of an employer who do not receive payment over and above their normal com-

pensation are exempt, as are advisers, consultants, or legal representatives.

Criminal Penalties

Not more than $10,000 or imprisonment for up to five years or both, plus civil remedies in the LMRA

Enforcement

Federal district court

The Equal Pay Act of 1963
Pub. L. 88–38 (EPA) (as amended)
[Section 3 of the Equal Pay Act of 1963 amends section 6 of the Fair Labor Standards Act by adding a new subsection (d). The amendment is incorporated into the revised text of the Fair Labor Standards Act.]

Purpose

To provide protections for employees and between employees on the basis of sex by paying wages to employees in any establishment "at a rate less than the rate at which [the employer] pays wages to employees of the opposite sex . . . for equal work on jobs the performance of which requires equal skill, effort, and responsibility, and which are performed under similar working conditions"

Whom/What the Act Covers

All employees of companies engaged in commerce in the United States.
    The exceptions are:

1. Where salaries or wages are paid pursuant to (a) a seniority system; (b) a merit system; (c) a system that measures earnings by quantity or quality of production; or (d) a differential based on any factor other than sex. However, an employer who is paying a wage rate differential in violation of the law shall not, in order to comply with the provisions of the law, reduce the wage rate of any employee.
2. Anyone employed in a bona fide executive, administrative, or professional capacity (including any employee employed in the capacity of academic administrative personnel or teacher in elementary or secondary schools), or in the capacity of outside salesman (as such terms are

defined and delimited from time to time by regulations of the secretary of labor).

3. Anyone employed by an amusement or recreational establishment, organized camp, or religious or nonprofit educational conference center, if (a) it does not operate for more than seven months in any calendar year, or (b) during the preceding calendar year, its average receipts for any six months were not more than 33 1/3 percent of its average receipts for the other six months of the year, except with respect to any employee of a private organization providing services or facilities (other than a private entity engaged in providing services and facilities directly related to skiing) in a national park or a national forest, or on land in the National Wildlife Refuge System, under a contract with the secretary of the interior or the secretary of agriculture.

4. Any employee employed in any aquatic form of animal and vegetable life, or in the first processing, canning, or packing marine products at sea as a part of, or in conjunction with, fishing operations, including the going to and returning from work and loading and unloading.

5. Any agricultural worker where (a) the employer did not, during any calendar quarter during the preceding calendar year, use more than 500 worker-days of agricultural labor, (b) the employee is an immediate family member of the employer, (c) the employee is a hand harvest laborer and is paid on a piece rate where a piece rate has been customarily and generally paid in that region, (1) the employee commutes daily from his or her permanent residence to the farm on which he or she is employed, and (2) the employee has been employed in agriculture less than thirteen weeks during the preceding calendar year, (d) the employee (other than an employee described in clause C of this subsection) (1) is sixteen years old or under and is employed as a hand harvest laborer, is paid on a piece rate basis in an operation that customarily and generally pays on a piece rate basis in that region; (2) is employed on the same farm as his or her parent or parent substitute; and (3) is paid at the same piece rate as employees over age 16 are paid on the same farm, or (e) if such employee is principally engaged in the range production of livestock.

6. Any employee to the extent that such employee is exempted by regulations, order, or certificate of the secretary of labor.

7. Anyone employed in connection with the publication of any weekly, semiweekly, or daily newspaper with a circulation of less than 4,000, the major part of which is within the county where published or counties contiguous thereto.

8. Any switchboard operator employed by an independently owned public telephone company that has not more than 750 stations.

9. Anyone employed as a seaman on a vessel other than a U.S. vessel.

10. Anyone employed on a casual basis in domestic service employment

to provide babysitting services or anyone employed to provide companionship services for individuals who (because of age or infirmity) are unable to care for themselves.

What Managers Cannot Do

1. Transport, offer for transportation, ship, deliver, or sell in commerce, or to ship, deliver, or sell with knowledge that the shipment or delivery or sale of goods where anyone was employed in violation of this law, or in violation of any regulation or order of the secretary of labor. However, this law shall not impose any liability upon any common carrier for the transportation of any goods not produced by the common carrier, and it shall not be deemed unlawful if any common carrier accepts goods for transportation if acquired in good faith and in reliance on written assurance from the producer that the goods were produced in compliance with the requirements of this law.
2. Violate any of the provisions of this law or any regulation or order of the secretary of labor issued under this law.
3. Retaliate in any manner against any employee because he or she has filed a complaint or instituted or caused to be instituted any proceeding under or related to this law, or has testified or is about to testify in any such proceeding, or has served or is about to serve on an industry committee.
4. Make any statement, report, or record filed or kept with knowledge that the statement, report, or record is false in any material respect.

Enforcement

The authority given to the secretary of labor in the Fair Labor Standards Act of 1938, as amended, is exercised by the Equal Employment Opportunity Commission for purposes of enforcing the Equal Pay Act of 1963.

Penalties for Willful Violation
(Among a Long List of Other Possible Penalties)

1. A fine of not more than $10,000 or imprisonment for not more than six months, or both.
2. Liability to the employee or employees affected in the amount of their unpaid minimum wages, or their unpaid overtime compensation, as the case may be, and an additional equal amount as liquidated damages.
3. Liability for such legal or equitable relief as may be appropriate, including without limitation employment, reinstatement, promotion, and the payment of wages lost and an additional equal amount as liquidated damages.

The Worker Adjustment and Retraining Notification Act (The WARN Act)

Purpose

1. To protect families and communities by requiring employers of 100 or more employees (excluding part-time employees, or 100 or more employees including part-time employees, who in the aggregate work at least 4,000 hours per week, excluding hours of overtime) to provide notification 60 calendar days in advance of plant closings and mass layoffs
2. To provide workers and their families some transition time to adjust to the prospective loss of employment, to seek and obtain alternative jobs and, if necessary, to enter skill training or retraining that will allow these workers to successfully compete in the job market
3. To provide for notice to state dislocated worker units so that assistance can be promptly provided

An employer who is not required to comply with the notice requirements of this act should, to the extent possible, provide notice to its employees about a proposal to close a plant or permanently reduce its workforce.

Who/What Is Protected?

1. Employees and their families
2. Communities in which a plant closing or mass layoff is to take place
3. Workers on temporary layoff or on leave who have a reasonable expectation of recall are counted as employees
4. Independent contractors and employees of subsidiaries that are wholly or partially owned by a parent company are treated as separate employers or as a part of the parent or contracting company depending on the degree of their independence from the parent
5. State dislocated worker units for failing to provide prompt assistance

What Managers Must Do

1. Give affected employees at least sixty days' written notice or voluntarily provide longer periods of advance notice. Where 500 or more employees (excluding part-time employees) are affected, the 33 percent requirement does not apply, and notice is required if the other criteria are met. By definition, plant closings involve employment loss that results from the shutdown of one or more distinct units within a single site or the entire site; a mass layoff involves employment loss, regardless of whether one or more units are shut down at the site.

2. Not order a plant closing or mass layoff until the end of a sixty-day period after serving written notice of such an order.
3. Decide who is the most appropriate person within the organization to prepare and deliver the notice to affected employees or their representative(s), the state dislocated worker unit, and the chief elected official of a unit of local government, for example, the local site plant manager, the local personnel director, or a labor relations officer.
4. Give written notice when it becomes reasonably foreseeable that an extension is required when the employer who has previously announced and carried out a short-term layoff (six months or less) requires an extension beyond six months due to reasonably unforeseeable business circumstances (including unforeseeable changes in price or cost) at the time of the initial layoff.
5. As seller, in the case of the sale of part or all of a business, take responsibility for providing notice of any plant closing or mass layoff that takes place up to and including the effective date (time) of the sale; the buyer is responsible for providing notice of any plant closing or mass layoff that takes place thereafter.
6. Give written notice if, in a sale of a unit or plant, the seller is made aware of any definite plans on the part of the buyer to carry out a plant closing or mass layoff within sixty days of purchase; the seller may give notice to affected employees as an agent of the buyer, if so empowered. If the seller does not give notice, the buyer is, nevertheless, responsible to give notice. If the seller gives notice as the buyer's agent, the responsibility for notice still remains with the buyer. It may be prudent for the buyer and seller to determine the impact of the sale on workers, and to arrange between them for advance notice to be given to affected employees or their representative(s).
7. Give written notice to each representative of the affected employees as of the time notice is required to be given or, if there is no such representative at that time, to each affected employee.
8. Give written notice to the state dislocated worker unit and the chief elected official of the unit of local government within which a closing or layoff is to occur.
9. Give written notice to representative(s) of affected employees, for example, the chief elected officer of the exclusive representative(s) or bargaining agent(s). If he or she is not the same as the officer of the local union(s) representing affected employees, the law recommends that a copy also be given to the local union official(s).
10. Give written notice to affected employees who may reasonably be expected to experience an employment loss, including employees who will likely lose their jobs because of bumping rights or other factors or to the incumbents in those positions. Even if part-time employees are

not counted in determining whether plant closing or mass layoff thresholds are reached, give written notice to those workers also.

What Managers Can Do

1. Reassign or transfer employees to employer-sponsored programs, such as retraining or job search activities, as long as the reassignment does not constitute a constructive discharge or other involuntary termination
2. Offer to transfer employees to a different site of employment within a reasonable commuting distance with no more than a six-month break in employment, or offer to transfer employees to any other site of employment regardless of distance with no more than a six-month break in employment, and the employee accepts within thirty days of the offer or of the closing or layoff, whichever is later
3. Give notice in ambiguous situations as a civically desirable and good business practice for an employer to provide advance notice to its workers or unions, local government, and the state when terminating a significant number of employees

What a Written Notice Must Contain

1. The legal name and address of the employment site where the plant closing or mass layoff will occur
2. The name and telephone number of a company official to contact for further information
3. A statement explaining whether the planned action is expected to be permanent or temporary
4. A statement explaining if the entire plant is to be closed
5. The date the first separation is expected as well as the anticipated schedule for conducting those and subsequent separations
6. A list of the job titles of positions to be affected
7. The names of the workers currently holding affected jobs
8. Some recognition of whether or not bumping rights exist

Conditions Under Which Notice May Be Given Less Than Sixty Days in Advance

1. The *faltering company* exception applies to plant closings but not to mass layoffs:
   a. If the employer has been actively seeking capital or business at the time that sixty-day notice would have been required, for example, seeking financing or refinancing through the arrangement of loans, the issuance of stocks, bonds, or other methods of internally gener-

ated financing; or the employer must have been seeking additional money, credit, or business through any other commercially reasonable method. The employer must be able to identify specific actions taken to obtain capital or business.

b. If there is a realistic opportunity to obtain the financing or business sought.

c. If the financing or business is sufficient, if obtained, to have enabled the employer to avoid or postpone the shutdown.

d. If the employer reasonably and in good faith believes that giving the required notice would have prevented his or her ability to obtain the needed capital or business.

2. The "unforeseeable business circumstances" exception applies to plant closings and mass layoffs caused by business circumstances that were not reasonably foreseeable at the time that the sixty-day notice would have been required.

a. If the circumstance is caused by some sudden, dramatic, and unexpected action or condition outside the employer's control.

b. If the employer exercises commercially reasonable business judgment that indicates that a similarly situated employer would make the same prediction with regard to the demands of its particular market. The employer is not required, however, to accurately predict general economic conditions that also may affect demand for its products or services.

3. The natural disaster exception applies to plant closings and mass layoffs due to any form of a natural disaster. Floods, earthquakes, droughts, storms, tidal waves or tsunamis, and similar effects of nature are natural disasters under this provision.

Enforcement

1. Civil courts
2. The Department of Labor can only provide assistance in understanding these regulations and may revise them from time to time as may be necessary.

Index

absenteeism vs. disability, 223–224
absolute privilege, 128
access laws, 129
accounting procedures, 292–293
advertising for job openings, 20
    example, 30–31
    permitted statements, 25–33
    restrictions, 23–25
affirmative action, viii, 24, 57–59, 121–122
affirmative defense, for sexual harass-
        ment charge, 182–184
African-American men, vii
Age Discrimination in Employment Act
        (ADEA), 14, 258, 305, 306, 336–338
    permitted actions, 310–317
    prohibited actions, 307–310
    summary, 307
age of job applicant, and job offer, 59–61
agency and employer liability, 181
AIDS
    discrimination, 227–229
    testing, 146–147
alcoholism, 216, 220
    accommodation for, 230–231
Americans with Disabilities Act of 1990,
        14, 39, 212, 222–223, 340–344
    casebook, 224–226
arbitrary placement, 309
arbitration, 259–261
Arizona Supreme Court, 291
arrest records, 36
at will doctrine, 255, 261, 268
    casebook, 275–280
    public exception, 290–292
attitudes, vii-viii
    testing, 89
audit systems, for performance appraisal,
        114–115

background checks, 93–94
    cost of, 97

BFOQ (bona fide occupational qualifica-
        tion), 15–16, 89
    in job advertisements, 25
    sound criteria for, 66
Biggert, Judy, 237–238
bilateral contract, 256
Boeing Company, 11
business decisions, and layoffs, 310–317
business grounds for hiring decisions,
        54–59

California
    Proposition 209, 58
    Supreme Court on lie detector tests,
        151
casebook
    employee action rights, 242–245
    Family and Medical Leave Act of 1993,
        175–177
    hiring, 59–60
    interviewing, 41–44
    negligent hiring, 93–97
    privacy, 146–160
    reasons for, 4–5
    recruiting, 32–34
    reduction in workforce, 318–325
    sex discrimination and sexual harass-
        ment, 198–210
child care questions, 70
child labor, 237
civil rights, 10
    legislation benefits, 15–16
Civil Rights Act of 1964, Title VII, 14, 63,
        103–104, 328–330
    and testing, 55
Civil Rights Act of 1991, 121–122, 260,
        333–336
Civil Rights Law of 1866, 14
Civil Rights Law of 1991, 11
Clinton, Bill, Justice Department under,
        11